Silent Boy

Torey Hayden

Silent Boy

He was a frightened boy who
refused to speak – until a teacher's
love broke through the silence

This book is based on the author's experiences. In order to protect privacy, names, some identifying characteristics, dialogue, and details have been changed or reconstructed. Some characters are not based on any one person but are composite characters.

HarperElement
An Imprint of HarperCollins*Publishers*
77–85 Fulham Palace Road,
Hammersmith, London W6 8JB

The website address is: www.thorsonselement.com

and *HarperElement* are trademarks of
HarperCollins*Publishers* Ltd

First published by Avon Books 1983
This edition published 2007

1

A catalogue record of this book is
available from the British Library

ISBN 978-0-00-781080-2

Printed and bound in Great Britain by
Clays Ltd, St Ives plc

To S. K.
for teaching me to cherish
the brutal privilege of being human

Part I

Chapter One

Zoo-boy. The legs of the table were his cage. With arms up protectively over his head, he rocked. Back and forth, back and forth. An aide tried to prod him into moving out from under the table but she had no luck. Back and forth, back and forth the boy rocked.

I watched from behind the one-way mirror. 'How old is he?' I asked the woman on my right.

'Fifteen.'

Hardly a boy anymore. I leaned close to the glass to see him. 'How long has he been here?' I asked.

'Four years.'

'Without ever speaking?'

'Without ever speaking.' She looked over at me in the eerie gloom of the room behind the mirror. 'Without ever making a noise at all.'

I continued to watch a little longer. Then I picked up my box of materials and went out into the room on the other side of the mirror. The aide backed off and, when I entered, she willingly left. I could hear the click of a door in the outer corridor and I knew she had gone behind the mirror to watch too. Only Zoo-boy and I were left in the room.

Carefully, I set down my box of materials. I waited a moment to see if he would react to a new person in the room, but he didn't. So I came closer. I sat down on the floor an arm's length away from where he had barricaded himself under the table. Still he rocked, his arms and legs curled up around him. I could get no idea of his stature.

'Kevin?'

No response.

Not sure what to do, I looked around. I was acutely aware of the audience beyond the mirror. They were talking in there, their voices indistinct, no more than an undulating murmur, like wind through cattails on a summer's afternoon. But I knew the sound for what it was.

The boy didn't look fifteen. Even wrapped up in a ball like that where I couldn't get much of a look at him, he didn't appear that old. Nine, maybe. Or eleven. Not nearly sixteen.

'Kevin,' I said again, 'my name is Torey. Do you remember Miss Wendolowski telling you someone was coming out to work with you? That's me. I'm Torey and I work with people who have a hard time talking.'

Still he rocked. I wasn't given even the slightest acknowledgment. All around us hung a heavy, cloying silence embroidered with the rhythmic sound of his body hitting against the linoleum.

I started to talk to him, keeping my voice soft and welcoming, the way one talks to timid puppies. I talked of why I had come, of what I was going to be doing with him, of other children whom I had worked with and had success. I told him about myself. What I said wasn't important, only the tone was.

No response. He only rocked.

The minutes slipped away. I was running dry of things to say. Such a one-sided conversation was not easy to maintain, but what made it more difficult was not Zoo-boy so much as the ghostly presence of those beyond the mirror. It was too easy to feel stupid talking to oneself when half a dozen people one couldn't see were watching. Finally, I pulled over my box of materials and sorted out a paperback book, a mystery story about a teenager and his girl friend. I'll read to you, I told Zoo-boy, until we feel a little more relaxed with one another.

'Chapter One: The Long Road.'

I read.

And read.

The minutes kept moving around the face of the clock. Occasionally there was the muffled noise of a door opening and closing beyond our little room. They were leaving, one by one. Nothing in here was worth wasting an afternoon to see. I was not a spectacular reader. The story wasn't riveting. And Zoo-boy only rocked.

I kept on reading. And counting the openings and closings. How many people had been in the room behind the mirror? I couldn't recall exactly. Six? Or was it seven? And how many had gone out already? Five?

I read on.

Click-click. Another gone.

Click-click. That was seven.

I continued to read. My voice became the only sound in the room. I looked over. Zoo-boy had stopped rocking.

Slowly he brought his arms down to see me better. He smiled. He was nobody's fool. He had been counting too.

He gestured at me, a small movement within the confines of the table and chairs.

'What?' I asked, because I couldn't understand what he was trying to communicate.

He gestured again, more widely this time. Only it wasn't just a simple motion. Rather, it was a sentence, a paragraph almost, of gestures.

I still couldn't understand. I moved a chair aside to see him better but I had to ask him to repeat it.

There was something he wanted me to know. The motions were poetic in their gyrating, wreathing urgency. A hand ballet. But they were no sign language I understood, not Ameslan, not the hand alphabet. I couldn't comprehend at all.

From under the table came a deep sigh. He grimaced at me. Then patiently he repeated his gestures again, more slowly this time, more emphatically, like someone speaking to a rather stupid child. He became frustrated when he could not make me understand.

Finally, he gave up. We sat in silence, staring at one another. The book was still in my hands, so in desperation to fill the time, I asked him if he'd like me to read a little more. Zoo-boy nodded.

I settled back against the wall. 'Chapter Five: Out of the Cave.'

Zoo-boy pushed the other chair slightly out from the table and reached to touch the cloth of my jeans. I looked up.

He had his mouth open, one hand pulling the lower jaw down. He pointed down his throat. Then dismally, he shook his head.

Chapter Two

For a little over a year I had been working at the clinic as a research psychologist. Most of my professional life had been spent as a teacher. While in education I had held a variety of positions, running the full gamut from teaching a regular first-grade class to teaching graduate-level university students, from working in an open-plan progressive school to working in a locked classroom on the children's unit of a state mental institution. I loved teaching. I always had; I still did. But then, as years passed, the general philosophies, particularly in special education, began to shift and I grew to feel like a stranger in my own world.

At that point I decided to work on a doctorate in special education. I'm not sure why. I never particularly wanted the degree itself, it would overqualify me and I could never return to the classroom with it. And no other aspect of education

appealed to me. I certainly would never make an adminis-
trator. But I went ahead and started the doctorate anyway.
In the final analysis I suppose it was simply something to do
while I tried to decide what direction my life should take
next.

In my deep heart of hearts I was hoping that the philo-
sophical pendulum would swing again in education and
I could return to the classroom without compromising my
own beliefs. However, as I dragged out my studies over four
years, the change did not come, and I was faced with the brutal decision either of actually getting the degree and slam-
ming shut the classroom door forever or of leaving the whole
thing messily unfinished and trying something new. In the
end, I chose the latter route because I just couldn't confront
the thought of never being able to return to teaching in the
future. So I moved away from Minneapolis and the university with nothing to show for my four years there.

Throughout my career I had been working on research into
a little-known psychological phenomenon known as elective mutism. This is an emotional disturbance occurring pri-
marily in children. The child is physically capable of speaking but for psychological reasons refuses to do so. Most of
these youngsters actually do speak somewhere, usually at
home with their families, but they are voluntarily mute
everywhere else. Over the years I had accrued a large body
of data on this problem and developed treatment methods.
Thus, when I saw an advertisement for a child psychologist,
a research position with some clinical work, it seemed a reasonable solution to the difficulties I was having with my own
field.

As the months passed, I found I was happy enough in my work at the clinic, but it was different from teaching. The children were parceled out to me, mostly by virtue of their language or lack of it, since that was my specialty. But they were never *my* children. In the few hours a week that I saw them, each individually, there was no opportunity for that small, self-contained civilization to develop when the door to the outer world was closed.

The clinic, however, did provide a lot of advantages. It was pleasant to be in the company of adults again for the major part of my working day. It wasn't so much because I preferred their company but rather for the side benefits. I could wear decent clothes and put on makeup and not worry if some kid was going to spit up on my dry-clean-only blazer or escape the room because I wasn't wearing my sure-grip track shoes. I could wear my long hair loose without worrying about someone pulling it out of my head. And perhaps best of all, I could wear skirts again. I didn't need the freedom of movement and washability jeans provided, more to the point, my legs were not covered with bruises from being kicked constantly.

Association with my new colleagues at the clinic was reason enough to take the job. All of them were well educated, experienced, intelligent and expressive. There was always someone to kick an idea around with. In addition, there were other good points. I had magnificent facilities at my disposal, including a large, airy, sunlit therapy room, brand-new toys and equipment, a video recorder that worked, a computer down the hall and a statistician to go with it who spoke genuine English. Moreover, I had recognition for my work.

I had a good salary. And I had more free time than I had ever had before. So, all in all, I was happy enough.

Then came Zoo-boy.

I hadn't especially wanted the case. Right from the beginning the hopelessness shone through. One morning a social worker named Dana Wendolowski from the Garson Gayer Home had phoned the clinic in search of me. We have a boy for you, she told me, and the weary despair was a little too clear in her voice.

His name was Kevin Richter, although no one seemed to call him Kevin. He had earned his nickname because he spent all his waking hours under tables, chairs lined up in front of him and around the perimeter of the table until he was secure behind a protective barrier of wooden legs. There he sat, rocked sometimes, ate, did his schoolwork, watched TV. There he lived in his little self-built cage. Zoo-boy.

But Kevin's problem went deeper than just an affinity for tables. He did not talk. He made no noise, even when he wept. The files claimed he had talked once upon a time, a long time ago. According to the sketchily drawn past in the Garson Gayer records, Kevin had never spoken at school when he'd attended. He was retained once and then twice because he did not talk to the teachers and no one knew whether or not he was learning. He had talked at home, at least that's what the report said. And then he'd stopped. First he stopped talking to his stepfather, then a little later to his mother. Supposedly, he continued to speak to his younger sisters but by the time he was committed to the first residential treatment program, at nine, someone noticed Kevin was not speaking at all. No one could say exactly when he stopped talking. One day someone asked, and no one could remember the last time they had heard Kevin. And no one had heard him since.

Far more apparent than his lack of speech were Kevin's fears. He lived in morbid, gut-wrenching fear of almost everything, his life was consumed by it. He feared highways and door hinges and spirals on notebooks and dogs and darkness and pliers and odd bits of string that might fall on the floor. He was too terrified of water to bathe; too superstitious of being without clothes to change them. And for the last three years Kevin had refused to set foot outside the door of the Garson Gayer residence. He had actually stayed inside all that time. Kevin's fears had trapped him in a far more secure prison than he could ever have built with tables and chairs.

As the social worker told me these things I braced my forehead on one fist, the receiver of the phone in the crook of my neck. With my other hand I filled the margin of the desk blotter with doodles. The woman's voice had a hurried desperation to it, as if she knew I would cut her short before she had said everything she needed to say.

Garson Gayer was a new facility, a model progressive institution. They had a full staff, including a resident psychologist, speech therapists, nurses and teachers. Why did they want me? I asked.

She had read about my work. She'd heard I worked with children who did not speak. I wondered aloud, Why, when there was so much wrong with this boy, had they decided to tackle his lack of speech? Well, you have to start somewhere, she replied, and her laugh was hollow. The phone grew quiet for a moment. Truth is, she said, it's not quite like that. Kevin would be sixteen in mid-September and here it was, already late August. Garson Gayer only took children up through their fifteenth birthdays, so the rules had already been bent for him to allow him to stay this long. The state had custody of Kevin. And so far nothing they'd done for him at Garson Gayer had produced any improvement. If they couldn't come up with something soon, well … She did not say it. She didn't have to. We both knew the places boys like Kevin went, who had no family, no money, no hope.

He sounded like a lost cause right from the beginning. He had a lousy past. Very little useful data was recorded in the Garson Gayer file but there was enough to make Kevin's childhood sound like so many others I had known. School failures, financial difficulties, physical abuse of Kevin and other children in the family, marital troubles, friction between Kevin and his stepfather, alcohol abuse, and perhaps most sinister of all, the fact that Kevin had been voluntarily given into state custody by his mother. What must a kid be like when even his own mother did not want him? Moreover, Kevin had spent seven years already in institutions, more than eight totally mute, and almost sixteen learning to feel comfortable being crazy. If that wasn't the portrait of a loser, I didn't know what would be.

I didn't want this case. As it was, I already had too many children to become involved with one who would obviously be a black hole – a maw to dump time and energy and effort into with no return. And as I sat and listened and drew geometric designs on the blotter, I had an even more shameful thought. This was a private clinic; we usually didn't get the welfare kids.

All I had to do to get rid of this case was mention money in a very serious way. While Garson Gayer would obviously foot the bill for my initial work with Kevin Richter, if I didn't want the case, well, that would be the easiest way. . . .

It was tempting. It was a good deal more tempting to refuse this case than I was ready to admit. Yet I couldn't. I could think such thoughts but I couldn't make myself act on them. It would have been so different in the schoolroom. Ed or Birk or Lew simply would have rung me from the Special Ed Office and told me, 'I've got a new kid for you.' And I would have groused because I always groused, and they wouldn't have noticed because they never did. Then he'd be mine, that loser, that kid with no hope, who couldn't make it anywhere else, and we'd try there in my room, amidst the battered books and the rummage-sale toys and noisy finches and the stink of unchanged pants, to build another chance. We didn't succeed very often. Our triumphs, when they did come, were few and small. Sometimes no one else even noticed them. But it didn't matter. I never thought of not trying, only because I never had the godly privilege of judging if I should. Or if I could. Or if I would. So, while not wanting this case, I took it and agreed to come. Given the option and seeing the odds, I sure wasn't keen about it. But I did not think that should be my decision.

Because of my classroom experience and my research, I had evolved therapeutic techniques which varied a little from those of my colleagues at the clinic. I preferred to see the more seriously disturbed children daily over a shorter period of time, rather than once a week over many months or years.

Also I often went to the child instead of having him come to the clinic, so that we could work in the troubled environment. In the initial sessions, I was very definite about setting up expectations for the child. From the beginning we both knew why I was there and what things we needed to accomplish together. On the other hand, the sessions themselves tended to be casual, unstructured affairs. This approach worked well for me and I was comfortable with it.

My research had yielded a reliable method for treating elective mutes. I set up the expectation that the child would speak, gave him the opportunity to do so and assumed he would. However, I was not sure what I could do for Kevin-under-the-table. While the technique had always worked before, I was concerned about its applicability to him. The most critical question, I thought, as I hung up from talking with the social worker, was whether or not Kevin *was* an elective mute. *Had* he ever really talked? To a worried or wishful parent, so many noises could sound like words. By my calculations, he would have been a very young child when anyone last actually heard him speak, and then it had only been his immediate family. Could a five-year-old sister be a trusted judge of speech? Could a mother assess the quality of her preschool son's words, if she only occasionally heard him talk at home? And there was no evidence at all that anyone who might be considered a reliable judge of normal speech had ever heard him. Kevin wasn't deaf; that had been checked repeatedly by the various institutions he had been in. He could gesture his basic needs but he did not know true sign language. Someone had tried to teach him at Garson Gayer, but a suspected very low IQ was cited when he didn't learn.

For all intents and purposes, Kevin was noncommunicative.
Whether his silence was the result of choice or of circumstances or of disturbance or of some organic occurrence in
the brain, no one knew.

So what could I do with him? How could I find out?

That first day in the therapy room had been vaguely reassuring to me. Despite his bizarre behaviors, he was aware
enough of his environment to do something as canny as
count the people leaving the room behind the mirror. That
wasn't a stupid boy's actions, whatever his reported IQ. And
yet he had let me in on the secret. When the others had left,
he stopped rocking and responded to me.

Another thing I knew he could do was read. In fact, according to Kevin's written schoolwork, he read startlingly well
for a boy educated in institutions as if mentally retarded. He
could comprehend a written text at a seventh-grade level.

Armed with these scanty bits of information, I decided to
plow my way right in, assume he could talk and try to get him
to. I settled on a tactic that had worked with other elective
mutes: I'd have him read aloud to me from the book we'd
started in the mirrored therapy room.

The next morning I returned to Garson Gayer. Gratefully, I
accepted an alternative room down near the ward rather than
go back to the room with the one-way mirror. The other
therapists needed that room, Miss Wendolowski said, and I
was quite glad not to have it. Kevin and I did not need the
worry of ghosts along with everything else.

The room we got was a bare little affair. It was small. I could
pace it in four steps either direction. The only furniture

consisted of a table, two chairs and a bookcase with no books in it. There was a vomit-green carpet, the kind that wears like Astroturf. One wall was half windows, a nice feature. A broad radiator ran along the length below the windows and uttered a small reptilian sound. All other walls were bare and painted white, a not-quite-white white, gloss two-thirds of the way up for washability and the rest flat paint. That was an institutional painting habit and I hated it. I always felt as if I were in a discreet cage and, when a teacher, I'd felt obliged to hang the kids' work up there on the flat part and get it mucky, just for the freedom of it. Here there were no pictures on the walls at all, no posters, nothing, save a black-and-white clock that audibly breathed the minutes. And the pale golden September sunshine.

I arrived before Kevin that morning. An aide escorted me down and then left to fetch him. I stood alone in the small room and waited. Beyond the windows I could see a little girl outside in the courtyard. She looked to be about eight or nine and was confined to a wheelchair. Her movements were spastic and her head lolled to one side. I could hear her crying for someone named Winnie. Over and over again she wailed, her voice high-pitched and keening. It was a lonely sound that made my skin crawl.

The door opened and the aide pushed Kevin in. Then, without entering himself, the aide asked me when we'd be through. Thirty minutes, I replied. He nodded, jangled his keys a moment and seemed ready to say something else. But he didn't. Instead he closed the door and I heard the key turn in the lock. That startled me. I had no key of my own to let us out and I hadn't expected to be locked in. A small twinge of panic pinched my stomach and I had to take a deep breath before I could accept the fact and turn to face Kevin.

He stood paralyzed with fear. His eyes darted frantically around the room. I was between him and the table and I could see him weighing the danger of passing me to get to safety.

He was a tall youth. It was the first time I'd had a real look at him, and he was a big boy, nearly a man, although an aura of youngness clung to him. He was at least as tall as I was, but thin and frail looking, like a winter cornstalk. Brown hair fell lank over his forehead. Adolescence had ravaged his skin, leaving him with lumpy features and cheeks smothered in acne. Thick-lensed glasses slid down his nose, in spite of a black elastic strap to keep them in place. His eyes were gray and lifeless as a city puddle. He wore church-box clothes, a hopelessly too-small red-checked flannel shirt and gabardine trousers that barely covered the tops of his socks. He looked more like a cartoonist's caricature of a boy than a real person.

God, he was ugly.

A moment of hopelessness washed over me as I looked at him. Stepping aside, I allowed room for him to pass. Relief flooded his features and he dived past me and under the table.

The chairs went up, seats facing outward, backs tight against the table. I stood watching while he fashioned his cage. He was not shutting me out. He smiled pleasantly at me and gestured in a friendly manner, and I knew it was not me that he felt so compelled to protect himself from. The disquieting fact was that there was no one else in the room, nothing but the walls and the pale sunlight.

I pondered how to work with him, whether to sit on the floor outside the makeshift barricade, as I had in the mirrored therapy room, or whether to join him under the table. After another moment of indecision, I dropped down on my hands and knees and crawled under the table too. He welcomed me with a pleased smile, moved over to make room, of which there wasn't much, until we both sat hunched together like gnomes in the semidarkness.

We were only inches from one another. He smelled rather gamey at that distance, and so I just sat for a few minutes, accustoming myself to the lack of light and the cramped space and the odor. Kevin began to rock slightly, his arms clasped tight around his knees, his chin resting atop. He stared at me without wavering.

Well, now what? I really was feeling awfully pessimistic at just that moment. Leaning out, I pulled my box of materials into the cage with us. Taking off the lid, I searched through it for the book we had been reading.

It's scary, I said to Kevin as I dug through the junk in the box, to start talking when one has been silent so long. But the easiest way to start is to jump right in.

There were other kids, I said, whom I had worked with, who hadn't been speaking either. I told Kevin about them, of how they had felt before they'd started talking again, of how scary it was the first time and how sure they'd all been that they couldn't do it. But they could. Every single child had been able to talk in the end, I said, and nothing bad had happened to any of them for it. There was nothing to be frightened of. They all were, because that was the way it felt in the beginning, but there actually was nothing to fear in the end. It was just a feeling.

I spoke in a slow, easy voice, letting it reek with confidence.

I lounged back to the extent one could lounge back while sitting under a table with a large fifteen-year-old, so that he could see how relaxed I was, how certain I was of success.

Opening the book, I feigned great interest in it, looking at all the illustrations and I kept talking, oozing self-assurance like a car salesman. Then I laid the book on the carpet. What we're going to do, I said to him, is have you read to me. Let's start here.

Kevin looked at me in alarm.

'Right here, I think,' I said. 'I read those chapters yesterday, so we'll have you start right here. Chapter Seven: The Tide Goes Out.'

Kevin grabbed my arm and shook his head violently. His eyes were dilated wide with horror.

'Yes, I know. It's not something you're used to doing. But that's okay. Nothing will happen. And everybody's a little afraid when they first get started. That's natural.' I tried to sound very casual, as if this were a most usual thing. Kevin, however, knew it to be highly unusual. He had the look of a frightened horse, that wild, whites-of-the-eyes expression, with his head turned to one side.

Smoothing the pages out, I pointed to the first word. 'We'll start with just this one word, okay? Forget the rest of them. Just look at this one. What is it?'

He rocked a little harder and the table shuddered.

'Here, look at it. This one word. Give it a try.'

Kevin regarded the page. He still had his frightened-horse look. Bringing a hand up, he rubbed his forehead and then pulled his palm down across his face, dragging it out of shape. Then tentatively, he put one finger under the first word.

Seconds passed.

'What is that word? Look at it. What is it?'

Kevin took a deep breath.

'The first word is always the hardest one. After that, it's a cinch. You'll see.'

He started to rock again. I could hear his breath coming shallowly, the fear rattling up through his throat.

'Only that first word. That word. How does it start? Come on. Get that word.'

Kevin was taking me seriously. He was going to try. Bringing his other hand down, he ran it along the perimeter of the book, then stopped it to steady the page. Cautiously, as if the book might leap up and nip him, he bent over it until he was hunched almost double. In the gloom under the table, that movement obscured what little light we did have on the page.

He took another deep breath. All the while I kept urging, kept talking to keep the silence at bay. I didn't want him to hear the silence and know it was stronger than I was.

A third big breath, shakier this time. He lifted his hand and wiped the sweat off on his shirt front. A wet stain had been left where his finger was on the page. Frantically he tried to erase it, and when he couldn't, he glanced over at me to see what my reaction was. Then he put his hand back over it to cover it.

He needed another minute to rock. It was not easy to do in his hunched position and the whole table shook.

'Let's go. Let's have a try.'

He opened his mouth. No sound, not even a breath. Seconds drew into minutes. He closed his mouth again.

My constant patter continued. Come on, come on, come on. Let's go. Let's try.

Again Kevin began taking breaths in preparation. His mouth opened and closed like a fish's as he would get ready to try and then lose courage. He started to tap the word with a finger, and that small steady, penetrating sound soon filled up the space around us.

'Have a go. Come on, Kev, you can do it. I know you can. This is just the way it happens, give it a try.'

A funny noise joined the cacophony of taps and tries. Kevin's teeth were chattering. At first I had to sit back a little to identify the sound, and that made him look over at me. I could see them chatter. I smiled. Kevin lurched back over the book again with determination. He had begun to believe me. He was going to get that word.

Sweat beaded on his upper lip. His hands shook. Big, dark circles dampened his shirt under his arms and down the center of his back, and the smell was incredible. Still he opened and closed his mouth in abortive tries. He made big, wide circles with it, as if trying to stretch it into working order.

Minute after minute after minute was filled with his grimaces and with my nonstop patter until I felt like we were caught in a time vortex. Kevin undoubtedly thought we were caught in hell. The cords of his neck were taut. Veins stood out at his temples. His face was crimson.

I could hear the mechanical respirations of the black-and-white clock on the wall. Leaning out from under the table, I looked up at it. Twenty-three minutes had passed.

The aide would be returning soon. In an attempt to startle Kevin out of this nonproductive cycle he'd gotten trapped in, I whacked the floor with the flat of my hand. Often enough that worked with other children and we would leap right over the first word. But not this time. Startled, Kevin only bumped his head on the underside of the tabletop. Rubbing it tenderly, he bent forward and attacked the word anew. He brought a hand to his mouth and tried to force his lips into the shape of the word. The word was 'every' and soon it required both hands to stretch his lips back into the shape of an *e*. Sweat dropped from his face down onto the page. The ever-present sound of his teeth chattering echoed in our enclosure.

I slid back out from under the table and sat up straight, rubbing the tense muscles in my back. The thirty minutes were nearly over and we weren't going to have success. If he hadn't been trying so desperately, I don't think I would have felt as disheartened as I did, but it was apparent Kevin cared. Unfortunately, caring wasn't enough.

'Well, we'll call it a day, shall we?' I said and reached in for the book. 'It's not such a big matter that it didn't work out this time. That happens lots. We'll try again tomorrow.'

He looked at me. Tears puddled up and then ran down over his cheeks.

Chapter Three

Puzzled, I drove back to the clinic after the session. Kevin appeared to be trying so hard. Very rarely had I had a kid who had tried like that right from the beginning. It made him enjoyable to work with because it was the two of us together against the problem. However, I was not so naïve as not to wonder why. Why would he appear to want to talk again so willingly, if he were able to speak, but was refusing to do so? That didn't make very good sense. What *was* his exact problem? How did his lack of speech tie in? Did his fears cause his inability to talk? Or did his failure to speak cause the fears? Or were they even related? Perhaps what nagged at me most was the uncertainty that Kevin could, indeed, talk. If he couldn't, that clearly would account for why he didn't. And it probably would account as well for why he was trying so hard, if he believed I could give him a power he did not possess. The lack of information on this boy who had been in and out of institutions for so many years was appalling. Was it possible Kevin had never spoken normally? Could he have been deprived of speech through some accident or organic factor? Was I trying to force him to do something he was physically or mentally incapable of doing? Had he some sort of insidious mental illness like schizophrenia which had stolen speech from him, as it sometimes does?

There were so many questions about this boy. Questions without answers.

'Someone phoned for you,' Jeff said when I arrived back in my office at the clinic. He was bent over *The New England Journal of Medicine* and did not bother to look up.

'Who was it? Did you answer it?' I asked. Jeff was loath to answer the phone under most circumstances. A child psychiatrist in his last years of training, Jeff shared a closet-sized office with me, which used to house rats and pigeons when the former occupant, Dr Kirk, was into his rats-and-pigeons phase. The room still smelled a little like a rodent-infested aviary. There were no windows, which did not help the smell any, but we were hardly cut off from the outside. Instead, we had three telephones between the two of us, all with different numbers. His, mine and ours. I had no idea why there were three since the room was too small to accommodate another desk and Dr Kirk, for all his cleverness, had not been training a zoological answering service. But there it was, that third phone, residing on a chair between our two desks, and an odd assortment of calls still came in over it. Consequently, the room was usually alive with ringing. Jeff, if he could help it, never answered any of the three.

I began taking off my jacket. 'I said, Jeff, did you answer it?'

'Yes.' His article must have been awfully riveting.

'Well, who was it? What did they want?'

'I don't know.' He looked up at last. 'They hung up.'

My silence was adequate reply.

'I did *too* ask! Don't look at me like that.'

I dropped my box of materials on the desk and slumped into my chair. All along my back the muscles were sore. I hadn't realized at the time how much I'd been empathizing with Kevin's distress. For several moments I just sat, letting the muscles relax, not really thinking at all. My eyes rose up the wall in front of me to the confusion of things on my bulletin board. It was kind of a portrait of my mind turned inside out–kids' drawings, a button in Welsh protesting nuclear energy, four photographs, my calendar with all its visual proof that I did not need a case like Kevin's, my rotation schedule sheet, a few brightly colored leaves, caught falling from the trees to fulfill that old superstition about good luck for twelve leaves caught in autumn, a gigantic poster of a Cheshire cat, the framed poem in childish hand by one of my former students. Kevin sat at the very back of my mind, pushed there by nothingness. I had meant to ask Jeff's ideas on the case but I was momentarily drained. I just sat.

Then the phone rang, shattering what little sense I had put back into my head.

* * *

We had a community program known as Big Brothers/Big Sisters which was designed to provide underprivileged children, especially those from broken homes, with the chance to enjoy a caring relationship with an adult. I had participated in the program before but had given it up when I was teaching because I didn't have enough time. Now without a class of my own, without my usual daily fix of rascality, I'd decided to rejoin.

The woman was calling to tell me that they had matched me with an eight-year-old Native American girl. She apologized for not being able to get hold of me sooner because that evening they were holding an open house for the new participants. She hoped very much that I'd be able to make it on such short notice.

She was a scruffy-looking little kid, a bit on the chubby side with grimy chipmunk cheeks and two Band-Aids on her forehead. She wore patched blue corduroy pants, a pink-striped polyester top covered in fuzz balls and a red cardigan with the top button buttoned. Her hair was in two long, fist-thick braids. And I suspect she had more teeth missing from her mouth than were in it. So she hissed like a snake when saying *S*'s and she sprayed.

'You my Big Sister?' she asked as I wandered into the room. We both had name tags on. Hers was upside down. I turned my head to read it. Charity Stands-On-Top.

'Yup. I'm Torey.'

She gave me a big, toothless grin. We sat down together on one of the long benches. I had a glass of cherry Kool-Aid and two cookies in my hands. Charity had obviously been imbibing already because she had a bright red mustache.

'Is one of them cookies mine?' she inquired politely. It hadn't been. I suspect she had probably already had her quota but I gave it to her anyway. Another huge, face-splitting grin.

'So, well then, what you gonna do with me?' she asked, and put the cookie whole into her mouth. 'Where you gonna take me? My other Big Sister, Diana, she used to take me to the movies. You gonna take me to the movies?'

'Maybe,' I said.

'Well, then, I got to have popcorn—buttered popcorn—when I go to the movies. And a big-sized Pepsi. Or maybe Coke. That'd be okay too. And one of them big suckers that lasts long. And a box of jelly Dots. Diana, she used to buy me all of them things. Every time.'

'I see.'

'She used to buy me other stuff too. You gonna buy me stuff?'

'What sort of stuff?'

She shrugged. 'Just stuff,' she answered ambiguously and eyed the remainder of my other cookie. 'Good stuff,' she continued when I offered no comment and no cookie. 'You know. Not clothes or anything. I ain't a poor kid. You don't have to go buying me no clothes. What I need's good stuff. Like once, Diana bought me this Tonka truck. You know. One of them real big ones that you can sit on and dig up the yard.'

'Oh. I see.'

'Her name was Diana. Did I tell you that? What's your name again?'

'Torey.'

'Oh yeah. I forgot. That's a weird name. Where'd you get a weird name like that at?'

'It's from Victoria.'

'Oh. That's an even weirder name.' Charity looked me over in a very appraising manner and I felt like a piece of livestock at an auction.

'I thought you'd be prettier,' she said at last.

Not knowing exactly how to field that one, I just shrugged.

'You got funny-looking eyes. Why are they that color? Do you wear contact lenses?'

'No.'

'Diana did. She was practically blind. And they kept falling out. Once they dropped right out and we had to look all over the floor at Woolworth's on our hands and knees and then this guy comes in and he goes *CRUNCH!*' Charity fell about with laughter. I finished my Kool-Aid.

'You don't got much to say, do you?' she said to me. 'You got a funny voice. Is that why? Are you embarrassed? Where did you get your funny voice at? Is something wrong with it?'

'I don't think so. I was born with it.'

There was a long, long pause while Charity regarded me further. Then she shook her head with resignation. 'You really aren't very interesting, are you?'

I could hardly have described Charity that way. Full of cheeky arrogance and a surety about herself that was intimidating, Charity was convinced she owned the world. Five minutes with her and I knew that. I also knew that if Charity had been the first kid I'd ever met, I'd probably not have chosen a career working with children.

I supposed she was a street kid, wiser at eight than I'd be at eighty. She had that streetwise air about her, the confidence that shifting for oneself gives. Yet she was terribly disarming with her chubby cheeks and her Band-Aids and her huge, gaping grin.

'So,' she said, her mouth full with a cookie she'd charmed off the refreshments lady, 'what do you do when you ain't here?'

'I work. With kids.'

'Oh? What kind of kids? Where at? Do I know 'em?'

'I work at the Sandry Clinic.'

'Ohhhhhh,' she replied with a wise nod. '*Them* kind of kids. What's the matter with your kids? They jump up and down? My brother jumps up and down and he wets the bed. He went to one of them places once. But you know what? It didn't do no good. He still wets the bed.'

'That happens sometimes.'

'So what they like, your kids? What do they do?'

I told her about Kevin. I would hardly have expected myself to, but I did. I told how this boy had lived in a treatment home all these years and how he hadn't talked in ever so long a time. I told how we sat together under the table and tried to read. The strength of Kevin's fears came back to me, and I tried to describe to Charity what it had been like being with him when he was so afraid.

Charity was leaning forward, her chin in her hands. She listened carefully. 'Why do *you* go to work with him?' she asked.

'Because that's what my job is.'

'He sounds weird to me.'

'He is weird. But that's okay. I don't mind that.'

'Can I meet him sometimes? Will you take me to meet him?'

'Maybe. Someday maybe.'

'He'd talk to me. I'd say, "Kid, you don't have to be scared of me. I'm just a little kid." Then he'd talk to me.'

'The trouble is,' I said, 'we don't even know if he can talk. Maybe we're trying to make him do something he can't really do.'

'How come you don't know?'

'Because we don't know,' I replied, feeling a little exasperated. 'That's how come.'

A look of disdain crossed her face and she leaned back on the bench. 'You're silly. That's the silliest thing I ever heard.'

'What is? Why?'

'Well, how come if you don't know, you don't ask him? How come you don't just say, "Kid, can you talk?" Then you'd know.' She smiled affably. 'How you supposed to know, if you don't ask?'

Chapter Four

The staff behind the front desk at Garson Gayer were beginning to recognize me. They called Hello to me from behind their glass partition as I came past. When I went in the back room to get a cup of coffee, I could hear one woman tell the other who I was: Zoo-boy's therapist. Come to try and make him talk, she said, and I could tell from her tone of voice that she didn't think it would happen. I hung up my jacket and went on down to the small white room. I didn't even have the secretaries fooled.

Kevin and I had no more success this second try than we had had the day before. The only variation was that the tears came sooner. Over his pimply cheeks, down onto his chin they rolled to drip off onto the book where he would rub them out furiously with his fingers, leaving big smeary blobs on the paper. However, never once did the tears deter him.

He kept trying. Long after I was ready to give up, long after the whole enterprise took on a dreary, somewhat perverse mood, Kevin kept trying, kept laboring away to get cooperation out of his voice and his mouth and his heart. And he kept failing.

The hell was not Kevin's alone. It had fast become mine as well. I felt as trapped in his fears as I did in the table-and-chairs cage. There was an odd, deviant feel to his efforts because, while he tried so hard, futility was draped over us as tangibly as a cloak. I could not shake it off. Like Sisyphus rolling his huge stone to the hilltop, Kevin continued to struggle but with the foregone conclusion that regardless of the effort, the stone would go rolling back down again. That was the perversity of it to me, that he could appear to try so hard and still emanate such hopelessness.

Every muscle in my body grew rigid. I had a headache from clenching my teeth too tightly. My own voice faltered. I had urged and coaxed and cajoled until even coffee could not lubricate my throat enough.

Kevin trembled. His shoulders shook. Even his head shook. I could hear fear-torn breath come through chattering teeth. And all the effort was in vain.

Finally I put my hand over the book. Our time was nearly up. 'We'll try again tomorrow, okay?'

He regarded me wistfully. His chin trembled a little more.

'We'll get it done, Kevin. Don't worry.'

But clearly he did.

'Kevin, I want to ask you something.'

He watched me.

'*Can* you talk? I mean, *can* you? Are you able to?'

His eyes fell. To the carpet. To the book. To his hands. A great silence loomed up which was both divisive, putting infinity between us, and binding. For a boy who said nothing, he certainly left nothing unsaid.

'Kevin?'

He gestured. I didn't understand. He gestured again and grimaced, frustration sharpening the movements of his hands. But I was stupid. Disgruntled, he smacked the floor with his fingers, and we sat again in silence.

'Can you, Kevin?'

His eyes came back to me, back to meet my eyes. He nodded.

'You can?'

He shrugged.

'You can, though. You *can* talk? You can but you don't? You won't? Is it something like that?'

An incomplete gesture with one hand and then he dropped it. He shrugged again and stared only at the carpet.

'Why don't you then?'

He began to cry, his mouth dragged down in misery. I thought to put my arms around him and comfort him but I didn't. I shouldn't. The silence between us told me that much, so I just sat, my hands in my lap. Kevin only wept harder, his big man-sized fingers locking and unlocking. His shoulders shook. But no sound came from him.

On my way back to the clinic from Garson Gayer, I stopped in town to pick up some labels from the printer's. As I was walking down the street toward the print shop, I passed a drugstore window filled with an array of Halloween decorations for sale. I had gone completely by the store before being pulled back to pause and gaze at the display. Black cats on pumpkins, honeycomb jack-o'-lanterns, glow-in-the-dark skeletons, ghost lapel pins, a book of Pumpkin carols and other *Peanuts* memorabilia lined the window.

A profound, aching nostalgia flooded me as I stood there. I no longer had any children to buy decorations for, no longer had a reason to make a room gay with orange and black crepe paper. Suddenly my life seemed so empty, cast adrift as I was in an all-adult world.

I could hear the kids. Standing right there on a city street in front of the drugstore, I could hear things like Robbie Cutmar's gleeful whoops when I had pulled that big, honeycomb pumpkin out of the bag. It had cost me $3.98 in a year when $3.98 was a lot of money to me but it had been such a glorious thing. We made legends about that pumpkin, about where it had come from, about the mysterious things it must have seen when our dingy little classroom was empty for the night. Halloween came and went and still we couldn't take that pumpkin down. It'd stayed with us in the classroom until almost April, until Tessa had accidentally fallen on it during a seizure and smashed it flat. And yet, for all its glory, that pumpkin wasn't nearly so splendid as any of these in this window. That was the problem, I thought sadly. I could now afford to buy whichever pumpkin in the window I wanted but there was no place in my life to put it.

The window display proved too attractive. I had to go inside the drugstore to look at the things more carefully. All the while a black-hearted little gremlin sat somewhere inside me and chided me for the irrationality of what I was doing.

After all, I had no class now; I might never have one again. I didn't have any children of my own. I had no excuse to buy things like this for myself. But at the same time I fingered the change in my pocket, counting how much was there beyond what had to be spent at the printer's.

I succumbed. I got a little package containing two cardboard bats with honeycomb bodies to be attached. With a piece of thread they could fly. Then I picked up a copy of the Pumpkin Carols. I'd always been an ardent *Peanuts* fan. One of the greatest pleasures of my career had been the last year I'd taught, when the kids had gone together and bought me a Snoopy wristwatch as an end-of-the-year present.

Paging through the songbook, I giggled aloud. Then I turned it over to see the price. One dollar. A whole crummy dollar for four pages and seven songs. What an awful lot of money for something like that. Especially when I did not need it. I put it back.

Aimlessly I wandered around the store and looked at other things, at birthday cards and ball-point pens. I walked through the aisles of shampoos and cotton balls and nail clippers. But I wasn't being very successful. I could actually hear the kids singing those stupid little songs. *But there aren't any kids now!* Still, I could hear them. And without half trying I could see their faces. Whoever said an active imagination is a blessing?

I returned to the display, lifted the songbook, flipped through the pages again. Then like a shoplifter, I slipped the book under my arm so that I would not have to acknowledge to my black-hearted little gremlin that I was doing such a stupid thing as buying it.

Back in the office I tore open the package with the two cardboard bats and punched them out of the sheet. Laying out the directions in case I got desperate enough to resort to them, I began assembling the things. It was no mean feat. A Ph.D. in engineering would have been the most helpful.

'What the *hell* are you doing?' Jeff stood in the doorway.

Having stacked three of his medical dictionaries on top of my desk, I was standing on them in an attempt to reach the ceiling. We worked in an old building and the ceilings must have been at least eleven feet high.

'I'm hanging these bats.'

He shut the door and came across to my desk. Skeptically, he gazed up. 'Escaped from your belfry at last, did they?'

I made a face at him.

'Where did you get the idea that we needed bats hanging in here?'

Finally I managed to get one thumbtack into the ceiling and then reached up to tie a thread around it. Even with three massive books under me, I was not tall enough.

'You're not intending on hanging any of those over my desk, are you, Hayden? They're not going over there.'

The thread was refusing to cooperate. Once I did get it around, it pulled the thumbtack out of the ceiling when I tried to tie it. That, along with Jeff's comments, was serving to stretch my vocabulary into a more colorful vein than I normally used.

Jeff's interest, however, was definitely aroused. He was leaning over my desk and staring up. 'Why don't you make a loop first?' he asked.

'Why don't you move off?'

'I mean, put the tack in, then make a loop and try to lasso it.'

'Don't worry about it, Jeff. I'll manage fine.'

Jeff went over to his desk and picked up his new edition of *The Physician's Desk Reference* and brought it back. He nudged my leg. 'Here, Hayden, move over. Let me do it.'

Within moments we were both balanced on books atop my desk with cardboard bats swinging from our hands.

I liked Jeff. Everyone liked Jeff. There was something about him which was innately likeable, but it was a mercurial, undefinable quality. He was tall but not particularly handsome, at least not in the classic handsome-doctor way. He was more what you'd call cute, like a boy you'd take home to Mother when you were in high school. His hair was brown and wavy, a few freckles were still left on his nose and he had never had his teeth straightened, so when he smiled, it came out a cheerful, lop-sided grin. He had an unsurpassable sense of humor, brash, zany and somewhat more juvenile than one would expect from a doctor. Secretly, I suspected that was the reason Jeff and I had been sequestered off together. Between the two of us, we pretty much comprised the clinic's contribution toward New Wave psychiatry. But for all his beguiling boyishness, Jeff was brilliant. Of all the people I had met in my career, I don't think I had ever come across anyone with as much sheer intelligence as Jeff had. It glowed from him. We all knew Jeff was brilliant, including Jeff himself, which made him rather hard to live with sometimes. But he had the golden touch. And while he wasn't modest about it, he took it casually, as if it were not something special. That made him likeable, that quality of off-handed genius, and it made the rest of us feel lucky to know him.

We were still standing there, nose to nose, atop books on my desk when Kevin weaseled his way back into my conversation.

'What do you think?' I asked Jeff, after telling him about the morning's experience.

Jeff paused, fingering the paper honeycomb of the bat's belly. 'What's he afraid of? Is he afraid of actually talking, do you think? Of hearing his voice?' Another small pause and Jeff looked at me. 'Or of what his voice might say, if he does talk?'

'I don't know,' I replied.

'Or is he maybe not afraid at all of that? Could it be that he doesn't *want* to talk and he's discovered fear makes a convenient cover? People might not bother you quite so much to do something if they think you're afraid of it. They no longer blame you and make you responsible.' Jeff then stretched up and tied the thread into place. The bat flew between us.

'I don't know. He's different from my other elective mutes. I don't know what's going on with him. I don't know what he's thinking.'

Jeff gave me an easy, very casual sort of grin. 'No. But then do we ever know that?'

Chapter Five

The one other person whose imagination had been cap-
tured by Kevin's enigmatic behavior was the Garson
Gayer social worker, Dana Wendolowski. She had been the
moving force behind obtaining permission to keep Kevin at
the home beyond the usual age limit and she had been the
one to go to the trouble of searching for someone with
expertise in psychogenic language problems.

I found a friend in Dana. She was an incredibly hard worker.
The only social worker for all of Garson Gayer's ninety-six
children, she still managed to keep tabs on the progress of
even the most hopeless ones and to do what she could to
improve their situations both inside and outside the walls of
the home. There never was a child I asked her about whom
she did not know personally. And there certainly wasn't a
single one of them she didn't care for passionately.

Although originally from a close-knit farm family in the distant rural reaches of Tennessee, Dana had been in the city since she had finished her graduate studies in social work. In her late twenties, she was a very attractive woman in a Scandinavian sort of way, although her fine, highborn features were at odds with her gentle personality.

In the past Dana had tried her own hand at working with Kevin and trying to get him to talk. She had repeatedly brought him into her office, tried to put him at ease by not forcing the issue and by being kind and reassuring with him. But she just had too many other obligations, and after a number of weeks of fruitless, one-sided interactions, she had been forced to give in. But she hadn't given up on him.

I met Dana when I came into the back room behind the office the following morning. She had been retrieving some typing from the secretaries at the front desk and I was headed for the coffeepot to make some milky coffee. The sessions with Kevin were killing my voice, and even though I didn't really like coffee very much, that seemed to be the only thing between me and hoarseness.

How was it going? she asked. All right? Was the room all right? Did I need anything? Did I have what I wanted in there?

I assured her I was fine.

She smiled hesitantly. 'Guess what we found Kevin doing last night?'

I shook my head.

'One of the aides went into his room unexpectedly and Kevin didn't hear him. Kevin was standing in front of his mirror. He was working his mouth. Con—that's the aide—said he thought Kevin was trying to talk. You know. He was pushing his lips into shapes of words. He wasn't making any sounds or anything but he was trying to form words with his lips.' She smiled at me, paused, studied my face. She had her typing clasped against her breast like a shield. 'That's a good sign, isn't it? Do you think it is? A good sign, I mean? That he wants to talk? That you might get him to?'

I returned her smile. There was anxiety in her voice. She'd been at Garson Gayer only two years – less than half the time Kevin had been there – and I could already hear the need for miracles gnawing at her. She'd invested a lot of herself in this brutal business, this job where there was always too much to do and too little to do it with. And I could hear it was weighing hard on a farm girl from Tennessee.

'Yes,' I said, 'I think it's probably a good sign.'

'Con came right down and told me. He told me what he'd seen and I very nearly called you. I wanted to. I was so excited. And I wanted you to know you were helping him.'

I worked my way down to the therapy room, balancing my cup of coffee on top of my box of materials and struggling to find the key in my pocket. It was a brilliant autumn day outside and when I opened the door to the small room, I was stunned by the piercing sunlight. It illuminated all the little dust motes floating through the air.

Dana's report of Kevin's making faces in the mirror was intriguing to me. It was hard to tell if it was much of a sign or not. I didn't want to put much emphasis on it in my own mind because there was no way of knowing what he had been doing. Just making faces at himself maybe. Or perhaps really practicing. Who knows. But I filed the observation away in the back of my head. So little was known about this silent kid that I appreciated every small notation.

I'd arrived with a new-hatched scheme that morning. Instead of laboring over the dreary story book we'd been using, I thought I'd have Kevin read from the Pumpkin Carol book. We could relax with that. I'd read him some; we could laugh over them; he could try one. It sounded pretty easy.

Kevin appeared at 9:30 on the dot. The aide opened the door and Kevin scuttled in, half walking, half crawling with his knees bent and his arms stiff at his sides. Once the aide retreated, Kevin dived past me for the safety of the table.

Pulling out a chair, I dropped down to the floor, too, and came under the table. Quickly Kevin grabbed the chair and set it up, back against the table, seat facing out, in the way he seemed to find most reassuring. There we were together in the daylight darkness. The dust motes continued gliding down through shafts of sunlight only a few feet away and yet they were a world removed from our murky hideout under the table.

Carefully, I brought the *Peanuts* carol book out of the box of materials and showed it to Kevin. Paging through the songs, I tried to explain how they had come about. He listened politely but I could tell he didn't get it. My account was lame, and humor dies under scrutiny.

Then he reached past me for the box. Opening it again, he took out the mystery story and thumbed through it for the page we had been warring with.

'I thought we might do this one instead. I think we need a change,' I said.

He regarded me a long moment, and I had no clue as to what was going on in his head. His eyes narrowed. The other book remained in his hands.

'Don't you want to try these? These are funny, see? They go to the tunes of Christmas carols. You know.' And I was suddenly stricken with the thought that perhaps he didn't know. Maybe his life had been institutionalized beyond a world containing Christmas carols. 'Do you want me to read you one?' My voice was beginning to sound a little pathetic even in my own ears. The whole morning was falling flat.

Kevin shook his head. Spreading the mystery story open on the carpet, he leaned over it. He brought a hand up and pushed his lips back to make an *e*. I heard the familiar breaths in preparation. Then he launched full-tilt into war. Kevin shook, chattered, sweated and physically tried to make his mouth into the shape of the word. He rubbed his throat upward to push the word out. He stretched his neck, as if about to gag. Nothing worked.

'Look,' I said, 'I got another idea. Come here. Come out from under there a little bit. I need more room.'

I crawled out from under the table. Standing up, I offered him one of the chairs. 'Come here.'

Kevin crawled to the edge of the table but not out from under it. I could not lure him farther. So, taking the chair, I sat in it myself. He was sitting, feet under him, about even with my knees. I bent over and put my hands on his throat.

'You know what I think we need? Some exercise. I think you're so tense that your muscles are all tight. We need you to relax so that it will be easier for your throat to speak.'

He shook beneath my fingers. And crikey, he was an ugly kid. I had sort of gotten used to that, but looking at him eyeball to eyeball, it was difficult to miss.

'Open your mouth. Wide.'

Sweat beaded up but he opened his mouth slightly.

'*Big!* Like this.' I demonstrated with a great big gape. 'I want you to do exactly what I do. And I'm going to keep my hands against your voice box there to see how your muscles are doing. Relax. Relax, Kevin, I won't do anything to hurt you.'

I made the exercises up on the spot. I had never used anything like them before nor was I certain where to feel for the voice box. However, where my hands were seemed to be a likely enough place. We both had our mouths wide open like preying sharks. It would have been a wonderful opportunity for a mouthwash commercial.

The whole thing was an incredible con game. Maybe most of psychology is. It wasn't a lie, really. While I maybe didn't actually have any special exercises, I reckoned any sort of exercise ought to help. And while I had no real idea where the voice box was, I still could feel tense muscles, and if he could relax, that surely would be a help. So, it wasn't really a lie, just a sort of middle-sized humbug. And probably nothing was wrong with that. But it was a little sobering to consider when one was sitting with one's hands around a kid's throat.

'Relax, Kev. You're all tense. Nothing's going to hurt you. Trust me. Relax. Here, put your hands on my throat. Feel what the muscles are like? Feel how relaxed? Here, now, touch yours. See the difference? We want to make yours feel like mine.'

So there we sat with our hands round one another's throats, as if we were in mortal combat. In a way, I suppose we were.

I had him open his mouth wide and move it around and around. He had to take deep breaths, hold them, let them out slowly. He waggled his head from side to side, felt my muscles, felt his, felt mine again, waggled some more to relax. All the time I kept talking confidently, like I did this every day, and I kept changing the exercises rapidly so that he had to concentrate to keep up.

'Okay, Kevin, now with your mouth open like that, breathe out real slowly, like this.' I demonstrated, putting enough pressure into my breath to make a very softly whispered *'haaa'* sound. Kevin, who had one hand around my throat and one around his own, also breathed out slowly. But there was no sound.

'Good. Do it again a little harder. Feel those muscles relax. That's what we're trying to do, relax those muscles there. Get down in your diaphragm, use that more. Do it again.' A bit of a lie there to distract him from the sound. I demonstrated, putting on a big show of using my diaphragm.

This time the sound was audible when he tried, but he was so caught up in what we were doing that he did not notice it. Quickly I tried to distract him further by letting him compare the muscles in our throats again. Were they the same? Yes. Good. Do it again.

I continued to breathe a whisper into the *'haaa,'* each time a little louder but still soft enough that it was as much a breath as a whisper. I wanted the gradations in loudness to be virtually undetectable.

Kevin kept up with me, imitating the same gradations of sound. His brow was furrowed in concentration. He had ceased shaking. In fact, both of us were so absorbed in the act of making our breaths comparable that I don't believe either one of us remembered at that instant why we were doing it.

'Okay, harder now. Feel your stomach so you can see if your diaphragm's pushing. Like this. *Haaaa.*' A definite whisper.

'*Haa*—,' went Kevin and then he caught what I had done. His whisper died midbreath. His face reddened, his eyes bulged. I still had him by the throat but he abruptly broke my grip. Back under the table he went.

I leaned down to peer at him. 'Hey? Come out of there. Come on. You were doing fine. Let's try again.'

Kevin was way back under there, rolled up in a ball as he had been on the very first day.

I slid off the chair and came down under the table too. Touching his shoulder, I smiled at him. 'You were doing just super. Did you know that? You were really doing a great job. Let's give it another go.'

Beneath my fingertips I felt muscles rockhard with tension, then there was a little tremble and Kevin exploded. *Bang!* Like a volcano he went off, leaping up on his feet and knocking the table backward off his shoulders. Chairs toppled. My box and all its contents flew. Around and around the room Kevin tore. He banged into walls, scrabbled over furniture, tripped and stumbled to his feet again.

Startled, I leaped up too. He was a great big kid and he made a frightening sight in that wild state. It was at that moment that I realized exactly how little I knew Kevin-under-the-table. He might as well have been an animal, like my dog at home, whose problems I could only guess at because our worlds were so different and we could not communicate much of anything to one another.

Back and forth Kevin went, the crablike scuttle still evident in his gait. He was screaming, at least he would have been screaming, if he'd made any noise to go along with it. His mouth was wide open and he grimaced violently but all that came out were staccato puffs of air. Tears washed over his cheeks. Snot ran down into his mouth.

Suddenly the door opened behind me and the aide stepped in. He muttered under his breath when he saw us and slammed the door again. Within seconds four men converged on us like a division of the Marines. They marched in, tackled Kevin and threw him spread-eagle to the floor. Behind them came a nurse. She had a hypodermic needle in hand. While the men restrained Kevin, she whipped down his trousers and administered the shot.

All the while, Kevin struggled. Thin and wiry as he was, he fought a good fight, and it took all four men to hold him down.

Unused to being rescued from my crises, I just stood there, struck dumb with surprise. I hadn't realized Kevin and I were so much out of control. He had been upset, sure, but we'd stayed in the confines of the room. He wasn't hurting me, or me, him. And he wasn't doing anything that should cause deployment of the Marines and the psychotropic tranquilizers.

Kevin was taken up to one of the seclusion rooms at the far end of the ward. It was a tiny room with a thick wooden door and long green things, which looked like futon mattresses, hanging from the walls. A padded cell. The only window was a small grate in the door. Kevin had been stripped to his underpants so that he would not hurt himself and was now flinging himself back and forth against the padding.

I went up to the ward and stood there, watching him for a few moments. Then I went down to Dana Wendolowski's office.

Dana gave me a sympathetic smile when I came in. 'I heard,' she said. 'But don't worry about it. He does that sometimes.'

'He does?' No one had told me that.

'No one knows why. They don't really seem to be tantrums. I don't know. He just has them. We give him a shot, put him in seclusion for a while and he gets over them eventually. They never last long. And he can go a long time between them.'

'Oh, I see,' I said and leaned back in the chair. I didn't see at all.

After another cup of coffee, I returned to the ward. A number of aides had collected around the desk there watching me as I came through the double doors.

'He does that,' one young woman said to me. That response seemed to explain everything to everyone.

'May I go in and see him?' I asked. I was beginning to feel restless and a little irritable without knowing exactly why. I didn't have the patience to stand there and chat with them.

One of the people broke away and went over to the seclusion-room door. She peered through the window for a moment and returned. 'Yeah, I guess so. If you want. He's just laying in there.'

The room was incredibly small, although perhaps not so small as it felt. Kevin didn't move when I came in. He lay face down on the floor, his face hidden in crossed arms. I stood over him a moment and did nothing.

While I was standing there, my mind was almost blank. I just stared at him without having any really conscious thoughts going through my head at all. He *was* a big kid. Naked except for his underpants, I could see how thin he was. His skin was sallow and waxy. He'd clearly been an abused child. I could see all the familiar little scars that lamp cords and lighted cigarets leave. They were all over his back and down his legs like the tracks of some small vermin.

I didn't love the kid. I didn't even really like him. He was too old. I didn't know what to do with adolescents. He was too far gone for my type of magic. I traded in a certain kind of innocence, in the belief that adults, just by being adults, could make things better. But he was too old. He already knew that wasn't true and that left us without anything, just two ordinary people.

Kevin stirred. He looked up at me. There grew between us a long silence.

'Did you think I was trying to trick you?' I asked. 'I'm sorry, if you did. If I upset you in there, I'm sorry because I didn't mean to.'

Kevin looked away. Still on his stomach, he brought his crossed arms closer and rested his chin on them.

'It must have seemed that way,' I said. 'It must have seemed like I was trying to catch you unawares and trick you. I wasn't really. I was just trying to help, to make it so you weren't so scared.'

He raised his head to look at me.

'I am sorry,' I said.

Kevin turned around and sat up. He gazed at me. I was still standing near the door, but the room was so small that we were scarcely more than a foot or two apart. He seemed oddly relaxed. The fear had fallen momentarily away from him and while he sat with his arms around his knees, it was a natural position. But perhaps that was just because of the tranquilizer.

'I have to go now,' I said. 'I need to get back to the clinic where I work.'

Kevin's face puckered. He gestured.

'I'll be back tomorrow, all right?' I turned and opened the door. Kevin rose as I let myself out. 'Good-bye for now.'

He came to the door, and it was hard shutting it on him. He put his face to the window and remained there, watching me. Even as I left the ward and let the two broad doors swing shut behind me, when I looked back I was able to see Kevin's face still pressed against the glass of the tiny window in the seclusion-room door.

Chapter Six

He had arrived in the small white room ahead of me the next day. The aide was standing outside the door when I came and he opened it for me. Kevin was already under the table.

I could hear him. '*Haa,*' he was going, '*haa, haa, haa.*' It was a breathy sound, not quite a whisper. It sounded like an engine coughing to life.

I bent down and moved a chair aside. Kevin started, looking up at me with great dark eyes. He did not smile his customary goofy grin and I felt like a trespasser. So I asked permission to come down and join him. He moved over to make room for me but then he turned his head away and continued with the sounds. I slid under the table and replaced the chair.

'*Haa.*

'*Haa. Haa.*

'*Haaaaaaaaa.*'

As on the other days, Kevin was self-motivated. I didn't need to be there at all. *Haaa. Haa. Haaaa.* There was a determined urgency to him this day. He was going to do it.

'*Haa. Ha. Haaa. Haaa. Haaaaaaaaaaaaaaaa.*'

He swayed.

Haa was not a good thing to have to keep saying over and over again. His intense work on the sound was causing him to hyperventilate. It made him sway with dizziness and occasionally he was forced to pause and let his head clear. I wondered as I watched him if he knew his breathing was making him feel like that or if he just thought it was the fear.

The fear was with us. Like a living thing, it sat upon his shoulders. He trembled. Sweat flowed in rivulets down through his hair and over his ravaged skin.

'*Haaaaa. Ha. Ha. Ha.*' Still there was no real sound to it, although it was very nearly a whisper.

The minutes passed. I sat, too, with my arms hugging my knees, my chin atop them. *Haa*, Kevin kept saying. My bad knee grew sore from sitting so long like that without moving but I was afraid to move.

'*Haaaaaaa. Haaa. Haa, haa.*'

Over and over he repeated that one sound. He seemed to need to hear himself say it because he kept his head cocked to one side. He would say the sound and then his eyes would narrow in concentration as if he was appraising the quality of it. I wondered if he had forgotten what his own voice sounded like. Or how it felt to speak.

'*Haaa. Haa, haa, haa, haa, haa, haa.*'

A deep breath.

'*Haaaaaaaaaaaaaa.*' The sound became a real whisper for the first time and the breathiness went out of it. Kevin jerked up, hit his head on the table. He cocked his head again. '*Haaaaaaaaaaaa,*' he went in a whisper. '*Hooo, haaa, ho.*' His brows knit. '*Ho,*' he whispered again and listened to the quality of the sound.

Now it was all whispers. He continued to repeat the sound, varying the vowels. '*Haaa, ho, heeee, huh, haaaaaaaaaaaa.*' Then back to the breathy *ha, ha, ha, ha* before returning to the softer whispered noises. He could hear the difference. With an expression of intense concentration, he tried the two, the sound and the whisper, side by side. Back and forth between the two he went.

He was like a piano tuner tuning a fine instrument. Hugging my knees very tightly, I tried to make myself as small and unobtrusive as possible. This was not my place. I had nothing to do with what Kevin was accomplishing. I was, if anything, an interloper into this private interaction Kevin was having with himself. But at the same time, I was utterly fascinated. It was like being in someone's mind, as if I had been given the privilege of actually being inside someone else, of seeing another person relating to himself in that personal, intimate way we discourse with ourselves.

'*Haaaaaaaaaaaaaa. HaaaaAAAAAaa.*' His voice broke through. It startled him and he froze, every muscle going tense. Sweat dripped off his chin onto his shirt. Silence roared around us.

'*HaaAAA?*' he said tentatively and froze again. '*HAA?*'

'*HAAAA,*' in a real voice. '*HAAAAAAAAAAAAAAAAA.*'

Kevin's muscles remained tense, the outline of them rippling along under his T-shirt, standing out like Roman columns in his neck. But his concentration did not break. '*Haa,*' he said aloud, listening to the sound. His voice was gravelly and hoarse from nonuse. '*Ha. Ha, ha, ha, ha,*' he said in short bursts. Intense concentration kept his features puckered.

'*Ha. Ha. Ha. Ho. Ho. Ho. Ha. Ha.*' He sounded like a machine gun, shooting the words out in sharp staccato. '*Huh. Huh. Huh. Ho. Ho. Hee. Hee. Hee. Ha.*'

I stayed small and silent. I did not know if he had forgotten me or not, but it did not seem like the moment to call attention to my presence.

'*Huh. Huh. Huh. Huh. Hup. Hup. Haa. Haap. Haap. Haap.*' He experimented with new sounds.

All of a sudden the life went out of him. He gave a great sigh of weariness and dropped his head down on his knees in exhaustion. Then, like a tree falling, he just tumbled over onto his side and lay in a heap. Again he sighed.

I watched him.

He was exhausted. Every last bit of energy drained out of him. I was feeling a great camaraderie with him just then. His success did not have anything to do with me, but I felt very privileged that he had let me share it. I was smiling, without even being aware of it.

'That was hard work, wasn't it?' I said. 'You must be dead tired.'

'*Ho,*' he said, and I could hear him repeat the sound a couple of times. '*Ho, ho.* I …,' he said, 'I, I didn't … *ho* … I didn't think I was going to do it. *Whew. Whooooow.*' His voice cracked and he cleared his throat. 'I didn't think I was ever going to be able to do that again,' he said softly from under his arms. 'I thought I never could do it.'

On Sunday afternoon I had Charity over. It was the first time we had seen one another since the open house. I had planned to make a kite with her and take her down to the field at the bottom of the road to fly it. The wind was excellent for kite flying, and it was a beautiful autumn afternoon.

Charity was unimpressed.

'What's this for?' she asked as she came into the kitchen. I had sticks and newspapers lying spread out on the table. I explained carefully, trying to make my own enthusiasm for the project contagious. I loved making kites, and it had grown to be a passsion when I had had my classroom.

'What do you want to do that for?' she asked earnestly. 'You can buy kites at the store. You don't have to make 'em, you know.'

'It's fun.'

'Oh.'

I bribed her with a chocolate-chip cookie, and we set about cutting and gluing and tying tails. Charity was a little scruffier looking than she had been on the night of the open house. Although her hair was in braids, they obviously had been slept in, causing long strands of hair to escape. Toast crumbs and bits of jam clung to the hair by her face. Her forehead was still patched up with Band-Aids, one across the other in an X, like a pirate's crossbones. She wore a faded T-shirt with an even more faded kitten on it and, up on the right-hand shoulder, a huge, glittery dime-store brooch. It had a big hunk of blue glass in the middle, surrounded by rhinestones. I commented on it.

'Oh this?' Charity asked, and went a little cross-eyed trying to see it. 'My big sister Sandy bought it for me. See, she gave it to me. It's an emerald.'

'I thought emeralds were green. Maybe it's a sapphire.'

'Nope. It's an emerald. A blue emerald. They're betterer than green emeralds. Green ones are common. These're *rare!*'

'Well, yes, I'd agree with that,' I said.

'It's real too.'

'Really?'

'Yup. It's worth at least a million dollars probably. Only I'd never sell it. Sandy gave it to me and it's a real, genuine blue emerald.'

'Do you have other sisters, Charity?'

'Oh yeah. I got Sandy, she's twelve. And Cheryl, she's ten. And Diana, she's eight.'

'Diana? I thought Diana was your Big Sister from the program.'

'This is another Diana. This one's my real, genuine sister. For real.'

'I see. And that's all? Are you the youngest?'

She nodded decisively. 'Yep. I'm the very youngest. When they got me, they stopped. 'Cause I'm the very best. They didn't want any more after me.'

I could understand that. For a moment I became absorbed in getting paper to stick to the side of the kite, then I looked over. 'Hey, wait a minute, Charity. I thought you said you were eight. If you're eight, how come Diana's eight?'

Charity looked flustered, but only for a fleeting moment. She smacked her forehead with one hand. 'Oh, I goofed. Silly me. Diana's nine. I forgot.'

'Oh. I thought perhaps you were twins,' I said, thanking God for not making two of Charity.

'Yeah! That's right! I forgot. We're twins.'

'But I *thought* you just said—'

'Well, see, Diana's the oldest twin and I'm the youngest.'

'I thought you said she was nine, though. And you're eight.'

'Well, yeah, I did,' she said, looking at me as if I were the one who was losing her marbles.

'Are you sure you know what twins are, Charity?'

'Of course I do. Do you think I'm stupid? I just forgot. I got a lot on my mind and I just forgot. Diana's just the oldest twin and I'm the youngest. First her and then me. So that's why she's nine. And I'm going to be nine pretty soon too.'

'Oh? When?'

'Next August.'

'But, Charity, it's October now.'

'Yeah, see what I mean? Any day now I'll be nine.'

Clearly this was a conversation best to be dropped.

Later we walked down to the field to fly the kite. The wind was good and even Charity's part of the kite held up well, despite its patches. Charity ran when I told her to run and stopped when I told her to stop and let the string out when instructed. When the kite was finally airborne, she sank gratefully into the grass and sprawled out. I sat down next to her.

She looked over. 'How come we're doing this?'

'Because it's fun.'

'Oh,' she said, quite interested. 'When does the fun part start?'

'This *is* the fun part, Charity.'

'Oh, it is?' Her forehead wrinkled. 'You do this for *fun?*'

I was a little disenchanted with this kid. After all, it was my Sunday afternoon too. 'Yes, I do this for fun. And I'm having it. Why aren't you?'

Charity looked startled. 'Well, I guess maybe I am,' she said. 'I just didn't know it.' And for the first time since she'd arrived, she fell silent.

Both of us lay in the grass and watched the kite. Charity rose after a while and walked around the field before coming back and settling down with me again. She chattered on constantly.

At the end of the day when I was preparing to take her home, she fished something out of her pocket.

'Here.'

It was an unidentifiable wad about three inches across.

'I brung this for you,' she said.

I took it and thanked her. There was a piece of thin paper around it which I attempted to unwrap. Inside was a squishy, gummy-looking lump. 'What is it?' I inquired politely.

'A piece of cake. Last Wednesday this girl had a birthday at school and she brang us all some cake. I saved it for you.'

'Oh.' That made me feel obliged to eat it and so I took a bite and tried to look like it was scrumptious.

'I ate a little bit of it. Just there at the edge. But I saved you the most.' She was smiling sweetly, her empty tooth sockets all showing.

'Well, thank you, Charity, that's awfully thoughtful of you.'

'Oh, that's okay,' she replied and shrugged. 'I tried to give it to our dog but he spit it out.'

Chapter Seven

Kevin spoke. In the way I had found typical of most elective mutes, he came back with full powers of speech – grammar, vocabulary, sentence structure – as if he had been speaking all along. In the very beginning, his voice was hoarse and gritty sounding from lack of use. We went through a truckload of throat lozenges and hard candies, trying to ease the roughness, but soon he became accustomed to speaking again and the soreness went away.

Kevin was not a hesitant conversationalist. For the first few days our communications were limited while he experimented with his voice. However, he was speaking easily before the following week was out.

Our conversations were none too brilliant in the beginning. After such an ordeal, I think one is inclined to expect profundity at the very least. Thus it was anticlimatic to have most of our conversations revolve around things like crossword puzzles or Kevin's day on the ward or my work at the clinic. I couldn't tell how much he was guarding from me because I just did not know him very well.

However, simply because we had conquered his lack of speech did not mean that we had solved all problems. We were a long way from it. His fear, for example, was still of the same magnificent proportions. The only difference now was that he could make occasional comments about it. But we remained trapped under that damned table. In fact, we seemed more firmly stuck under it than before.

I compromised on the table issue, by not always going under it myself. Instead, I pushed the chairs to one side and sat down on the carpet just beyond the table. This was more comfortable because there was more room and I didn't have to hunch up. But it did not entice Kevin out and he would not talk to me if I got very far away from him. So mostly, I lay on the rug on my stomach, half of me under the table, half of me out.

Kevin was able to make me captive to others of his fears, too. For instance, one morning someone had left a box of old schoolbooks sitting on the empty bookcase in the room. It was a largish cardboard carton, and when I noticed it, I could see old readers and workbooks sticking out of the top but I gave no thought to it. Kevin, however, focused on it right off.

'What's in that box?' he asked from under the table.

'Some old schoolbooks, I think,' I replied.

'What kind of books?'

'I don't know. I didn't look.'

A worried expression crossed his face. 'Go look.' He nudged me. 'Go look for me. Tell me what's in it.'

When I didn't move, he became more agitated. His speech gave him a new power over me because now he could be sure I understood what he wanted. Sweat beaded up on his face.

'There might be spirals in there,' he said in a hushed voice. 'On notebooks. There might be spiral notebooks inside that box.'

'I don't think so, Kevin. I think there's just old school-books.'

'But sometimes there's spirals on old books.'

'No, I don't think there are.'

'There might be. You said you didn't look. So you don't know. There might be and you just can't see them. They might be under there. Spirals might be in that box. Go look and find out.'

He could not concentrate. Once the terrifying thought had entered his head, he became obsessed with it. He *knew* those small, metal, springlike spirals were in there, lurking, waiting to shoot out and get him. All the little manifestations of fear began, the trembling, the chattering, the sweating, the shallow breathing. He wrapped himself up in a small ball way back in the safety of his table and rocked. Nothing I could say would relieve him. Tears welled up. His knuckles went white. And in the end I got up, took all the stuff out of the box, showed him all of it, just to prove that it was entirely safe with no spiral-bound notebooks to be found. Only then could he relax.

For the first few sessions after Kevin began to talk, I told no one. I'm not sure why. It seemed a secret trust for a while. But once his speaking began to take on all the proportions of normalcy and was no longer such a special achievement in and of itself, I started the usual procedures to generalize it to include other people.

Normally, I was able to quickly generalize an elective mute's speech beyond the two of us. However, in Kevin's case I soon realized that Kevin's choice to speak had little to do with me, personally, and my techniques. Consequently, I had no ability to make him speak to other people. It quickly became apparent that I had not caused him to speak. Instead, he had simply opened his private world of one to include me.

And Kevin chose forthrightly not to speak to anyone else. That drastically narrowed the scope of our first victory.

It drove me mad for a while because I could do nothing. I had told Dana and the staff and Jeff what had happened, that Kevin was speaking to me, but try as I might, if Dana or someone else came into the small white room, I could not get Kevin to talk to them. I tried. There was war between us for a while. I tried my usual approach. I tried my backup techniques. I tried other methods afterward, which I had used with some success with other children. I tried other people's recommendations, the things I read about in journals. When those all expired from overwork, I invented a few new techniques on the spot. In the end, I hoped to wear him down just by the sheer quantity of tries, if nothing else. But I didn't. Nothing worked.

Nothing worked for a very simple reason, I suspect. Kevin wouldn't let it. This was a very different kind of battle than the one that first week. Then, it had been him and me against the silence. Not so now. It was Kevin against me.

Finally I gave up. It had grown to be a power struggle between us and nothing more. I don't know. Perhaps if I had persisted I might have worn him down eventually. But if I had, the objective would have been tarnished. To dominate, I would have had to let the real objective fall to the wayside, stripped of its integrity. So reluctantly I gave in. When the days passed and I could not generalize Kevin's speech to other people, I had to face defeat. It was miserably hard to back down, but for whatever reason, this apparently was not the time for it to happen.

Undoubtedly, the most irritating aspect of the lack of generalization was that I don't think everyone believed me when I said Kevin talked to me. I took a terrible drubbing from Jeff. He was absolutely merciless for a while until I actually got angry with him over it. But with Jeff, no matter how irritating, it was pure jest. He knew that if I said the boy talked, he talked. However, the staff at Garson Gayer really got under my skin. They made half-joking remarks and clustered around the door of the small white room and grew very keen for tapes and recordings, so that they could hear for themselves. Everyone knew that under normal circumstances I did a lot of video-recording of my work. That I wasn't doing so with Kevin seemed to only strengthen the likelihood that I was fabricating the entire thing. But I couldn't record. There was no way to disguise a recorder in the bare little room and even if I could have, I don't think I would. It would have been a kind of betrayal to Kevin, who feared the world beyond the door so much. Winning the power struggle with him or asserting my position with the staff shouldn't be worth that much. So I just held my tongue, stayed out of earshot when I could and pretended not to hear the insinuations or feel them.

So, as the hazy days of October passed, it remained just the two of us alone under the table.

One of the most remarkable things about Kevin was his almost nonexistent personal history. Previously, I had always considered files a nuisance. They prejudiced people against kids before they even met. They were filled mostly with bureaucratic nonsense and the self-important mutterings of little gods. But nonetheless, all my kids had come with them in one form or another and I had always read them. Usually, the worse the kid, the thicker the file. One time I had a fourteen-inch-thick file in my cabinet for one ten-year-old. For Kevin, however, this was not the case, a very remarkable fact in light of his long history with the state.

His folder was a small one, squashed amidst the fatter ones of other children. There was an intake sheet. His mother's name was given and his stepfather's. No mention was made of a natural father. A tick mark indicated that he had siblings, but they weren't enumerated. Most of the rest of the sheet was blank, owing to the fact that he had been in state care rather than at home. There were a number of data sheets and anecdotal records of things that had occurred since Kevin had been living at Garson Gayer. They made interesting reading: accounts of his various fears, of his refusal to go outside, of his 'tantrums,' which had required seclusion and medication. But by and large, they were unremarkable. There were some medical reports of bouts with flu and ingrown toenails. Nothing special.

The only detailed report in the whole folder was his school report. Kevin had attended kindergarten at the far south end of the city. After the first year, he was retained because he didn't talk. Since he still did not talk at the end of the second year but appeared to be progressing adequately, he was passed to the first grade. That whole next year was disastrous. First grade is designed for children who speak. Kevin didn't. Subjected to behavior controls, tests, inquiries, Kevin failed to respond. He just sat and watched.

In this first-grade section of the report there were a few notes about Kevin's home life. In a questionable state, the report said. Kevin had bruises and other evidence of physical abuse. I flipped to the front of the report. It was dated prior to the time when reporting child abuse to the authorities became mandatory. And apparently this abuse had never been noted. Scars. Burns. A bruise on the face. The teacher got salve to put on his broken skin and washed his sores, but she told no one. Only people like me, ten years on, found out. Kevin had a sister, a five-year-old at the time, in kindergarten. They were close, Kevin and this sister, and the teacher thought she had overheard him talk to the sister out on the playground. He was very protective of the child. The only time the teacher had seen him react was when someone threatened the little girl. A good sign, this teacher felt.

Unfortunately, by the end of that first year in first grade Kevin had given no evidence of learning. If he could read, he didn't show it. The school psychologist was called in and Kevin was tested.

The report broke down then, the entries becoming sporadic. Kevin went on to a special-education class the next year. He was eight. At the end of that year he was reported to have a testable IQ of 40, which put him in a very low, uneducable stratum. He was institutionalized for the first time during this period, and from then on, it seemed to be nothing but a string of group homes and juvenile centers and residences. He was even in the children's unit at the state hospital for a short time before being deemed too retarded and moved into a state-run program for the mentally handicapped. It was not clear when he was where or for how long or why he was switched from one place to another so frequently. But whatever the reason, it did nothing to liberate his power of speech.

There was nothing current in Kevin's file except updated Garson Gayer reports of height and weight and that sort of thing. There was nothing more to tell why he had been institutionalized in the first place or where his fears had developed or why he had come to Garson Gayer, a residential treatment center not given to taking in severely retarded or welfare kids. And perhaps most sinister of all, there was no explanation anywhere for the single line penciled across the top of the intake sheet: *Voluntary termination of parental rights. Made ward of the state.*

When I inquired, I found no one knew much more about Kevin. Almost none of the staff had been there as long as he had because Garson Gayer, like most institutions, was a victim of high staff turnover. Dana, who was my usual source of information about everything, had been at the home less than half the time Kevin had. She'd never thought much about his lack of history. With ninety-five other children to worry about and with a cast-iron belief in dealing with only the here and now, she was unbothered by it. Stay in the present, she'd repeat over and over to me. You're living today, deal with today. And in my heart I knew she was probably right. The staff psychologist only shrugged when I asked him. What do you want? A leather-bound biography? There's as much in his as in anybody else's file.

What did I want? That was a stupid question. I wanted answers. I wanted to know why this kid behaved like this. I wanted to know how to fix him. I knew a file wouldn't tell me those things, even if it had been thick as an encyclopedia. But I still wanted it, for me perhaps more than for Kevin. After all these years of casting my lot with the liberals and the freethinkers, saying how damaging such files were, how they fueled self-fulfilling prophecy, I guess I should have willingly taken a dose of my own medicine. But it felt awful. It left me feeling adrift in a wide sea with no chart. As the days passed, I thought how much nicer it would have been to be adrift with even a bad chart than with no chart at all.

We were reading a cookbook. It was a children's paperback featuring different dishes of the world. I had used it with my kids in the classroom when I was teaching, and after I'd told Kevin about how we used to cook sometimes, he'd asked if I would bring the book in. So we were sitting on the floor, browsing through the pages together.

'What's that?' he asked, pointing to an artist's illustration.

'Spaghetti with tomato sauce on it, I think.'

He was thoughtful a moment. 'It looks kinda like brains.'

I hadn't noticed that particular quality about spaghetti before and examined the picture more carefully.

'Have you ever seen brains before?' Kevin asked.

'Yes. The grocery store up on 12th Street sells them sometimes. I guess you scramble them up with eggs or something.'

'No, I mean real brains.'

'Those are. From cattle, I think. Some people eat them. I guess they're supposed to be very good but I haven't been that brave myself yet.'

'No,' said Kevin. 'I mean *real* brains. Like you got in here.' He tapped his forehead. 'People's brains.'

I paused. I had seen human brains before. When I was a biology student in college there were some pickled in formaldehyde up on a shelf in the science building. There'd been pickled babies up there too.

'I have,' Kevin said before I could comment. 'They're all red and sort of yellowish and bumpy. Like that spaghetti.'

'Hmmm.'

'Does that make you sick?' he asked, studying my face carefully.

'Is it supposed to?'

'Does it?'

'It's not one of my favorite things to think about, if that's what you mean,' I replied.

He was still regarding me very closely. It was a penetrating expression and I could not tell what he was trying to glean from me. Then he looked back at the book. 'I couldn't eat spaghetti,' he said. 'Not if it looked like that—like brains, all squashed out.'

I nodded.

Relaxing a little, he sat back. 'Let's turn the page,' he said. 'Let's look at something else.'

But mostly the days of October were a quiet time. The frantic first weeks when I had tried so desperately to get Kevin to talk passed and we grew familiar with one another. I learned his fears and how to ease them. He weathered my moments of restless impatience. I started bringing him things from the outside, things he liked to do, like paper-and-pencil puzzles and coloring books. I brought him candy bars and magazines and things he hadn't seen in years. He talked to me mostly of little things, of all the personal minutiae he had saved up over so many years of silence.

Slowly, slowly we managed to creep out from under the table. It was not a fast change at all. I just kept moving back, a fraction of a step a day and Kevin, intent in conversation, would move toward me. Eventually we were both outside the perimeter of the tabletop, and once we were, we stayed. Kevin still couldn't rise from the floor. He always had to remain there where he could dive for safety if he needed to. But under normal circumstances, he stopped finding it necessary to hide all the time.

The fear began to drop away from him too. Once inside the small white room, when the door to the outer world was shut, I noticed he would sit in a fairly relaxed position and talk to me with great animation. He then would look for all the world like any other sixteen-year-old might look. However, should someone appear at the door or a noise occur outside the room somewhere, the fear would leap up and hood him. His face would go pale, his pupils dilate, his breathing quicken. And he'd go silent. That never changed. He relaxed a little but he always remained alert, always wary.

I had brought him a joke book. Elephant jokes. They were horrid ones, so awful that you couldn't even groan convincingly when you heard them. But Kevin relished them all. He had quite a sense of humor for a kid in his circumstances, more than I often encountered. So it was fun to joke with him. At the moment his favorite story had to do with frogs in blenders, and I had heard it at least twenty times, so I brought him the elephant joke book.

I had snatched some pillows from the therapy room down the hall. Pushing them up against the radiator under the window, I leaned back while Kevin sat cross-legged and read me the jokes. There must have been about thirty pages in the book with a joke or two per page. Kevin read them all to me and when he had finished, he went back through and read again the ones he liked best. They were so dreadful that I couldn't even remember the answers the second time through, so I entertained him by making up my own, equally horrible.

'Where'd you get this?' he asked me when we finished.

'Out at the mall. In one of those little cardshops.'

'Do they have others?'

I nodded. 'Not elephant jokes. But other ones with jokes in them.'

He regarded me for a moment. 'Would you get me one? Another one?'

'Yes, maybe. Later on. They cost a lot of money for their size. But I'll get another one when I can.'

He continued watching me. It was a bright day and the morning sun flowed through the window. It grazed the side of his face and illuminated his eyes. Even in the sunlight, his eyes were a true gray. There was no other color in them at all.

And still he watched me. 'You don't hate me, do you?' he asked softly.

'No, I don't hate you.'

A curious half smile touched his lips. 'I didn't think you did.' His gaze wandered from my face. He looked above me to the window. Then slowly he rose up on his knees to see out. He stayed that way a minute or two before dropping back down.

'You know,' he said and then paused. He flipped through the joke book. 'You know, I talked to you.'

I nodded.

'I talked to you. I wanted to talk to you.' He looked up. 'You see, I knew you didn't hate me.'

'No, I don't.'

'I knew that. Even from the beginning. You didn't hate me and I could tell it.' The strange half smile was back, and once again he looked over my head to the sunlight. It was in his eyes but he didn't squint. It bathed him. He sat and stared into it like a lean Buddha.

'Kevin,' I said, 'may I ask you something?'

He looked back to me.

'How come you talked? How come you decided to do it at all?'

He sighed and gazed into the sunlight. 'Well, I talked to *you* because I said. Because I knew you didn't hate me. I said that.'

'But why'd you decide to talk at all, after all these years?'

He was silent. He remained silent so long that I thought he wasn't going to answer me. He just stared into the sun.

'I used to have a cat,' he said at last. 'But it's dead now. It's in the ground. It's just bones and dirt.' He regarded me. 'How can I talk about that?' He looked back into the sun. 'How can I not talk about it?'

Chapter Eight

There were two matters with Kevin that were going to have to be tackled sooner or later. First was Kevin's hygiene. I realized right from the beginning that part of his difficulty with cleanliness was tied to his numerous fears. For instance, he was so afraid of water that there was no hope of getting him into a bathtub. However, lack of good hygiene made him generally so unpleasant to be with and so unattractive that I felt it should be given some priority. Beauty may be only skin deep but the judgments founded on it tend to go a lot deeper, whether we wished they would or not. No one was going to take to a kid who looked like the aftermath of Mount St Helens and smelled like a locker room after a game, regardless of how clever I or Dana or anyone else might be about changing his behavior. Ordinary people just aren't that accepting.

Kevin never would set the world on fire in the looks department. He was sort of your basic model ugly kid. But if his hair hadn't looked like someone had tested their lawn mower on it and his clothes fit and he washed, he had the potential to be a whole lot closer to average.

Unfortunately, I quickly learned that many of Kevin's problems were beyond my control. His hair, for instance. It was the old buzz job up the back and around the sides, leaving one long lock hanging over his forehead. It looked like a grown-out Mohican. Unfortunately, all the boys at Garson Gayer looked like that. Zoe, the cook, brought in her clippers once a month and gave all the fellows a workover. But there wasn't much to be done about it. She was free and she was there. I didn't know any barbers at all, particularly ones who made house calls. And I couldn't cut hair myself. I had tried once when I was a teacher at a state hospital, and one of my boys complained about looking like a girl. So I took the school shears from my desk and gave him a trim and, while he no longer would be mistaken for a girl, it ended any ideas I might have had about a potential future in hairdressing.

Kevin's clothes were about as bad as his haircut. They were obviously thirdhand and at least ten years out of style. This wouldn't have mattered much if it weren't that they were so small for him. One shirt's sleeves couldn't be buttoned because they came so far up on his wrists that the cuffs wouldn't fit around that part of his arm. He owned no pants that covered the tops of his socks. Worse, the pants were all too tight in the crotch. In the beginning, I had thought he was constantly masturbating. As it turned out, he was simply trying to pull the pants down a little to allow himself to sit comfortably. This daily torture was almost more than I could bear to watch.

Perhaps worst of all was Kevin's skin. It could have kept a dermatologist in business for life. He had acne everywhere, undoubtedly aggravated by the fact that he did not wash. There were pimples on his cheeks, on his nose, on his chin, on his forehead, even on his ears. In the bad places, his pimples seemed to have pimples. It was gruesome to have to sit really near him, forced to view such devastation at close range, and I could only imagine, if it repulsed me, what it would do to strangers.

Clearly Kevin's appearance and hygiene were areas for some definite overhauling, and as we grew more comfortable with one another, I mulled over methods of approaching it. However, before embarking on any wild schemes of improvement, I wanted to enlist the cooperation of Dana and the Garson Gayer staff who supervised the rest of Kevin's day.

We were in a team meeting when I brought it up. I pointed out my reasoning on the matter, that it would make him more pleasant to be with, that it would reduce people's negative image of him, that it would eliminate some of the prejudices surrounding this boy because he looked so retarded and disturbed when, indeed, I would not be surprised to find his IQ quite close to average, and that undoubtedly it would improve Kevin's own self-esteem, since no one likes to think of himself as ugly. These were reasonable objectives, I said, if we all worked together. Certainly, there must be a physician affiliated with Garson Gayer who could prescribe treatment for his skin. There had to be state money coming in for a clothing allowance. When had his eyes been tested last? And his hair ... well, I inquired politely, could we give Zoe a vacation from that task for just a little while?

Here was an area where I met unexpected opposition. Or rather, apathy. Dana said forthrightly that she had been looking at Kevin for so long that she'd gotten used to him. Not too much under there anyway. He never would be Mr America. No, I agreed, and I didn't expect a Mr America. But there was no reason for him to look like something off the back ward at the state hospital either. Someone at the table shrugged when I said that. He shrugged again when I looked at him. Why bother? he said. That time would come soon enough.

Dana had another counter, one which I couldn't so easily dismiss. Why get him new clothes when he refused to wash or even change without a struggle? They'd be ruined in a few weeks. How would you get him to a dermatologist or an opthalmologist when he wouldn't leave the building? Why put him through all that hassle when he didn't care?

How did we know he didn't care? I bet he did, I said, and my voice sounded weak in my own ears. We didn't know. Kevin seemed quite happy in his filthy, unkempt state. He certainly never remarked on it to me. Maybe it didn't matter. So, for the time being at least, I gave up that effort. Maybe I just realized what everyone else there had known, even though it wasn't said. What did it matter to a kid like Zoo-boy? Where was he going anyway?

The other issue was less easily dismissed. Fear.

Fear lived with us like a third party. It had a life of its own. It ruled us; it tyrannized us. I came after a while to think of it

not as a part of Kevin but as a separate entity. It bullied him
and it bullied me. And try as we would to overcome it, if we
ventured too far—*whap!*—it drew us up sharp like misbehav-
ing puppies on leashes. Kevin would immediately be reduced
to a shivering, quivering, teary mass and the next time he
would be terrified to try whatever had frightened him the
time before.

The fears were funny things—funny-odd. I never knew
from one day to the next what things might evoke fear in
him. Like the spirals on the notebooks that he'd imagined
were lurking in that box. Or door hinges. He could go berserk
with terror over a squeaky door hinge. Or squeaky chairs.
I became a master at improvising squeak-stoppers. I used
everything from pencil lead, ground fine between my fingers, to lipstick. And smells were terrifying. Sharp, pungent
odors frightened Kevin and odors are an almost impossible
thing to get away from. More than once I resorted to carefully stuffing bits of cotton up his nostrils so that he would
not be able to smell some infinitesimally faint odor in the
room.

After a point I felt like a squirrel on a treadmill. Yet, how
ever bad it might have been for me, no doubt it was much
worse for Kevin.

'Sometimes, I lay in bed at night,' he said to me one day.
'You know how it is when you're in bed and it's dark. They
leave a light on in the hallway but we can't have them in our
rooms after ten o'clock. And it makes shadows. That light in
the hallway does, and regular things, they stretch all out.
I lay there and I look at them and I think, you know, these
are just regular things. That's just my desk. Or that's just a

chair. But they don't look that way then. They look like something else.'

He turned to glance briefly at me. His voice, as always, was
very soft. When Kevin spoke, it sounded more as if he were
talking only to himself, half aloud, and not to me at all. It was
always in such a quiet, almost dreamy manner – the way my
thoughts sounded when I heard them inside my head.

'They look the way people look,' he said. 'You know, people you thought liked you who suddenly you know don't really.
The chairs and desk and stuff, they change in the darkness.
Like people change. And I lay in my bed and I think, you
know, this is the way the chair really is. The way it looks in
daytime, that's just a foolie. It looks that way to make me
think it's all right. But it's an ugly thing, a chair at night is.
And I know even in the day that it's ugly underneath. It will
be ugly again, when I'm alone with it. When it's dark. The
chair'll be ugly.'

A small silence came between us. Morning sun bathed over
me and I was warm.

'I'm scared of chairs,' Kevin said. When I said nothing, he
glanced at me. Then down at the floor where he fiddled with
some unseen thing in the carpet. 'I try not to be scared of
things. I try to fight it. But I'm not good at it. It's everywhere
at once. It's like fighting the night.'

November came. Without the holidays to mark the passing
of time as they did in school, the days and weeks got away
from me and the months could pass softly without my ever
remembering when one started and the other one ended.
The sharp sunny days began to fade and grow gray and fitful.

All the summer's leaves were dead in the gutters and the final peace was made as the world lay down in winter.

Kevin and I kept at our work. Somewhere along the line, thirty minutes just wasn't enough, and I extended my time with him to an hour. I couldn't easily afford it with the other kids at the clinic, and it meant I had to work into the evening because I was still coming to see him every day. Kevin continued to talk to me and to no one else, although we had laid that problem to rest for the time being. All in all, it was a quiet period, spent sharing little moments.

We were coloring. Kevin had a thing about coloring, and I didn't mind it because it was relaxing and it was the mindless sort of activity I found best for allowing us to talk without its being apparent that was what we were doing.

I had brought us one of those huge posters from the discount store which one colors in with felt-tipped markers. This poster depicted a spaceship out among the stars.

Kevin was coloring the crew at the window of the rocket and I was doing the sky because it was large and boring to color, so Kevin didn't like it. I was not especially enamored of it myself.

'You know,' I said after what seemed like an interminable amount of coloring, 'I'm not so keen on doing this either. I wish I had a broad-tipped marker instead of this one.'

'Well,' replied Kevin matter-of-factly, 'you have to do it.'

'We could split it,' I suggested, looking at all that was left.

There was a long, long silence as Kevin stared at the poster. I saw his knuckles go white as he gripped the pen harder. His breathing tightened. They were the same old signs, and I glanced around the room quickly to see what could possibly be frightening him.

'No, you have to do it,' Kevin said. His voice was low. The muscles along his jaw tensed.

I stared at him because I could see his fear coming up on him but I didn't know what was causing it. Then I looked back at the poster, thinking perhaps I could distract him from the fear.

'Why don't we just leave it blank? There's too much coloring. I could do the stars instead and outline them in black. Then they'd stand out good.'

'No,' he said very quietly.

I looked at him. He looked squarely back at me. Fear had dilated his pupils but there was an intensity behind them that I did not recognize.

'What's going on, Kevin? What's wrong?'

'You have to do it. You have to color that sky.'

'Why?'

He began to tremble. His whole body arched away from me slightly. 'You *have* to do it.'

I watched him.

His voice was only a whisper. 'You have to. Because I've told you to, do you hear?'

I shifted positions. I'd been sitting on my feet and the circulation was going, so I moved them.

'*Awk!*' Kevin screamed when I did. His marker flew out of his hand. Abruptly, he dived for the safety of the table.

'Kev?'

'I didn't mean it!' he shrieked and covered his head, as he rolled into a ball. 'I didn't mean it, I didn't mean it. You don't have to!'

Stunned, I only gaped at him.

'I'm sorry, I'm sorry, I'm sorry. I didn't mean it!' He was in tears already, rocking and sobbing. 'Please, please, please, I didn't mean it. Honest I didn't. Please. I'm sorry.'

'Kevin, I don't mind. It's not that big a deal. Don't be frightened. I'm not angry. You want me to do the sky? I don't mind. I'll do the sky. Okay?'

'Please, please, please, please, please,' he begged. 'Oh please don't think I meant it. I didn't. Please, I'm sorry.'

'*Kevin?*'

He was beside himself, rocking and weeping, crying for me to forget and absolve him. I was too astonished at having caused such a furor to really think about what was going on. On my hands and knees I crawled across the carpet to try and talk him down from his hysteria.

WHAM!

Leaping to his feet when I approached, he threw the table off over his back. 'Get away from me!' he shouted. His face grew red, terror glazed his eyes. 'Get away! Get *away!*'

Before I could gather my senses, he had picked up one of the chairs. He hurled it at me with keen precision and it didn't really miss. Painfully, I staggered to my feet.

The room was too small for Kevin to be able to elude me to his satisfaction, and clearly it was I who terrified him. He reacted to me as if I were the Devil Incarnate.

Because the room was so small and he could not get away from me, Kevin felt obliged to keep me at bay by throwing things at me. He needn't have. I was quite sufficiently panic-stricken myself and was perfectly willing to stay out of his way. This frightened, I knew he was dangerous. And looming up to his nearly six-foot height, he made an awesome sight when he held a chair aloft.

There wasn't much for me to do. I ducked. A lot. Kevin threw anything and everything he could get his hands on. Chairs, pens, the poster, my box, its contents, even the table. His terror gave him improbable strength. And I, like a circus performer, jumped and ducked and dodged. The most painful things turned out to be the numerous small wooden blocks I had had in my box. They were two-inch square colored counting cubes with surprisingly sharp edges, and Kevin fired them like missiles.

Frantically I looked around for a call button or some other method of summoning help. There was none. I did have a key to the door, which the stupid aide persisted in locking. Still, with Kevin in this state, I did not want to chance turning my back on him for long, especially in front of an exit. But what else to do? Through my mind whirred all the alternatives I could think of. Would I be able to talk him down from this? Would he wear himself out before he splattered me? Should I just keep dodging and hope my strength held out longer than his? I don't think he was dead serious on really hurting me. All he wanted was to keep me away from him. But that made him plenty dangerous. Every move I made was interpreted as an attack and provoked another frenzy of panic and missiles. But it was a vicious cycle. When I moved, he threw things. When he threw things, I had to move again to avoid being hit.

Around and around and around we went. He was screaming now, ripping at his clothes and throwing himself against the walls in an attempt to escape me. When he came to the door, he jerked at it violently, but of course it was locked.

In the end, I confined myself to the two bare walls and stayed away from the windows and the door so that he would not think I was blocking any exits from him. I held a wooden chair in one hand and fended off what he threw the best I could. He began to scream when I kept the chair in hand because I think he thought I was planning to attack him with it. He screamed and screamed and screamed.

That did the trick. They heard us. Within moments a crowd of faces pressed against the small door window, frightening Kevin even further. Next came the frantic rattling of a key in the lock. Kevin tried to run from the door and fell face forward over the table. His hysteria mounted as he scrambled to his feet and threw himself against the windows.

The door burst open. People spilled in. Relieved to be rescued, I slumped back against the far wall and slid down to the floor. They swarmed over Kevin and tried to pull him from the window. He shrieked louder and fought like a wounded tiger. The Marines were there and they had his legs and his pants. They pulled his shoes off as they tugged him down from the sill. I heard the sound of cloth tearing as they struggled to lift him. There were six of them this time, six big burly men with tattooed arms and Charles Atlas muscles rippling under their shirts. Still they could not maneuver Kevin. They got him down from the windows but now he was on the floor, wiggling and squirming. Kevin escaped their grasp and, like a caged bird, battered himself against the window again. Two more men came and then a nurse. Dana was there too. So was the psychologist and two people in business suits whom I did not recognize. I stayed away from them all, clear over to the far side because I was still afraid I would only add fuel to Kevin's delirium, if I approached. In the end, it took nine men to defeat that one cornstalk of a boy and bear him out. All the way down the corridor I could hear him screaming, the pitch of it high and hysterical.

Dana came over to me, righting chairs and the table as she came. Of all the people in the room, she was the only one to come to me in the aftermath of the commotion. I was rolling up the sleeve of my shirt to look at my arm.

All of me hurt. There was no point in denying that. Now that Kevin had been borne away, I was feeling sorely in need of a little comfort myself.

The chair had hit my arm, and already a red-and-purple bruise stretched out along the upper half. Dana touched it gently.

'They'll have a doctor in for Kevin,' she said. 'You ought to have him look at that before he goes. Does it hurt?'

I nodded.

'You've got a scratch on your nose too.' She fingered it and then refocused her gaze on me. 'What happened?'

'I wish I knew for sure. I don't.'

'He just went off?'

I shrugged.

I intended to stay until Kevin quieted down and then go talk to him. However, when I went up to the ward, he was still in the seclusion room, still screaming and throwing himself against the walls. So I went down to see the doctor. There normally was not a physician at the residence, but to increase psychotropic tranquilizers in emergencies and to put an individual in seclusion with the door locked, the affiliated psychiatrist had to come over and sign orders. Thus, when I was unable to go in and see Kevin, I went down to where the psychiatrist was sitting in the back of the reception office, drinking coffee. He was a big, heavyset fellow in his late fifties, white haired and very jolly. He set me awash with antiseptic and plastered Band-Aids all over me while telling me about the king-sized sunflowers he had grown in his garden for a competition. Afterward, I treated myself to a can of Dr Pepper and went into Dana's office to begin the nasty job of recording all this in Kevin's chart. Most of the staff I encountered had a wry smile for me, a manifestation of the sort of gallows humor one develops working in such places. At least, they said, they had all heard Kevin now.

When I went back up to the ward an hour later, Kevin had been given a second tranquilizing injection. He was still banging around in the seclusion room, however. Briefly I gazed through the window in the door. He was entirely naked. Everything had been removed to prevent him hurting himself, even his glasses. He careened from side to side of the padded cell, knocking himself against the walls, bouncing off, falling into them again. His movements were woozy from the medication or perhaps just from sheer exhaustion but he kept at it. He was still screaming, although it was just a banshee cry now, thin and reedy and keening. His eyes were closed, his head back as he staggered around. With his hands he clawed at his face and his chest, as if to rip them open.

I stood at the window but stared instead at the grain in the wood of the door. It felt eerie to know I had the power to frighten somebody that much. One of the aides came up beside me. She said nothing but stood very close to me and I could feel the warmth of her body, while still not touching her.

'He's psychotic,' she said. She spoke gently, as if they were comforting words, and I suppose she meant that they should be. My own emotions were in an awesome state. They pressed outward against my ribs and chest and upward until they almost forced tears into my eyes. I wanted to cry without really understanding why. I wasn't disappointed by what had happened. It was natural enough. Nor was I depressed. I had no special expectations of this boy. In fact, I don't think my emotions were even over Kevin, himself. But I was so near to tears. My arm hurt. I was tired and feeling very vulnerable. The single thing I wanted most just then was for that unknown aide standing next to me to put her arms around me. I needed comfort. I could not even give conscious thought to what was hurting so much inside of me. It was too deep, too complex for words.

Finally, I had to leave. I couldn't wait any longer. That perhaps was the worst of all, having to leave Kevin like that. But there wasn't any choice. I would be late as it was for my next commitment, and Kevin's siege showed no signs of abating. So I left him there alone in his padded cell, alone with his fear.

Chapter Nine

The next day Kevin did not come. I sat in the small white room, waiting. Finally an aide arrived to tell me Kevin would not be there. When I asked why, the aide said he was ill. I asked if I might go up and see Kevin. The aide couldn't see any reason why not.

I had never been in Kevin's room before. It was a small cubicle in a larger dormitorylike room, Garson Gayer's attempt to give each child some privacy. They felt themselves quite progressive in this matter and advertised it in their brochure.

Kevin lay on his bed, his back to the door, when I entered. I glanced around the small space. It was as bare as our little white room.

'Kev?' I said softly, in case he was still going to be frightened of me. He had been or still was weeping and he had his hands over his face. It was a heavy, silent kind of misery. Sitting down on the edge of the bed, I ran my hand along his arm. 'Kev, it's our time together. Don't you want to come down?'

He shook his head.

I leaned against him to see his face. 'Look, Kevin, I know things didn't work out so well yesterday. Things went wrong. But that's the way of things. They do go wrong sometimes. But it doesn't matter so much. We'll get over it.'

He shook his head again. I could see the tears running down along his fingers as he continued to cover his face from me.

'Sure they will. Right now it doesn't seem very much that way. It feels like the whole world came to an end, doesn't it? But it hasn't. I'm here, aren't I? I wouldn't have come back, if I hadn't wanted to. But I do. Because I like being with you so much.'

Kevin did not respond.

I tried again, telling him things would be all right and that I was all recovered from what had happened the day before. Kevin did absolutely nothing but lie there with his hands to his face. I feared perhaps he had decided to stop talking to me.

'Kevin, won't you come down? We only have half an hour left. Come on. Get up and come down and we'll do crossword puzzles together. You like crossword puzzles. Okay? All right?'

He refused to budge. He refused to move, to respond, to even look at me. After another five minutes, I rose. Another day, I said. We'd try again another day, another time.

On my way out of the ward, I stopped at the nurses' desk to get Kevin's chart. Because he was institutionalized, I was obliged to record all my activities with him on a running chart. I took the chart and went across the hall to the staff room. Sitting down at the table, I opened it and began to write.

Kevin appeared in the doorway. I was alone in the staff room. I sat at the table amid the chaos of dirty coffee mugs and notebooks of staff activities and tons and tons of loose paper. He simply came to the door and stood until I became aware of someone watching me and looked up.

The ravages of the previous day showed on him. His face was swollen all up one side. He had bruises everywhere. I smiled when I saw him. 'Hi.'

He said nothing.

I looked down at the chart, back at him. The silence between us was fragile, the way silences often are after arguments, in the aftermath of great anger. Except, for me at least, there had been no argument, no anger.

Kevin stared at me.

I fingered the pen I had been writing with.

The silence breathed between us.

'Can I sit down?' he asked me.

I nodded and indicated a chair across the table from me. He came into the staff room, pulled out the chair and sat down.

Again the great, lengthening stillness, like cotton over a tender sore. I bent and began to write again. *Kevin came to the staff room to see me after I had left him in his room. He sat in a chair rather than on the floor. He does not appear to be afraid.*

Out beyond the room were the noises of the ward. Aides and other kids moved around. Nurses chatted. I lived in mortal terror that someone would walk in on us, demand to know what Kevin was doing in an off-limits place like the staff room and destroy the fellowship between us which was so carefully weaving itself back together in the silence.

Kevin crossed his arms on the table and laid his head down.

'Is the Thorazine still making you sleepy?' I asked.

He nodded.

I went back to writing.

'You know what he did to me once?' he said, as much to the silence as to me.

'No. What?' I didn't even know what he was talking about.

'I used not to eat my oatmeal. It was the only thing in the whole world I used not to eat. My mom, she used to make it for breakfast. Every day she made it. Then he'd tell me to eat it. He'd make me sit at the table and stay there until I ate every bit. And if I fussed, he went and got more.'

I said nothing, not daring to.

'If I didn't eat it and I had to go to school or something, he'd save it for lunch for me. And once, this one time, the oatmeal got to be about two days old. It made me sick to look at it.'

He paused, drew a breath. I was so scared someone was going to interrupt us.

'He grabbed my hair and pulled it until I opened my mouth. Then he stuffed it in. Well, I sicked it all up again, right there at the table. I couldn't help it. It had mold growing on it. It was awful. But you know what he made me do? He made me eat the sick.'

I continued to write.

'It was the only thing I never liked to eat. I ate everything else. I made a special point to eat everything else. But I guess it didn't matter very much.'

'It must have made you awfully mad,' I said and looked up. Perspiration had made huge stains on his shirt.

'He made me mad all right. He made me want to kill him.' Kevin looked at me. His eyes narrowed. 'And I will someday. When I get out of here. He won't be able to tell me what to do then. And if he does, I'll carve his body into little bits.'

'And so,' said Charity, reclining back on my couch and putting her feet up on the arm, 'you know what happened next? Well, we got to sleep outside on the porch, me and Sandy did. And so we took our blankets out there and we got to sleep.'

'You slept on the porch in November?'

'Yup. Camping out, we was. Just like on TV. Mom let me do it 'cause Sandy was with me. Sandy's twelve. So my mom said it was okay.'

'Wasn't it a little chilly?'

'Gosh no. We had lots of blankets.' Charity lay all the way back on the couch and kicked her feet up. For a few moments she bicycled in the air. 'And the next morning we got up and baked pancakes, me and Sandy. Sandy's twelve. She can touch the stove.'

'I see.' Actually I didn't. I couldn't imagine when Charity was finding time to do all these things, since she seemed to have moved in with me over the past few weeks. When I would come home from work, there was Charity, hunched up on my doorstep, still dressed in her school clothes. She would stay until supper and eat with me, if I'd let her. Then down in front of the television she'd go. Or if I was writing, she would stand in back of my chair, feet on the rung, and read over my shoulder, all the while making my desk chair sway. She couldn't read worth a hill of beans, so mostly she just shouted out letters she recognized. *B! R! H!* would come the constant chant behind me while I tried to concentrate on wording a technical paper about bilingualism and psychogenic language problems. Charity would stay until I chucked her out every night. On weekends I was even luckier. One Saturday she arrived at 6:15 in the morning.

Charity's family seemed quite pleased with the arrangement. I must admit, if I'd had Charity I probably would have too. In the beginning I demanded that she have permission and could prove it before she could stay. But that was hopeless. The family had no phone and the couple of times I had bothered to pile her in the car and drive her home for consent, no one there had even missed her. I suspect they'd realized she'd found a place to go and someone to feed her and were satisfied to let her milk the situation for all it was worth. I was irked by the imposition; it was like having acquired a stray cat. But as with cats, I was too soft to ignore her and send her home hungry.

Truth was, of course, that Charity's family was full of problems of their own, not the least of them, Charity herself. They lived well below the poverty level in a small dingy place down by the river. I had met Charity's mother only once when I had brought Charity home. She was a young woman but she looked ancient. Her body was riddled with the stigmata of a rough life, and I suspected they went clear through to her heart. The house was constantly jammed with relatives, and they all seemed to live there on a more or less permanent basis. While Charity had no father, there was no lack of males in her home, but their exact position in the household was something I never knew for sure.

Charity herself continued to be a personal challenge to me. A master of the unintentional put-down, Charity had done more to devastate my ego in three months than most kids had in a lifetime. I have no doubt that if I had encountered Charity earlier in my career, I would have become a medical technologist like my mother wanted.

Still she had an innate charm about her. She would be standing there on my doorstep complaining loudly or would be struggling with some mishap, like the time she had polished her fingernails and then couldn't get her mittens off, and I'd think to myself, what's the matter with you? You're supposed to be an *authority!* Sixty pounds of sheer challenge was Charity.

It was a Wednesday evening, when she lounged across my furniture and gave me more excruciating details of life with Sandy.

'Can I eat supper with you? What we having?' she asked when I rose with what must have been a suppertime look on my face. She was off the couch in a second and skipping out into the kitchen ahead of me, her body dancing side to side like an excited puppy.

'Stew,' I said. 'Stew and salad and bread.'

'Is that all?'

'That's all.'

'Why don't you ever keep any good stuff around?'

'Like what?' I asked.

'Like ice cream or Cokes or something?'

'Because that's not what I make my suppers out of.'

'Oh well,' she said good-naturedly. 'If that's what we gotta have, then that's what we gotta have, huh?'

I nodded.

I gave her the lettuce to wash and the carrots to slice. *Touché* she shouted to herself and stabbed the knife into the air at unseen dangers. I took it and the carrots and let her shake the dressing instead.

And then as I was putting the stew into bowls, Charity came bounding over and leaned across my arm to see what was happening.

'Tor?'

'Yes?'

'Can I spend the night with you?'

'No, I don't think so. It's a school night.'

'So? What difference does that make? I'll still go to school.'

'You need to go home and get a bath and—'

'Why?' she interrupted, looking down at herself. 'Am I dirty? Don't you got a bathtub here?'

'That's not the point. It's a school night. You ought to be home in bed and then be able to get up and put on school clothes and get there before the bell rings. It would be too hard from clear over here. We're practically across town. And I have to leave for work a lot earlier than you have to go to school.'

'It wouldn't be so hard. I could do it. I could wear these here clothes. They ain't dirty. I could get up real, real early. Okay? Can I? Please?'

I shook my head and handed her a bowl of stew. 'No, not on a school night, Charity. Maybe some weekend. But not on a school night. End of conversation.'

Carefully she carried her bowl over to the table. Setting it down, she climbed up onto the chair. 'You gonna have a man over here tonight, is that how come I can't?'

I looked at her. 'No, Charity. That isn't how come you can't. I told you how come you can't.'

She had already started shoveling her food in, so she just shrugged. 'Well, that's all right. I understand. That's when my mom works too. Every night but Mondays.'

The next morning dawned dark and gray, and when I drove to Garson Gayer at 9:30, the streetlights were still blazing.

Kevin had arrived in the room ahead of me. When I came, he was standing at the window looking out. It was the first time I had ever seen him just standing without being in the process of getting somewhere, unless of course I counted the day before, outside the staff room. He appeared to have momentarily put down the burden of fear.

He did not turn when I entered but continued to stare out of the window. The day was so gray, a bitter November day that spoke only of winter and made the icy darkness ahead of us seem millennia long. It was not snowing. It was doing nothing outside at all. It was silent, motionless and cold, like death.

I came up behind Kevin, put my box down on the radiator below the window and did not speak. I had to admit feeling a little afraid of him, standing there. The other day was not long enough past. I was still sore, and he had demonstrated his strength so well. This wasn't like it had been with the little children. I was a physically strong person myself and even with the older children, with the boys ten or eleven or twelve, I could easily subdue them when I had to, no matter how out of control they might have been. I had always had the confidence to act without much regard to physical danger because I was tall and in good condition and strong and I knew it. But things were different with Kevin. He wasn't a child. He was a man. I found it scary to know all I had to rely on were my wits. They didn't always feel so sharp.

Kevin still did not turn from the window, and something about him made me unwilling to break the silence. I too looked out the window. The small courtyard was without life.

Kevin stood quietly, his shoulders back, his hands interlocked behind his back. The side of his face was still swollen, turning bluish green at the jawline where the bruise appeared deepest. As I watched him, I could see that he had not necessarily put his fear aside but rather some other thing had superceded it. He seemed suddenly very old to me, a thing Kevin had never seemed before. And he seemed weary.

'I wish I could see more,' he said at last.

'What do you mean?'

'Beyond this window. This isn't a very good window. It doesn't let you see anything except where you are. I already know where I am. I wish I could see more.'

Then the silence again.

The silence grew very long. I was uncomfortable with it, I think only because I feared to break it. Kevin was clearly somewhere else, and I did not know if I should call him back or not. This was a different Kevin; he had changed from the boy under the table. I did not know him.

He turned slightly, glanced at me. 'They pay you, don't they?'

'Who?' I asked. 'For what?'

'To come here.'

I nodded.

'You come here and do this with me because someone pays you to.'

'It's my job, if that's what you mean.'

Silence.

'You knew that,' I said. 'You knew all along.'

He shrugged, a half shrug really, just one shoulder. It lent an air of indifference to the gesture.

'What's eating you, Kev?'

'Nothing.'

'I can hardly believe that.'

Another shrug. Then the silence. He was a master at silence. It protected him as effectively as chain mail. But I wasn't bad at the game myself. I too said nothing and we stood together, staring out into the heavy grayness. The minutes passed.

'I thought,' he said softly, 'that maybe you came because you wanted to.'

'I do.'

'But not because you got money for it.'

'That's secondary. I do come because I want to. I wouldn't come, if I didn't. Nobody can pay me enough to go where I don't want to go. So the money's not the issue.'

He shrugged. 'Doesn't matter. I'm used to it.' He looked over at me. 'They told you I got no family, didn't they? They told you that I just got brought here and left and I've never seen them since.'

'No, they didn't exactly tell me.'

'I guess I was just thinking,' he said, 'that it would have been nice to have at least one person in the world who didn't have to be paid to like me.'

Chapter Ten

The days grew eerie. It was mid-November. Usually this was a time for pale white skies and large, floating snowflakes, when winter came upon us tenderly and beguiled us. But not this year. The temperature dropped to just above freezing. The clouds hung low and dark, making it necessary to leave the lights on all day. However, they gave up no rain. As the days strung out lifelessly, one behind the other with no change, a fog began rising up from the land. It cloaked the deathly pallor of the days in a soft, white shroud. It was what they would have called *Mabinogi* days in Wales, days for spirits to come alive and for ancient things no longer in the present world.

Kevin seemed to take on the same secret nature as the weather. He never recovered from the blowup over the rocket poster. Whatever had happened then had been complete. Kevin changed.

Kevin's behavior remained especially enigmatic over a period of about ten days. He talked to me little; he did very few of the old things which had given him pleasure. No more crosswords or activity books or games with small toy cars. He grew up very suddenly in those ten days, and the aura of youngness which had clung to him vanished. Instead he was restless, spending most days before the window or pacing up and down the length of the small white room. The most mysterious change of all, in my opinion, was that his fear seemed to have fallen away from him, shed like a reptile's old skin. His chart indicated that he was still fearful on the ward and in the schoolroom and still protected himself with tables and chairs, but when he came to me, he put his fear away. He now walked into the room, he sat in chairs, on the table, on the radiator below the window. His shoulders were held back and he seemed an altogether different person than he had before. But the fearlessness had been replaced with a different sort of burden, a kind of weariness about him, which made him seem very old yet without vulnerability. Perhaps it was a type of depression. I didn't know. But it emanated from him, this heavy, heartless tiredness.

I did not understand what was happening to him. I made no pretense to. I only came, wary and watchful. I was no longer afraid of him, as I had been the first couple of days after the explosion. But because I had so few concrete clues as to what was happening to him, I remained vigilant. It was a vaguely anxious period for me, the way it is when one awaits a tornado after the watch has been sounded, although at the same time, it was intriguing.

* * *

'I drew you something,' Kevin said to me when I arrived. As on other days, he had come into the room ahead of me. He was at the window, perched on the radiator, but as I entered, he came to the table. He walked. Like a man, he walked, with big, powerful strides. No more crouching or cowering. Pulling out a chair, he sat down. 'Look,' he said. 'See what I drew for you.'

He had a piece of brown paper, a sack that had been cut open as carefully as possible to expose the maximum amount of unwrinkled space.

'It isn't very good,' he said. 'They don't let us have pencils on our own here, so this one I had to steal from the schoolroom when I was having lessons. It was easy. They don't watch me under the table. But see, it's just a grubby little thing. And I had to use a crayon for the red. If I had colored pencils, I could have done it better. But I don't. I'm sorry it isn't so good.'

It was good enough. In fact, it was hideously good. On this piece of opened sack was an expertly executed drawing of a man lying on a road. He had been disemboweled, the curvy, squirmy coils of his intestines strewn across the tarmac. A bird—a crow, I think—sat upon the protruding bone of one leg and pulled forth a long, sinewy bit of meat from the body cavity. Blood had spilled everywhere, puddling in the road, trickling through blades of grass. On one side I could even see the red footprints of some vermin which had trailed through the blood and off the side of the paper.

It was a horrible picture, shocking in its photographic accuracy and demonic in its incredible attention to detail.

That Kevin's obvious talent was unsuspected made the entire thing more sinister.

'It could have been better,' Kevin said quietly. 'If I'd had real pencils.'

'It's very good as it is. I hadn't realized you drew so well.'

'I draw *very* well,' he replied and the note of confidence in his voice was menacing, the way it is when one knows precisely the power of one's abilities.

'I can see that.'

He was studying me carefully, hoping to see, I think, if the contents of the picture shocked or sickened me. It had, more by virtue of its unexpected excellence than anything else, but one could hardly ignore what the picture was about either. It was the detail that unsettled me the most, especially those bloody rat footprints. However, I did the best I could to show no reaction at all. That seemed best.

When I looked over, Kevin smiled. It was the same, easy grin he's always given me, a slightly foolish expression that made him look retarded, although I knew full well by now he wasn't.

'That's what I'm going to do to him,' he said. 'I want to see his stupid body split open and maggots eating his guts.'

'Oh,' I said and realized I didn't even know who it was that should suffer this fate. I asked.

'My stepfather, of course.' His forehead wrinkled, as if he expected that I should have known that fact, as if he thought he had told me and was now disappointed that I'd forgotten. But he hadn't told me.

Again he scrutinized my face very, very carefully, looking me fully in the eyes without turning away. I wasn't sure this time what he was searching for. Perhaps I had unsettled him by not knowing who the picture was about and he was assessing my value. Perhaps he was simply trying to figure out how much he could reveal to me, how relaxed he could become. I was unable to tell. But he stared at me for the longest time, his eyes slightly squinted behind the thick glasses. I felt probed to my soul.

At last he turned away, looking down at the drawing again. 'This is what I'm going to do to him. Only it won't be just a drawing someday.'

The next day the drawing was back. He had folded it up in a little square and stuffed it down his T-shirt. With no one bothering him about bathing or changing his clothes, it had been undetected. I'd checked the charts before I went down to the small white room. There was no mention of a picture, so no one else must have seen it because that wasn't the sort of thing which would have failed to make an impression on the staff. It would have been charted. But it wasn't, so I knew the drawing was our little secret.

When I came into the room, Kevin had the drawing with him. He sat at the table and carefully flattened out the wrinkles. As I sat down next to him, Kevin examined the picture at length. With one finger he traced over particular parts, over the exposed internal organs, over the blood puddling beside the corpse. Then he turned away and stared out the window. Minutes seemed to pass and all he did was stare out at the murky, misty stillness in the courtyard.

'This is a good place,' he said so softly it could have been a thought said aloud.

I did not reply.

'This is the best place.' He still did not look at me. There was a long pause and then he spoke. 'You're magic, aren't you?'

I didn't understand what he was saying.

'Nothing happens to me in here when you're here. You're magic, aren't you?' he said to me. 'You keep bad things from happening to me.'

That was a very difficult thing to reply to. Because I did not know what might be behind his words, I simply echoed them. There was too much I didn't understand.

'You feel safe here,' I said.

He nodded. Caressing the paper, he nodded again.

And the day after that, the drawing was back.

'You hate him pretty bad, don't you?' I said as he sat tracing bits of the drawing with his finger.

'He's a fucking bastard,' Kevin replied. It was the first time I had heard Kevin swear.

I nodded.

'I'm going to get him,' Kevin said. 'When I get out of here, I'm going to get myself a knife and I'm going to find him and I'll get him. You just see if I don't.'

'You want to kill him.'

'Kill him? I want to murder the motherfucker so his stupid brains are all over the floor. So his grungy insides are splattered all over the cement like dog food.'

And the following day, the picture returned. Kevin was obsessed with it. It was all he wanted to talk about. He had added a new part. Up in the corner he had penciled in another skull, crushed. The brains were splashed over a distance beyond the fragmented skull, rather as one sees the remains of animals run over on the road. This, too, Kevin had gone over in detail with me. His conversations were terse and tight, his body rigid. Tension crackled around us like the air before an electrical storm.

For the first few days I simply sat with him, echoing his sentiments and trying to figure out what the hell to do next. I watched him carefully, desperate to sort out what was happening to him, to glean some form of understanding from his face, his posture, his behavior, his words. In the back of my mind increasingly was the concern that he might be dangerous. Had I created some sort of Frankenstein's monster by letting him loose from his self-imposed prison?

The myriad of paralyzing minor fears were gone, at least here in the small white room. And replacing them was what I began to suspect the fears had been protecting all along: hate. As the days went by and Kevin became increasingly obsessed with the brutal drawings of murder and talk of violence, I started to believe that he had used the fears as a method of controlling his hate. Indeed, that was perhaps the reason behind his many years of silence as well. If one did not speak at all, one did not run the risk of letting out dangerous thoughts. Kevin had simply been doing the best he could to manage his emotions. If something proved hazardous and aroused his feelings too much, he became afraid of it, he didn't talk about it. In the end he had become like a drug addict. It took more and more fears to contain his feelings and more and more silence to keep the things unsaid until suddenly he was trapped and the fears and silence ruled him. But fair dues to the kid. Zoo-boy had done the best he could in the circumstances. He'd caged the responsible party.

This also lent an air of insight to the explosion over the rocket poster. He had dared to make his own feelings known in the situation and perhaps more significantly, he had dared impose his will on me. Then like the proverbial straw on the camel's back, the resulting fear had proven too much.

But in the end he had survived and so had I. I think he had summed it up well that one day. This small white room was safe. Whatever magical powers he was imbuing me with I had no doubt would pass, but this room, itself, was proving safe. He'd ventured to talk. God had not struck him dead. We had had that horrific explosion over the poster. We both survived. Now he was able to bring in his drawings and say the things he had kept silent and nothing was happening to him. Slowly but surely, Kevin was discovering that the world was a safer place than he had believed, or at least this small part of it was.

This was, of course, all conjecture on my part, the type of introspection I did not usually indulge in about the kids. But it seemed a possible enough conclusion. These were rather rough waters we were riding through at the moment but, on the other hand, it was good to see him put away a little of his fear.

After almost a week of obsessive, rage-torn conversation over the drawing, Kevin still appeared unsated. We were sitting at the table on Friday morning when the aide arrived to escort him back to the ward. The aide had come a little earlier than usual and, thus, startled Kevin when he rattled the lock. Kevin's shoulders slumped, his head ducked down, he fell protectively over the picture. By the time the door opened, Kevin was plain old loopy Zoo-boy, slithering off the chair and onto the carpet. He dragged the paper and pencil down under the table with him.

'Won't you ever get out from there?' the aide asked as he came across the room to fish Kevin out from under the table. We must have looked an odd pair to him because I was still sitting in a chair at the table and Kevin was now under it. There was a note of good-natured despair in the aide's voice. 'Come on, Kevin. Time to go. Madge is going to murder you if you're late for O.T. again. Come on, get up from under there. Hurry up.' He put a toe under the table and nudged Kevin.

Kevin dragged himself up. As he prepared to go, he pressed the drawing, now folded up into a small square, into my hand. Obviously, he had not wanted to risk having the aide see him tuck it into his T-shirt. Then he slunk out the door.

Still sitting at the table, I opened the drawing up again for a private look at the thing. There, scribbled hastily across the top, was a note.

Bring me paper! And bring me pencils. Collared pencils, please. I need them!

The following morning I arrived with three sketchpads and a box of twenty-four colored pencils. Kevin was already there, sitting on the floor on the far side of the room. He turned when I entered.

'Here,' I said, coming over and sitting down beside him.

Kevin's face lit up. 'Did you get these for me?'

'Yes.'

'Because I told you to, huh? Just for me?'

I nodded.

He took the bag and ripped it open. Gleefully, he riffled through the sketchpads and then flipped the top off the box of pencils. He touched the points. 'Hey, these are good.' He pulled one pencil out and scribbled a bit on the edge of the sack. 'Yeah. Yeah, these are real good. I want to try them, all right? Can I take them out and draw with them?'

'They're yours. You can do what you want with them.'

'Yes.' He dumped the entire box of pencils out onto the floor and opened the sketchpad. 'Here, I'll make a picture for you. What do you want me to draw? You name it. I'll draw you anything.'

I paused in thought. From where I was sitting on the floor, I could see out the window. There was a large tree just beyond the pane, some sort of cottonwood, I think. Weak sunlight had broken through the clouds and was shining among the bare branches. For a moment the flicker of light and shadow transfixed me and I did not answer immediately. When I turned back, Kevin was already bent over the pad drawing. I leaned forward against his arm to see what it was.

It was a young girl, maybe six or seven, with long rather stringy brown hair and parted lips.

As I watched her come alive under his pencil, I was again awed by his obvious artistic talent. How had he gone so many years without anyone noticing? Or had he? Kevin appeared aware of the power of his talent. And he knew good materials and how to use them. His work, too, was undeniably sophisticated. Somewhere, somehow, some way, had his talents been nurtured?

Like the grisly drawing before it, this one had a photographic quality. Given the advantages of color, the picture soon took on subtle shadings and overtones. The child stood startlingly close to real life, yet at the same time there was a mystical quality to her, brought out by the colors.

She was a haunting-looking child, not really pretty, with her straggly, uncombed hair. She was not smiling. Instead, she gazed out intently at us from the drawing, as if we were intruders. Her lips, especially, I noticed. Parted, they were full and rather pouty and gave her an overall sort of infantile sensuality. It was an amazing picture, as accurate as a photograph yet as subtle as only art can be.

'Who is that?' I asked.

'Carol.'

He continued to draw, his hand going rapidly back and forth across the page, almost as if the picture couldn't get out fast enough. The child reached closer and closer to life.

'Who's Carol?'

'My sister.'

'She's lovely.'

He nodded.

There was an infinite silence, disturbed only by the sound of Kevin's pencil on the paper. I turned around so that I was facing him and leaned back against the wall. I watched him; I studied the way he moved as he drew.

It surprised me to realize as I sat there that he really wasn't such a bad-looking kid. Not really an ugly kid. He was relaxed over the drawing. The tension of the past few weeks had slipped away from his body and, absorbed in what he was doing, he assumed a freer, more natural posture than I had ever seen him in before.

I wondered about him as I sat there. I wondered what it felt like to be him. I wondered what thoughts he had in his head. More than any other kid I had been with, I was mystified by him.

Still he worked on in silence. I glanced up at the clock. Over at the window. I fiddled with the cuff of my shirt. The quiet wore on, nibbled at by the sound of his pencil.

Finally Kevin held the picture out at arm's length to examine it. He turned it so I could see it too, but before I got a good look, he was bent back over it to soften one line with his finger.

'Yeah,' he said half aloud. Then he glanced up. He smiled. It was a funny little smile, soft and reassuring. Then he returned to the drawing.

'You know,' he said, 'once I was going to buy Carol this boat. Did I ever tell you about that?'

'No.' He had never even told me Carol existed before now.

'Well, I was going to buy her this little boat. You had to go down to the corner store by the garage and they had these little plastic boats you could float in the water. You know. Like in the bathtub or something. But you had to ask to see them. The man there, he kept them up on a shelf behind the counter 'cause otherwise the kids used to steal them. They were good boats.

'Anyway, they cost $2.98. I had $3.10 and so I told Carol I was going to get her one of them boats. So I went down. And I went in. I thought to myself, now you're going to ask this guy to see one of them boats. But I couldn't do it. You know. I had to *ask*. I just couldn't. I had to walk out of the store and sit on the curb for a while. Then I got back up and went back in and thought *now* you're going to ask that guy to see one of them boats. But I couldn't. So I went back out on the curb and sat down for a while more.'

Kevin never looked up from his drawing. I closed my eyes a moment and I could see the little girl in the picture. She looked like so very many of my children had. I could see her with her straggly long hair and her shabby clothes and that provocative expression of self-made dignity that street kids have. I could see the little boy too, who could not work up the courage to speak.

'And after a bit,' Kevin continued, 'I thought to myself, now you *are* going in and ask that guy to see one of them boats. So I went in. But I couldn't. I just stood there and I could see he thought I was one of the kids who came in to steal and he said, "What do you want, kid?" and I got scared and I ran back outside. And I sat down on the curb again. I kept telling myself, you got to be able to do this. You promised Carol you'd get her that boat. You *got* to, you stupid idiot. So finally, I said to myself, now you are *going* to go in there and ask that guy to see one of them boats and so I walked in and I said, "Can I see one of them boats?" and he showed me one and it was red and Carol hated red, so I said, "Can I see one of them blue boats now?" and he said, "You got money, kid, or you just looking?" And I said, "I'm going to buy one for my sister." And so he showed me a blue one and I liked it and so I bought it. And I took it home and gave it to Carol.

'But later when I was outside, my stepfather came up. And Carol comes around the side of the house and she's got the boat in her hand and he said, "Where did you get that from?" and she said, "Kevin bought it for me from the shop by the garage." And he said that was a lie. He said, "You couldn't've bought it, Kevin, you must've stole it." I knew he thought that because I didn't talk to him, I wouldn't be able to talk to the guy at the shop either. But Carol said, "Yes, he did too buy it for me." And he told her to shut up. Then he took the boat and he put it on the ground and he stepped on it.'

Again Kevin held the picture out to examine it.

'Anyway, Carol cried. Not because of the boat or anything because she didn't cry about things like that. But because of me. She felt sorry for me. I think I could have stood it on my own. But I couldn't then. Why did he have to make me feel like that? In front of Carol? Why did he have to make Carol cry for me?'

Then he turned the page of the sketchbook over and began another drawing. I came up beside him to see what he was making. Beneath his hand the long, lean line of a body formed. The red pencils came up and blood spilled down. The blue pencil etched in the long, spidery fingers of the mesentery as it grasped at exposed organs. When the silver pencils started, I could see the gleam of slime along the tender coils of intestine.

I sat too amazed at what was happening to him to do anything other than just watch it. He clutched at the sketchpad, drawing in rapid, accurate strokes. His body was bent over the paper in frenzied tension, his face feverish with involvement. Releasing the picture became desperately important.

'I'm gonna kill him. I've gotta,' Kevin whispered under his breath. 'I'm gonna get a knife and murder him.'

'That might not be the best way of solving things, Kevin,' I said. 'Look what would happen to *you*, if you did . . .'

'Yes, I know,' he interrupted. 'I'll go to prison. I'll get life, probably. It's premeditated murder. I'd probably get life.' He looked up over the sketchpad at me. 'But *I* don't care. It'd be worth it to me. And what the heck? I've already been locked up half my life. And I haven't even ever done anything.'

Chapter Eleven

Then the impossible happened.

Because of a conference being held in town that week, I had notified Garson Gayer that I would have to come in earlier than my usual 9:30 to 10:30 slot to see Kevin. So on Monday I arrived in the bitterly cold half-darkness of a December morning. I had intended to flop down in Dana's office for a chat and a cup of coffee first, because I hadn't seen much of her lately and because the night before an old boyfriend had turned up and we had stayed up until four in the morning talking and drinking plonk in commemoration of times gone by. So I was half dead with want of sleep and had decided only the evil potion Dana brewed specially was going to make me human again.

'Hey! There she is! Dana, there's Torey!' shouted one of the secretaries from behind the glass of the reception area. The other woman came out and looked at me.

I had no idea what was going on.

'Torey's here,' I heard someone down the hall say and two aides appeared. Then Dana materialized.

'Well congratulations to you,' she said, and her face broke into smiles. When my expression remained blank, she smiled all the harder. 'Didn't they tell you?'

'Tell me what?'

'Kevin talked.'

Kevin *had* talked. Not just a word or two. He talked. As if seven years of silence had not happened, Kevin had casually responded to a comment Dana had made to him on Sunday afternoon. It was soon apparent that was no isolated incident. He answered everything put to him and by evening he was speaking spontaneously, volunteering his own thoughts to the staff and the other children.

Dana was ecstatic. Indeed, the entire Garson Gayer staff was in a holiday mood. *Kevin talked!* And they greeted me like a returning hero.

Kevin talked? The whole occurrence caught me completely by surprise. This made no sense at all to me. After all these months of silence during which I had tried so desperately to get him to talk to other people, why had he chosen now? What had made him suddenly change his mind? This really was an extraordinary thing, completely unexpected to me. And because it was so totally unexpected, it left me unsettled. The whole deal had an uneasy, slightly sinister overtone for me.

But how could I say that to Dana? Or the staff? They toasted me with strong-smelling coffee and sticky Danishes. They thought it had all been my doing; they called me the Miracle Worker. I sputtered over the coffee and said it had taken me as much by surprise as it had everyone else, that I hadn't expected it either. I said that I feared I had had very little to do with it. But even in my own ears it sounded like false modesty, when in fact it was nothing other than brutal truth.

I stayed long enough with Dana and the others to be pleasant but then excused myself to go down to the small white room. Kevin wasn't due for quite some time because I had come so early, but I had to get away from the staff. His talking had had very little to do with me, I suspected, at least in the way they were interpreting it, and I was uneasy having them believe I was as much in control of things as that. Indeed, there in the small white room, it occurred to me that I was quite out of control with Kevin. Putting my box on the table, I went to stand in front of the window and stare out into the courtyard. I dug my hands deep into the pockets of my jeans. Kevin was now doing things I didn't even anticipate. He had gained his own steam. I might have given him the push initially but now he was running under his own power and in his own direction. And it dawned on me that I was not necessarily even keeping up.

Outside the morning had brightened. Our stretch of gray, changeless days had broken around Thanksgiving, and now it was more as it typically was at this time of year, the days brilliant, the nights cold, the trees standing in naked splendor against a sky so sharply blue it looked brittle. I stood, hands still in my pockets, and watched the dead leaves whirl around the foot of the cottonwood. What was happening? It was like putting a puzzle together with so many pieces still loose that one didn't know what the picture was supposed to be and then suddenly discovering that half the pieces were for some other puzzle entirely. What was going on? And why?

Kevin was as pleased with himself as Dana was with him. He came into the room boldly, a smirk across his face. Like a benign king, he dismissed the aide with a wave of one arm. Coming over to the window, he hoisted himself up on the radiator. I was still standing there, so he was quite close to me, physically.

'I guess everybody told you,' he said. Then he got down and went over to the box on the table. Opening it, he took out one of the sketchpads and an ordinary lead pencil. He closed the box and returned to the radiator.

'Yes, they told me.'

'I kind of wanted to tell you myself. But I knew they'd get to you before I did.' He began to draw.

'Well, everyone's excited. It's understandable. You know how it must be for them ...' I stopped the conversation half-finished because I ran out of things to say.

Kevin glanced up briefly when I said no more. He gave me another one of those smirky smiles and then returned to his drawing. There was no fear with him whatsoever. Outgrown and shed, it had been left behind by an entirely new person.

I would not have recognized him as that frightened, rocking boy under the table only three months earlier. But in a way, I had been much more comfortable with Zoo-boy.

'So, are you proud of me?' Kevin asked. 'That I finally talked like you wanted?'

'Was it hard?' I asked.

He lifted his head, turned, gazed out the window for a moment. Then he nodded. 'Yes, it was hard. I knew I could do it. You know what I mean? I'd been thinking about it a lot lately. But actually doing it was hard.'

I nodded. For some unknown reason I was feeling strange. It was a physical sensation, very weird. The hairs along the back of my neck were prickling. I was feeling defensive too, as if this change in Kevin were not to my acclaim but rather my fault.

'So,' he said again, 'are you proud of me? It's what you wanted out of me, isn't it?'

I regarded him, trying to see in him what I was not seeing. Yes, I *had* wanted it. Once. I wasn't so sure that I wanted it now.

Kevin was watching me too. He was bent low over his sketchpad, pencil still poised, but he was watching me, searching, no doubt, for the very same sort of information in my face that I was trying to find in his. We were intimate strangers, each of us having believed we knew the other far better than either of us did.

'Why did you do it, Kev?' I asked. 'Why did you decide to talk now?'

'Because you wanted me to.'

I shook my head.

His lip twitched. He looked down at the pad. 'Well, because I thought it was time to.'

'Why?'

'Because I knew if I didn't talk, they'd never let me out of here. And I knew if I never got out of here, I . . .'

'Could never kill him?'

The silence between us was granite hard. If I had reached out, I'm sure I could have touched it.

Then he nodded. 'Yes. I could never kill him.'

As the days went by, one after the other, I watched Kevin's hate come unmasked. I realized that in most part it was my fault that it was happening. This small white room was safe. These sixty minutes were time out. I continued, as I had from the beginning, to have a most unusual sort of relationship with Kevin. He talked to me, almost as if I were part of him and that while he was telling these things to me, it was more as if he was simply revealing them to himself. In a way, I felt almost invisible. I had no identity as a person to Kevin, other than as a reflection of himself.

Yet, for me, this experience was beginning to take on the proportions of a horror story, like some dark novel penned in the deepest part of the night. Was he dangerous like this? That was a very real question. I had to ask myself that over and over again in the days and weeks that followed. Kevin's murders and violence provided a mordant backdrop to the Christmas season.

I wasn't in control of Kevin. I knew that. Would he take it into his head to actually experiment with what he drew in pictures? Would he accidentally displace some of this rage on an unsuspecting aide or nurse? Or another child? Or me? Would he suddenly overcome his petrifying fear of leaving the building, the way he had his fear of talking, and decide to run away? Like so many of his other fears, might he trade it in for action? Did he know that if he stepped outside the Garson Gayer building, he might not be able to contain his murderous rage?

These types of thoughts were with me constantly. Would he? Could he? I didn't know. That was the horror of it. I honestly did not know. I think I now understood how Frankenstein must have felt.

Yet, despite those uncertainties, I was hesitant to say too much to the rest of the staff beyond an occasional note in the chart. I had no real evidence that Kevin might be dangerous. Drawings and verbalized feelings were not enough. In fact, they alone would be viewed as a very acceptable way of working out such emotions. Every person at one time or another has such feelings anyway, and with Kevin's background, it was reasonable to expect him to have cause for rather more than an average amount. So his drawings were no cause in and of themselves to believe he would carry such things out.

But then who was I to judge? They were pretty dynamic emotions he was venting. What if he truly was dangerous? What if he went out and hurt someone seriously? How could I ever justify it to myself, if I had suspected and yet never properly alerted anyone to the possibility?

It was an agonizing time for me. Warily, I watched what I had created and I grew more and more weary with the burden of it. I think the worst was that the Christmas season was in full swing and it was impossible for me to balance the two. All my frustrations with Kevin I wanted to vent on the inanities of the season. I wanted to leap out of my car and mug the ding-a-ling Santas on the street corners. I wanted to bash in the stupid speaker in the elevator up to my office with its nonstop carols. Most of all, I wanted to scream. I wanted to stand on the street corner in the middle of all the shoppers and just scream. Scream what, I don't know, but screaming appealed to me a lot in those weeks.

If Kevin wasn't bad enough on his own, Charity was adding her little bit of fuel to the fire. She had gone from visiting me frequently to visiting me continuously. Not only did this deprive me of what small bit of solitude I had, especially at Christmastime, it also made any likely association with men virtually impossible. The few fellows who braved meeting her on the doorstep were usually impaled shortly with those dreadful off-the-wall remarks only Charity seemed capable of making. Or worse, they got stories full of typical Charity-like exaggeration about my previous liaisons. Before long, Charity managed to completely clear the deck, and it was just the two of us alone.

One night after an especially grueling day, not only with Kevin but with a kid named Fletcher Forbes, who had a vacuum-cleaner fetish and had just trapped me into an hour's intimate discussion about attachments and dust bags and the personal lives of Hoovers, I came home to be greeted by Charity sitting on my front steps. The day, so bright and sunny, had turned into a rather typical December night, and by the time I finished work, it was already dark, the wind blowing up fallen leaves in blustery gusts. Charity sat huddled in the lee of the porch.

'Whew,' she said when I climbed out of the car. 'I thought you were never getting home. Where were you anyhow? How come you're so late?'

Nerves and sheer tiredness left me without a lot of desire to cope. All I wanted was peace and quiet. 'What are you doing here?' I asked.

'How come you were late?'

'I was at the store getting groceries.'

'Oh good. What we having for supper?'

I fumbled with the keys, looking for the one to the house while I balanced the grocery bag.

'I said, what we having for supper?' she asked again. 'Something good, I hope. Pizza? Did you get us pizzas?'

'Who said you were eating with me? What are you doing here anyway? It's got to be twenty degrees out here. You'll catch your death one of these days.'

'I'm always here,' she said cheerfully and reached to take the grocery bag from me to see what was in it.

'Yes, I *know* you are. That's what I'm asking. How come?' I flung open the door and turned on the hall light. 'Why don't you ever go to your own home sometime and leave me alone?'

''Cause I like it here,' she said, as deaf as ever to what I was saying.

'But you don't *live* here. I do.'

I went out to the car to get the other bag of groceries and returned to the house. Charity was still standing on the porch, her eyes dilated to blackness in the half-light cast out from the hall. She held the door open for me. I put the groceries on the hall chair. 'Charity, does it ever occur to you that you're over here an awful lot? That maybe I have other things to do sometimes?'

'Well, I'm not stopping you from doing them.'

'Yes, you *are*. I want to do them alone.'

Her forehead wrinkled. 'You don't want me?' Her voice grew suddenly small.

That was right. I didn't. I wanted to be able to go in and sit down and have an evening to myself for once, maybe run a hot bath, jam up the stereo until the floor vibrated, drink something warm and soothing and lose myself in some mindless book that wouldn't suffer if dropped in the bath. I knew I couldn't do any of it with Charity there. Yet, seeing her face drop as she stood there in the wan hallway light, I didn't have the guts to tell her to get lost.

However, Charity took my pause for what it was, affirmation that she wasn't wanted. Abruptly tears welled up. She looked positively grief-stricken and I felt rotten to the core.

'No, no, no, of course I want you, Char. Come on in. I'm just tired and had other things on my mind, that's all.'

But Charity refused to move. She put her hands over her face to hide her tears.

I came down on my hands and knees to be closer to her height. 'Look, Charity, I was rude. I'm sorry. Of course I want you. Come in and we'll make supper, okay?'

'I even brang you my good school papers,' she sobbed through her hands. Then she fished out a grubby little wad from her pocket. 'I thought you might wanna see how good I done at school. And now you don't even want me.' And she wailed melodramatically.

'I said I was sorry, Charity. Now come on, don't worry about it. Listen, I got us fish sticks for supper. You like fish sticks. Let's go fix them for supper.' I had my arm around her but she wasn't willing to accept my comfort.

No luck. She howled louder.

'Okay, all right, suit yourself. I'm going in. We're heating the whole out-of-doors standing here like this.' I dragged her through the doorway and shut the door behind her. Then I left her and lugged the groceries into the kitchen. Dumping them on the counter, I began to put them away.

While I was reading the directions on the fish-sticks box, Charity came trailing in. Her nose was running, and she rubbed at her eyes in great, dramatic swipes.

'Do you like me?' she asked as I knocked the fish sticks out onto a baking sheet.

'Yes, of course I like you.' I touched her head as I went by.

'You still going to be my Big Sister?'

I stopped to look at her. 'Yes, of course, I am. People do get tired, Charity. And it makes them a little short-tempered sometimes. But it had nothing to do with you. It's not your fault that I'm tired.'

'Can I have a cookie then?' she asked, and the old gleam was back in her eye.

'You can have one after supper. We'll be ready to eat when these things are done.'

'My mom always gives me a cookie if I stop crying.'

'I have no doubt she does. But I'm not your mom, am I?'

'No,' said Charity and climbed up on the counter to sit beside me. 'But I wouldn't mind if you was.'

* * *

Charity settled down in front of the television with three cookies, half a can of Dr Pepper and a bowl of popcorn. I went off to the bedroom to go through my file cabinet. I had been reading a lot on the treatment of kids who hate and I thought I had cut out an article from a psychiatric journal and filed it somewhere.

It was a mistake. Opening the middle drawer of the cabinet, I came across all my old teaching materials. Folder after folder of teaching ideas, overhead-projector templates, pictures from bulletin boards, ideas snipped from teaching journals, handouts I'd gotten and handouts I'd given, magazine articles that had caught my eye and even not-quite related bits and pieces, like an editorial by a newspaper columnist, describing the grief he had suffered at the recent death of his wife. They were all stuffed together in intimate, idiosyncratic order. And there, too, were the folders of schoolwork from old pupils. Taking those out of the drawer, I sat down on the floor and began paging through them, paper by paper. Sheila was there and Cliffie and Joyce. Stephen, Sandy, Tommy, Adam, Lucio, Yolanda, Leslie. Each one, their pictures, their notes to me, their stories, their classwork, many of the papers already yellowed a little by the passage of time. The carefully handprinted letters dissolved away from the pages into the rich fabric of my memory.

I had a gifted imagination. From the dog-eared school papers I could re-create my world then so vividly that it paled the world around me. My adrenaline, already high from dealing with Kevin of late, surged. It was a feeling I had grown so accustomed to in those years spent in the classroom. It was like a drug fix, I think. I got hooked on the feeling all that adrenaline coursing through my blood brought, and it took me years to get used to living without it when I had finished with special education. Even now, with all my concern over Kevin, I did not have the long, sustained, hour-by-hour involvement I'd had then that kept my heart always running a little fast and gave me the privilege of eating a 3000-calorie lunch and never gaining weight. Re-created in my mind as I sat on the floor of the bedroom were those children, those days, those months, even the smell of those classrooms. And my body responded without any outside stimulation, sending that familiar tingling sensation rushing along my arms until my hands shook so badly that I couldn't hold the paper any longer.

What had happened to teaching? Why wasn't I there any-more? I was an unwilling exile. As I fingered the schoolwork, lifeless except in my imagination, I ached to turn back the clock, to return and appreciate a little more what I had had before I lost it.

Those had been simpler times. I hadn't thought so then. But, looking back, the difference in responsibility was great. Closing my classroom door and creating my own small world in the eye of the hurricane, I had felt in control. In a small way, maybe I had been. But mostly, I hadn't. By and large the school district decided who came to my room and who left and how long they stayed. They even decided if *I* would con-tinue to exist.

Here, it was very different. Suddenly I actually had the control I had wanted in those earlier years, not only over my fate but over other people's as well, over the innocent people

Kevin might injure or kill, if I guessed wrong, over the children I could have been working with, if Kevin proved hopeless and was sent to permanent hospitalization or imprisonment, and of course, over Kevin himself in a very real way. His fate depended on me, literally. I could do things and say things that would steal away years from his life, maybe his entire lifetime. Conversely, but much less easily, I could give his future back to him, if we were lucky.

That was too much responsibility for any person. Playing God was a good name for it because God we were being, doing this sort of work, and playing at it was all we were capable of. Yet I knew someone had to do it. I just wished it had never had to be me.

Among the papers in my lap was a little poem written by one of my children years before.

A parrot is a funny bird,
I wonder, when it talks,
If it knows it speaks in human words
But still has parrot thoughts.

That was me, the Parrot of God.

Chapter Twelve

We barreled on full tilt through December. I became more and more vigilant, more and more absorbed in Kevin's drama, as I tried to maintain some semblance of control. It eventually grew to be like riding a runaway horse. On one hand, one is terrified of falling off; yet on the other one develops sort of a nervous, challenged giddiness after a while, which feeds upon the terror, and sooner or later, one develops a taste for it. My adrenaline mounted. My weight dropped. My sleep was poor. Yet there was something addictive about it. I kept coming back, day after day, to see the thing I had let loose.

January arrived with a deep snowfall and sub-zero temperatures. When I came in the office one morning after my sessions with Kevin, I found Jeff sitting in his desk chair with his head hanging down between his knees. I had to shed a couple of layers before I was able to speak.

'What on earth are you doing?' I asked.

'I have a headache. I'm letting all the blood rush to my brain so that it'll go away.'

'And *you're* a doctor? Heaven help us. Why don't you just take an aspirin? I have some in my desk.' Still wearing my jacket and trailing a muffler, I went over to rummage through a drawer for the bottle. It had been in there quite a long time and smelled like vinegar when I uncapped it. 'Here.'

He kept his head on the floor. 'I don't want to pollute my body,' he replied.

Jeff never failed to amaze me. What a hypocrite. He regularly drank beer, which he and his roommate brewed up in their bathtub. 'Take the stupid aspirin, Jeff.'

'I'm just tired, that's all,' he said and sat up. He took the pills from me. 'I was up almost all last night at the hospital.'

'Here, I'll fetch you a glass of water,' I said. When I returned, Jeff had smashed the aspirin into powder in his palm with the eraser end of a pencil. He was the only doctor I knew who couldn't swallow pills.

'So what was going on down at the hospital?' I asked.

'Cheri Bennett. Once again.' And he rolled his eyes.

Returning from taking Charity home that evening, I heard the phone ring as I was putting the car in the garage. Madly, I fumbled with the keys to get the door open, but by the time I reached the telephone, it was too late.

Although it was just a little after nine, the long weeks were beginning to tell on me and I decided to run a hot bath and go to bed early. Just as I lowered myself below the surface of the water, the phone rang again.

It was Jeff. He'd had more than a headache that morning; he had strep throat. Now at home with a 103-degree fever, he wondered if I could take over any emergencies for him. Standing shivering and dripping wet at the phone, I was willing to agree to anything. Then I returned to a less-than-hot tub.

Jeff must have known what was coming. Less than an hour later when I was warm in bed, reading, the psychiatric unit of the hospital rang up. Could I come down? Cheri Bennett had gone on a rampage through the unit and was now holding the nurses at bay with a broken light bulb.

Wearily I rolled out of bed. It was almost ten-thirty.

I knew all about Cheri Bennett. She was fifteen and had, I think, a mad crush on Jeff. She was also a very seriously disturbed girl who made persistent and dangerous suicide bids. Nothing Jeff did seemed to affect her perilous course toward self-destruction. When she had been committed to the unit the previous Monday after leaping from the Seventeenth Street flyover, Jeff was almost tearful with frustration.

Although I had never seen Cheri Bennett, she wasn't too hard to recognize. She was the one up on the windowsill, her back to the glass, bravely thrusting at the air with her light bulb, like a fencer.

'Who the hell are you?' she hollered at me.

'Dr Tomlinson's sick,' I yelled back over the ruckus of the aides and nurses.

'But who the hell are *you*?'

'I'm Torey Hayden. I'm one of Dr Tomlinson's colleagues.'

'Are you a doctor?'

'No. I work with Dr Tomlinson. I'm here in his place. He's sick. I'm here to help you.'

'Who said I wanted your help? Who the fuck cares who you are anyway. You aren't even a doctor. How do you expect to help?'

It was not an easy night. Cheri was one of those kids who instantly endeared herself to me by her wild, anguished bravado. But unfortunately, the same was not true in reverse. It took me more than an hour just to get her to come down off her perch on the windowsill and sit on the bed.

I stayed all night. It took several hours to calm her down enough to get rid of the light bulb and the nail file and the bathrobe tie and all the other weapons she had managed to devise. After all that, I didn't have the heart to turn her over to the hospital staff to be drugged out of her misery and left in the dark, waiting for sleep or whatever else comes in the night. So once I had her calmed down and more relaxed, we talked.

The night shift changed. The morning crew came around, all full of laughter and good cheer. I didn't leave until breakfast arrived, and when I did, Cheri did nothing more than shrug her shoulders after me and turn away to eat.

At 8:20 in the morning I returned home again. It was just in time for Jeff to call again. He sounded horrible as he croaked a few directions to me regarding stuff at the office. A few things, he said, that he'd left undone at work. When I got there, I found he had left more undone than done. I couldn't face any of it. I rang Dana at Garson Gayer and explained what had happened. Then I stopped in the office and told Shirley that as far as I was concerned, Hayden, Tomlinson & Co. were closed. Then I went home and slept the rest of the morning away.

* * *

When I arrived the next morning, Kevin was subdued. He was there ahead of me as usual, perched on the radiator by the window, one knee up, his cheek resting against it. He was staring out the window and did not turn as I entered. He said nothing.

I put my things down on the table.

'Where were you yesterday?'

'Dana told you, didn't she?' I said. 'I had to be at the hospital the night before. Did she tell you?'

He nodded and slowly turned his head to look at me. 'But that was in the night. Why weren't you here yestereday morning?'

'Because I was so tired. I had been up all night, so I went home to sleep.'

'But you could have come here first.'

'I was too tired. I wouldn't have been any fun at all.'

'But you could have. It was only for an hour. Not like it was all day or something. Or all night like that kid took.'

'I'm sorry, Kevin. But it just didn't make me feel good to have been awake that long. I needed to sleep.'

Kevin turned away and looked out the window. He said no more.

I couldn't get him to talk to me again. He sat in moody silence and refused to turn or get down from the radiator or speak. So I put my things on the table, opened the box, and took out a crossword puzzle book. For twenty-five minutes I sat at the table and did a crossword. When next I looked up, Kevin was watching me.

'You ready to join me?' I asked.

He turned away.

I went back to the crossword.

'I made something for you yesterday,' he said.

I raised my head. He was regarding me but immediately turned back to the window. It was like a ballet, this head bobbing and turning we were doing.

'I made something for you and you weren't even here.'

'Do you want to show it to me now? Do you have it with you?'

He shrugged.

'You're pouting, Kevin. You're angry because I didn't come. I'm sorry, Kev, because I spoiled things for you, but it couldn't be helped.'

No answer. I returned to the crossword.

'It's almost time to go,' he said.

'Mmm-hmm.'

'Can I stay longer today? To make up for yesterday?'

I shook my head. 'That'd make you late for Mr Gardner's class, wouldn't it? We can't do that.'

The aide's key rattled in the lock and Kevin stood up. He studied me a minute. 'You know,' he said, 'I really don't like you very much.'

I had expected the whole thing to have blown over by the following day; however, Kevin was again sulky and sullen. I had arrived in the room early and positioned myself against the radiator so that he could not easily seek refuge in the window. This upset him slightly and he paced the room. In the far corner he stopped and watched me. Rummaging through my box, I pulled out one of the sketchpads and skimmed it across the floor. A pencil followed.

'Here, draw.'

Kevin regarded me. Then slowly, he knelt and picked up the pad. The temptation proved too much and he sat down on the carpet. Opening the sketchpad, he thumbed through earlier drawings until he finally located a blank page. The pencil poised, he stared at it. Then he looked up at me.

'What do you want me to draw?' he asked.

'I dunno.' I shrugged slightly. 'Anything. Make a world for yourself.'

He continued to watch me.

'I used to do that. When I was your age. I didn't draw. I wrote instead. And I could make a whole world for myself, just the way I liked it. I wrote stories about it. Stories and stories and stories. But you can draw. I think that's better. Because then people can see what your world looks like. I always wished I could have illustrated my world so that other people could see the things the way I saw them.'

Kevin's gaze never wandered from my face. 'Did you really do that? Make yourself a world?'

I nodded. 'Yes. And it had people in it and everything. And it was just the way I decided it to be.'

'Do you still do that?'

'Sometimes. I still write myself little stories and they're always my best ones. Because they're for me.'

There was a pause. Kevin fiddled with the weave of the carpet. 'Well, you know something?' He paused again. 'Something I never told anybody else? Never anybody?'

'Yes?'

'Well, I sort of got one of them worlds too. I guess I always had it. I never drew pictures of it or anything. It was just inside me.' He smiled and pulled at the carpet again. 'Well, see, there's sort of inside me this other guy. I call him Bryan. Bryan's a strong name, I think. The sort of name a strong guy would have. And well, here inside just stupid old Kevin, there's this real neat Bryan. And sometimes I think how I'm really Bryan. Not on the ouside maybe, but on the inside I am. But nobody knows it but me. Nobody knows I'm really special inside but me. It's my own private world sort of, like yours was. It's always been a secret about Bryan because I don't want anyone to know. They wouldn't believe it, and I don't want them to take Bryan away from me. I don't want to share with anybody.' He glanced over at me. 'Was your world like that too?'

'Yes, pretty much.'

'I've never told anyone this before.'

I smiled.

'But you knew, didn't you? You know everything, don't you?'

Again I smiled and shook my head. 'No, hardly. It's just that everybody has a private world inside him. Everybody does.'

'You wouldn't tell anybody else, would you?'

'No.'

'Not write it in the charts or anything? It'd just be between us, wouldn't it? Our secret?'

'Yes, just our secret.'

He smiled warmly at me. 'You know, I don't really mind you knowing. Maybe you could even call me Bryan, sometimes. Kind of like when we're in private. Like now. You could call me Bryan, like I really was. Like I wasn't Kevin at all.'

I nodded.

'Do you think you could?'

Again I nodded.

He smiled. 'Then do it, okay? Call me Bryan right now. Let me hear you say I'm Bryan. All right? Okay?'

'Okay, Bryan, I will.'

I felt good. I glowed in an idiot's paradise, as we sat there chatting while Kevin doodled on the pad. Then, glancing up at the clock, I noticed we had only five minutes left before the aide returned.

'Time's almost up,' I said. Kevin looked up from his drawing. There was a small, edgy pause, and I half expected him to ask for more time. That would have spoiled my momentary belief that we had accomplished something worthwhile, because it would have reopened the issue of my absence. But he didn't ask. After one last, long look at his work, he closed the sketchbook and rose to put it in the box.

'You know what?' he asked, smiling at me, 'I'm glad I get to come here.'

'Good. I'm pleased you enjoy it.'

'It's better here than all the rest of my day put together.' He went to dump some bits of paper in the wastebasket on the other side of the room. Halfway over something slipped from the pocket of his pants. It was a long object, wrapped in brown paper.

Kevin halted abruptly when he saw he'd dropped it. He bent and retrieved it.

'What's that?' I asked.

'Nothing special.'

'What is it?' I rose from my place and came over.

Kevin had taken it from his pocket again and was palming it. I could tell he was unwilling to show it to me, but at the same time he was still caught up in the warmth of our earlier camaraderie. The half smile of pleasure over a shared secret creased his lips.

'It's something I made,' he said and there was pride in his voice. 'Do you want to see it?'

I nodded.

Carefully, he unwrapped it. With tender deftness his fingers moved the paper. His love for the object was obvious, even in the way he removed its wrappings.

I didn't know exactly what it was. It was about eight inches long, a piece of blue-painted metal. One end was pointed, the other rounded. My lack of comprehension must have been clear.

'It's a knife,' Kevin said gently, as if explaining to a child. 'I made it from a piece of metal I took off my bed. See. I've been rubbing it against the wall in the TV room where there's bricks.'

When I did not say anything, he smiled, still with that gentle patience. Then he reached over and took hold of my arm, turning it underside upward.

'See, I made it sharp, so it can cut.' And he ran the point sharply along the skin of my inner arm. A scratch appeared and little points of blood welled up.

'Yes, I see,' I said and pulled my arm against my body.

He was still smiling, an odd sort of smile with just one side of his mouth curled up. There was nothing especially sinister about it, or there wouldn't have been if this all hadn't followed so shortly on the heels of our earlier fellowship. But now I felt violated. All I saw was someone who could turn my arm over and cut me and keep smiling.

Kevin raised the knife and studied its edge. 'I'm going to get him. What you got to do now is teach me how to go outside again. And then when I do, I'm going to split his guts all over the ground.'

He must have sensed that I was going to object, because he jerked back to me and brought the knife up under my chin. He smiled again. 'Remember us talking about secrets earlier?'

'Yes.'

'Well, you got another one you better keep. You wouldn't tell anyone I made this, would you?' It wasn't a question. It was a threat.

'Why should I tell?'

Again he grinned.

The knife came down. He fondled it, examined the edge, sighted against the point. 'It's a good knife. It's sharp. It'd kill real easy.'

'Kev?' I said. 'Give me the knife. To keep for you. You can't keep it here. They'll find it.'

'I've been keeping it. I got a good hiding place. They'll never find it.'

'Oh, they would, Kev. Sooner or later. And they'd take it away. Let me keep it for you. Like I did the picture, remember?'

He looked at me. 'You wouldn't bring it back.'

'Sure I would. Why shouldn't I? You can trust me. I keep my word. And they'd never take it away from me, not if I had it.'

'No.'

'Yeah, let me. I'll bring it every session. I promise I will, Kevin. Let me keep it.'

He turned the piece of blue metal over and over in his palm, caressed it, felt the point, the sharpened edges. He was right about one thing. It would kill. It was a crude but effective little weapon, perhaps all the more effective for not being immediately recognizable as a knife.

Cold sweat had begun to trickle down my back; it felt awful, all damp and tickly. I was worried that the click of the aide's key would come any moment now and startle Kevin before I had the knife.

He raised it, put it under his own chin and flicked it outward. Again he put it under my chin. He smiled. 'I really do think I could kill someone, you know. I think I might even enjoy it.'

'That's a good knife, Kevin. I like it. But let me keep it for you so they don't take it away. We wouldn't want that to happen, would we?'

Still he stood, contemplating. I said no more. I feared sounding overenthusiastic. Or overanxious. Beyond us the sun shone through the window with a springtime brightness. We could have been on the brink of May by the looks of it, not sliding into the cadaverous shadows of winter.

'Here,' Kevin said finally and put the knife in my hand. 'You can keep it for me.' He smiled again. 'I trust you.'

Chapter Thirteen

I was in over my head. I think I had known I was for some time, although I hadn't been willing to admit it. Kevin was an angry youngster in a deep and brutal way. There had been a lot of violent kids over the years. I had been kicked, hit, bitten, beaten and threatened and it was all part of the job description, part of what I had bargained for when I took it. So I wasn't easily shaken. But there was something different about Kevin. He spooked me. Never before had I actually been frightened of a kid. Certainly I had gotten into situations that had scared the liver out of me, but never before had I actually been frightened of the kid himself. With Kevin I was. It remained a somewhat heady fear, the kind I suppose skydivers or hang gliders must feel. In a way it intoxicated me and that kept me from acknowledging it for what it was. I was like the mouse trapped in the cobra's glare – terror-stricken but too fascinated to escape.

However, as I sat at my desk in the office and fingered the sharp edge of the homemade knife, I knew Kevin was unequivocally dangerous.

So what now?

When I went to see Kevin the next day, I took the knife with me in the pocket of my cords. Could he see it? Kevin asked, first thing. So I showed it to him. He examined it, turned it back and forth between his palms, felt the edges, the point. And smiled. It was his smile that always scared me the most; it was so goofy, so full of an idiot's innocence and yet I knew now, as he knew, that it had always been only a game of sorts. Then Kevin gave the knife back to me, I repocketed it and we went on about our usual things, as if the knife did not exist.

It was an eerie session. Kevin remained cheerful and agreeable, playing with little Matchbox cars he found in the box, fiddling with the puppets, laughing at them and me and himself. Covertly I watched him the entire time. What an incredible boy. In hardly four months he'd shown me so many sides. Yet, I knew none of them.

After the period was up, I went up to the staff room to chart. I needed to put something decisive in Kevin's records. Sitting down at the cluttered table, I opened the chart and began to write. *I am concerned about Kevin,* I wrote, *I think he's...* What? Dangerous? The kid makes knives out of parts of old beds? The kid draws pictures of intended murder victims? The kid cuddles hate the way the rest of us cuddle kittens? Could I say that? And then what? What would they do if they read that? Kevin already was in an institution. Where did you go from there? Garson Gayer was clean and bright and warm but hardly a model of freedom with its locked doors and padded cells. Would Kevin be sent from here? And where? The state hospital? A security unit? Would they think him crazy? Or just violent? Or both? And was he?

I didn't know. I crossed out what I had written and tried again. Again I crossed it out. The page couldn't be thrown away because other people had charted on it, so I just kept trying and crossing out and writing 'error.' I sat, staring at the paper. And in the end I put: *Tendencies toward violent behavior exhibited in therapy sessions. Monitor carefully on the ward.* The safety of jargon.

Mozart's flute music drifted through the clinic corridors. It was past 5:30 in the evening and all the offices were closed and darkened. Only the security lights remained on in the halls.

Dr Rosenthal was hunched over paperwork at his desk, and although he sat with his tie still in place and his suit jacket on, he had allowed himself the luxury of a cassette player in front of him as he worked. The music rippled out.

I knocked tentatively, and he did not turn immediately.

'Just a moment,' he said at last, still not looking up from what he was writing. With the other hand he gestured for me to sit. Putting my jacket down onto the arm of the huge, overstuffed chair beside his desk, I sat.

Dr Rosenthal was the director of the clinic. He was one of those big, grizzly sorts of men, all gray and frizzy around the temples, the type Hollywood always casts as older lovers. He wasn't especially handsome but he had an aura about him, the sort of virile attractiveness intellectual men have. He was a very tall man, well over six and a half feet, and very formal, always wearing a suit and a tie and calling us Hayden and Tomlinson, if we were younger, or simply doctor, if we merited that. Dr Rosenthal and I were very different sorts of people. Our perceptions on psychiatry and psychology were at almost opposite ends of the spectrum – the theist and the atheist. He was fanatically Freudian. I was fanatically uncommited. His concepts were based on theory. My concepts were based on my own experience in the outer world. He explained. I accepted that there weren't necessarily any explanations, or at least we didn't necessarily know them. Yet for all that separated us, I think I held few other persons in higher esteem. He had a mind as wickedly sharp as splintered glass, and I never saw his equal when it came to laying open the heart of a matter.

So I sat in the big leather chair and listened to Mozart while he finished what he was writing. Beside me was a bookshelf, crammed to overflowing with psychiatry texts. Dr Rosenthal's specialty was infant psychiatry, a branch I had not known existed prior to my arrival at the clinic. But Dr Rosenthal had written two books on the subject himself, and I saw in his bookcase many other volumes as well. It still amused me a little to think on it. He was such a terribly big man, so gruff and professional, so careful with appearances and proprieties and formalities, that I could hardly picture him with babies at all. But he was magic with them.

At last he turned around in his desk chair. I had come to him about Kevin. Dr Rosenthal had been closely following my work at Garson Gayer for some time, and I came now because I had nowhere else to go. I needed help.

To the strains of Mozart we carefully went over eveything, over Kevin's previous life as I knew it, over his traumatic fears, over his abrupt changes, over his failure to speak and his sudden revival. Just talking about it soothed me. I had begun to have very fatalistic thoughts because I knew if I gave up, no one else was likely to come in and take my place. But at the same time Kevin had grown so disconcerting that I was scared of continuing too, in case he might do something to me or himself or someone else.

We talked on and on. Dr Rosenthal asked me about my research, about other elective mutes I had worked with and how they compared with Kevin. He asked me small, nitty-gritty details of my work. He asked about my conceptualizations of the syndrome and of how I perceived Kevin's problems on a large scale, across the length of his life.

Then our conversation wandered away. Dr Rosenthal paused, opened the cassette deck and flipped over the tape. Did I like classical music, he asked? Yes, I replied. What kind? he inquired. Then he reached for his pipe. Did I mind if he smoked? He was trying to stop. He had two young children at home and he knew it wasn't good for them. He didn't smoke at home at all anymore. And he'd tried to stop during the day, here at the office. But did I mind if he did right now? No. And how about a cup of tea? he suggested. A cup of tea would be nice, wouldn't it? Pulling open a lower desk drawer, he produced a pot, tea bags and an immersion heater. I went to fetch my mug. The air around us swelled with music that made me think of green pastures in summer.

Then as he puffed on his pipe and leaned back in his desk chair, Dr Rosenthal studied me. Why was I in the business? he asked me. What need did it fulfill in me? Had I ever asked myself that question?

Yes, lots of times, I replied. And I couldn't give an answer honestly, I said, because it was such a complex question. Then silence came between us. He continued to puff and to regard me thoughtfully. I just stared into space, lost in my own thoughts. The tea was warm and strong and tasted lovely. Then I looked back to him. It was the challenge, I said, that put me in the business mostly. I had always been an undistinguished scholar throughout my long career as a student. I had found learning easy and then grown restless and impatient with the schooling process. It wasn't until late in my college career that I chanced upon work with emotionally disturbed children in a volunteer job and it captivated me. It was the ultimate challenge. Here was the brave new frontier. No matter how clever or educated or creative a person might be, he would never be able to conquer it all. There was always more to learn, more to guess at, more to think about. You could think forever, to the width and breadth and depth of your capacity and there would still be more. I loved that, I said. Like Columbus's New World, it was a tangible dream.

Dr Rosenthal just smiled.

And then we went back to Kevin. He was a little more tangible than I wished he was. But by now, Dr Rosenthal had an idea. What about Tomlinson? he asked. Would I feel better if Tomlinson joined me in the sessions for a while? He could provide some insight and if the worst happened, well, he said, Tomlinson's a good size. He ought to be able to handle the boy, if need be.

It seemed a viable solution. Jeff had been my primary confidant throughout the case with Kevin and so he was well informed. Moreover, Jeff and I complemented one another in our methods. By virtue of his training, Jeff was much more firmly grounded in the traditional, theoretical aspects of therapy whereas I tended to have a more practical, reality-based approach. We had worked together on other cases and found that rather than these differences causing us trouble, we were usually able to integrate them. So, yes, I said, I thought that was an excellent idea and I welcomed it.

Jeff was pleased. Kevin was such a different kid that I knew he would be a challenge for Jeff too. Jeff had expressed curiosity on other occasions about what could be done with him. And I immediately saw the other advantages. After the initial adjustments, we could split the load, and I would no longer be tied down to five hours a week at Garson Gayer. In this unusual setup using two therapists to remedy a problem Jeff and I had the premise for further professional research. And perhaps most of all, here was the opportunity to introduce Kevin to a warm, mature male model, someone who would not beat or torture him, someone who knew the greatest strength came from gentleness.

Unfortunately, Kevin did not think it was a good idea at all. He was outraged.

'You're going to bring someone else in? What do you mean you're going to bring someone in? What for? How come?'

'Jeff works with me, Kev. We do the same sorts of things. I just thought it would be nice for a change to have someone else with us.'

Kevin paced the length of the room. He stopped on the far side and turned to face me. 'Did you ask me? Did you ask to

find out if I thought it would be nice?' With one hand he ruf-
fled through his hair. 'No. No, you didn't. You didn't even
stop to think how I might feel. Nobody asks me. Nobody
ever asks me anything.'

Over to the window he went. He leaned forward until his
face was against the pane. Sun through the cottonwood
threw a mottled pattern over his skin.

'This is *my* place,' he said softly to the window and his
breath clouded the glass. 'This was my very own place.' Then
he turned to me. 'And now you wrecked it.'

'It'll still be your place. Jeff won't change that.'

'Yes, he will. I won't be able to talk to you anymore. I won't
be able to talk to you like I did because *he'll* be here and *he'll*
listen. And I don't want him to.'

'He won't change things. Jeff's just like me, Kev. He's real
easy to talk to. You'll see.'

With a weary sigh, Kevin pushed himself off the
window-sill. He paced again around the perimeter of the
room but more slowly this time. Finally he dropped down
onto the floor near where I was sitting. He said nothing.
He began picking little threads from the cuff of one shirt
sleeve.

I watched him and did not know what to do. Suddenly I
felt terribly bad. His life was so tragic. I forgot that sometimes in the noise of day-to-day happenings. But here he
was, his whole universe held up behind locked doors, his
world confined to a small bare white room with yucky-
colored carpet. I had to be careful to remember regardless of
what I thought, that I never could conceive of a life like that.
It was his; he knew it. I did not.

Stretching his arm out, Kevin lay down on the floor. He was at an angle to me, so I could not see his face. He fingered the rough surface of the carpet.

Kevin moved his head to look at me. 'Torey?'

'Yes?'

'How come he's going to come?'

'I wanted some help, Kev. I wanted to make sure I was doing everything I could to make things better for you so that someday maybe you can get out of here. But I wasn't sure I was doing it good enough on my own.'

'Did I do something wrong?'

'No, not really. No one did anything wrong.'

Silence. Kevin still lay on the rug, his eyes focused on some invisible point.

'Tor, can I ask you something else?'

'Yes, sure.'

'Do you like me?'

'Of course I do, Kevin.'

'I was just wondering. You know, sometimes I close my eyes so I can't see anything, can't see where I am. And I pretend. I pretend I'm a person. A real person. You know. I just wondered if you did that too sometimes, if that was how come you could like me?'

'I like you just for you, Kevin. And you are a real person.'

'No. I'm not. I mean, a real live person. Someone real. Not this. Not me. Not here.'

Chapter Fourteen

The first few sessions with Jeff were hell for all of us. Kevin was angry and uncooperative, refusing to talk to Jeff, refusing even to look at him. But he was much more seriously angry with me. Throughout our entire time together, Kevin and I had had an unusual relationship. Rather than my drawing him out into my world, he had absorbed me into his. It was he who had decided he would talk to me and he who did it and he who chose when to share his private world. Kevin had treated me more as just a part of himself, trusting me not to do anything he would not do. It had been an odd relationship, more one-sided in that way than others I had had with kids, but now it shattered. I had betrayed him. I had brought Jeff. Now Kevin was forced to see us for what we were, therapists, outsiders. Both Jeff and me. And the small inner world Kevin and I had built within the walls of the little white room crumbled.

Kevin had come too far to be able to retreat back into his fears and his old ways under the table. This left him temporarily naked and he cast about for several days for a way to deal with Jeff and me. When it became apparent that he was not going to adjust easily, we finally moved out of the small white room with its associations and down into the mirrored therapy room. That certainly didn't fool Kevin. He knew Jeff was there behind the mirror watching. And in a way it made him angrier, because he knew I hadn't liked that room either, just as he hadn't, and now I was using it the way the staff did. Just another sign I had turned against him. However, down there I could momentarily distract him because Jeff wasn't physically present, and it would be like old times for a few minutes before Kevin's restlessness and anger with me resurfaced.

Jeff, for his part, wasn't a whole lot better.

'God,' he said after the first session. 'He's the ugliest kid I've ever seen. Jesus, he looks like something a sheep threw up.'

'Oh, don't make a case of it. He's not *that* bad.'

'You've been looking at him too long, Hayden.'

When Jeff appeared on the scene, Kevin's hate retreated almost immediately. After all the weeks in November and December and the first part of this month when all I saw were brutal drawings and all I heard were grisly stories, it surprised me to realize that three or four days went by before I even noticed the tales were gone. I suppose I was just wrapped up in the trauma of Jeff's arrival. Perhaps Kevin was too.

We went through most of the snowy weeks of midwinter before Kevin gave even the smallest signs of settling down again. We continued to meet in the therapy room, first with just Kevin and me doing what we always did. Then later I started shouting at the mirrored wall, holding up our puzzle books or our games and talking to Jeff behind the mirror as well as to Kevin. Then Jeff started shouting replies. Kevin never joined into this high-decibel discourse but he finally began making remarks to me to pass on to Jeff. At long last, after February dawned and Jeff had been behind the mirror for a couple of weeks, he was able to come around for part of the session and join us. Kevin still did not talk to him but he would talk to me in front of Jeff and he would let Jeff talk to him without ignoring him entirely.

The content of our sessions were commonplace, even dull on occasion. It went back very much to what Kevin and I had been doing in the very beginning before the rocket poster blow-up–things like coloring and joke books and other rather untherapy-like activities. Mostly Kevin directed what we did and he preferred to navigate as far away as possible from personal things.

Then abruptly Kevin changed again. In mid-February, his distrust of Jeff subsided sharply. Within the space of a week he turned eager and talkative, speaking directly to Jeff. His manner was charming, suddenly, as if Jeff were an old, long-forgotten friend he'd just rediscovered. Kevin was warm to me but he became especially enamored of Jeff.

This time I could not detect a reason for the sudden change, although it was as sharp a change as his shift from fear in November and from hate in January. But whatever it was, Kevin changed. He grew friendly and outgoing. He and Jeff became buddies. Kevin forgot his knife (which he had never mentioned again after Jeff arrived), he forgot his sketchbook, he forgot his stepfather. He forgot all the weeks of sulky opposition. Instead, he leapt with both feet into affable camaraderie with Jeff. Jeff, in his turn, responded. He taught Kevin how to play Monopoly and checkers and they took turns crucifying me because I was routinely awful at both games. Jeff unearthed two books full of Little Moron jokes and Kevin literally rolled on the floor with laughter. Jeff discussed the finer points of male adolescence with him: shaving, food and girls.

I was ignored. I was ignored so thoroughly for a while that I got a little out of joint over it. And when I wasn't being ignored, they ganged up on me. They played 'get Torey.' It was make Torey the butt of the moron jokes, beat Torey at this game and not just by a little – cream her. Kevin wanted to really do me in in the games, push me into crushing bankruptcy at Monopoly or cow me with five kings at checkers. I think I understood what was going on. In a deep, subconscious way what he was doing was understandable and I realized it had to happen, but on the surface, I had to admit it hurt and the games ceased to be much fun for me. I had a very difficult time not becoming hyper-competitive myself and trying to cream him back.

During this period I had several opportunites just to sit back and watch the action because he and Jeff would get caught up together in one of their activities. When I did that, Kevin amazed me. He was such a complex character. He had altered completely over the five months we had been together, but they weren't the subtle chameleonic changes that I was used to seeing in kids. He could, instead, alter his personality entirely. For him it was more like the turning faces of one of those mirrored globes, reflecting first one image then another. I did not believe Kevin had multiple personalities. In my gut I felt he had to be very close to being able to control these changes, that he did them with, if not malice aforethought, then at least thought aforethought. And in my deep heart of hearts I could not shake the belief that Kevin had always been one jump ahead of us. From the very beginning, he had. Even while rocking under the table he had managed to count the number of openings and closings of the observation room door. For all that I did not know about him, one thing I did know for certain: We had all vastly underestimated his intelligence and even more so, his canniness.

Watching Kevin during these weeks, I grew increasingly uneasy. When we were back in the office alone, I tried to tell Jeff that something felt wrong to me about Kevin but my words never came out right. What exactly? Jeff would ask. Give specifics. But I couldn't. It was just in my gut. Jeff listened to me but eventually he would just sit at his desk and shake his head when I brought the topic up. I was just jealous. Kevin was going through a very trying stage of therapy and working out some strong feelings about me and probably about his mother, he said. That was why he so persistently attacked me in the games and verbally. That was why he sided with Jeff on everything. It was understandable, Jeff said, that it would all get under my skin after a while but it was critical that Kevin have the opportunity to work these feelings through. No, I said, there was something else. But I couldn't tell him what. The words just never formed in my head. It's in my gut, I would keep saying to him, and he'd tell me to forget it. I made more decisions with my gut than any other part of me, he complained. I was the only person he knew who did all of her thinking with her stomach. Give it a rest.

I remained disquieted for a while longer but then other thoughts began to take over. Jeff was right about one thing. I *was* jealous. Kevin seemed to grow so close to him so quickly. After all the work I had put into this kid, I hadn't brought Jeff in to take it over from me entirely. It hurt. Rapidly he and Kevin had jokes between them and special references of which I had no part. So I had to agree; Jeff was probably right in his assessment.

Kevin made marvelous progress at last. Maybe knowing a spirited, caring, interested man who could model appropriate male responses to things was what had been missing all along and something I clearly could not give him. My gut shifted about a little longer, but by the time the first winds of March came, I too had closed my mind to the other Kevins I had known. It was too hard to resist him and Jeff and their antics. After a while I felt only guilty for my feelings and for being such a wet blanket, so soon I joined them and then I couldn't remember anymore what my worries had been about.

Kevin sailed. Like a long-captive bird, he struggled to move his wings and then was airborne. Suddenly the world came alive for him. He wanted to know everything at once. What was beyond the walls of the Garson Gayer estate? What were the streets like leading up to it? How did snow form? What made a girl like you? Why does your stomach feel so funny when you're scared? Where is India? Had I ever been there? Were there elephants there? What is it like in a rain forest? Did I think Linda, the new aide, was pretty?

Kevin was forever on his feet in the small white room, running back and forth between Jeff and me, a book in his hands as he read some amazing fact. Look at this! Listen here! Listen to what I've found! Or he'd plaster himself to the window, nose against the glass. See that? See that part of the building? Do you know that kid out there? Do you know what her name is? That's Kelly. She lives in 4D.

His improvements quickly spilled over into other areas outside the small white room. For the first time his schoolwork progressed. He took a desperate interest in books. He wanted to learn games that the other kids played: table tennis, volleyball, wrestling. And he wanted to play with the other kids. For the very first time he actually wanted to socialize with the other children. Dana and the staff were delirious with this change.

Jeff kept pumping Kevin full of wonderful stories about the outside world in hopes of finally breaking through that barrier, one of the last of Kevin's great fears. The way Jeff talked, he made everywhere he'd ever been sound wonderful. Where would you like to go most? he'd ask Kevin and then tell about the zoo or the science museum or our office or the theater or the amusement park. Later, back in the office, Jeff would still be dreaming. We'd give the world to Kevin, if only he'd let us.

There certainly was a lot to accomplish, however. Kevin was not lacking for things to work on. The one other immovable fear, besides that of going outside, was Kevin's continuing terror of water. He absolutely refused to be submerged in even the tiniest amount. He couldn't even be persuaded to soak his foot when he had an ingrown toenail. Consequently, he had gone God knows how long without bathing or even really washing.

Jeff took over this segment of Kevin's therapy and in the end he hauled Kevin under the shower, clothes and all, and stripped him there. That worked reasonably well. Kevin survived the shower. If the water didn't run too fast and there was plenty of room to back out of it, if he wanted, and the drain worked well so that no water collected, he could tolerate it. Just barely, but he could.

This left us with the next problem: clothes. Now that there was a way to get Kevin reasonably clean, he had nothing to wear that matched his new state of hygiene. He owned a total of three shirts and two pairs of pants, all of which had been donations to the home. So we rooted about in the Garson Gayer books until we unearthed his clothing allowance and then Jeff and I went out to the shopping center one evening, armed with Kevin's measurements.

What a hoot. We were hopeless together. All we did was argue. If I wanted one color, Jeff wanted another. If I thought this size was right, Jeff was convinced it wouldn't fit. If I wanted to get it because I liked the style, Jeff groaned and said boys hadn't been wearing that since 1934. Or it looked like a preppy golf bag with buttons. I said *I* thought I knew what teenagers were wearing. Women paid more attention to things like that than men did. Jeff said I was sexist. Besides, he had *been* a teenage boy, hadn't he, and he should know no self-respecting guy would get caught dead in something like that. The saleslady thought we were married and shopping for our son. With all the arguing we were doing, that didn't say much for her ideas of marriage. Worse, it meant she couldn't tell that both of us were under thirty and would have been about eleven at his birth. But she did end up selling us three wrong-sized pairs of jeans because Jeff insisted that I had measured Kevin's inseam wrong. We also got a range of colorful, easy-care T-shirts and Jeff found a white muslin shirt he insisted we get, which ended up making Kevin look like Mahatma Gandhi.

But while the clothes and the showers made a tremendous change in Kevin's appearance, the best improvement occurred when Jeff was able to get his own barber to come out to Garson Gayer. Kev got the whole works—a wash, a cut, a style and blow-dry. Jeff and I had to pay for it out of our own pockets but it was worth it. It didn't exactly transform him into Robert Redford, but Kevin was so proud of it. When the session was over, Jeff and I stood in the doorway of the small white room and watched Kevin go back to the ward with the aide. He strutted like a rooster, his scrawny chest thrown out, his too-long jeans rolled up, the smell of Old Spice trailing after him.

'He's still kind of ugly,' Jeff whispered to me.

'I dunno. I was sort of thinking he was kind of okay looking.'

Jeff paused. A smile touched the corners of his lips. 'Yeah, I guess he sort of is, isn't he?'

A week later Jeff and I decided to split the workload. It was mid-March and almost two months had passed since Jeff had joined us. The strain of coming every day was beginning to tell on both of us. So we reduced our visits to three times a week. On Mondays Jeff came, on Wednesdays I did and on Fridays we came together.

Kevin was surprisingly unperturbed by this change. We explained it to him and he nodded. That sounded okay to him. For the first time I realized that he actually had grown in therapy and was perhaps already beginning to outgrow us. A few months more perhaps, and Kevin would not need us.

'Kev?'

It was evening. I'd come in my free time because I had promised to help Kevin with a school project. We were making a papier-mâché map of the U.S. for the school-district science fair. I had told Kevin about the fair and the map was his idea. Garson Gayer students did not normally participate in such events, but Kevin thought it might be exciting to do so, to be the first kid to try. He'd gotten the map idea out of a book his teacher had, and I'd offered to come in my free time and give him a hand, since I'd used papier-mâché with my kids in the classroom.

So there we were, both on the floor of the small white room, our sleeves rolled up, a bucket of soaking newspapers between us. I was mangling the Rockies of Colorado. Kevin was intent on straightening out the Great Plains.

I said his name. He answered with a grunt. Most of his attention was on Kansas.

'You know what sounds good to me?' I said.

'What?'

'Hot chocolate.'

'Mmm, yeah,' he agreed without taking his eyes off Kansas. 'Let's go get some.'

Kevin looked up. There was a blob of the Northern Rockies on his nose where he had been leaning too close to his work. 'What do you mean? The cook won't let you in the kitchen. It's not a mealtime. That's a rule.'

'I wasn't thinking of the dining room. Every day when I come here, I go past a Frosty-Freez. It's just down the road. On the corner of Hill Street and 23rd. I thought we could go there.'

Kevin straightened up. His eyes narrowed. 'What do you mean?'

'I mean, let's go down there to the Frosty-Freez and get some hot chocolate.'

His eyes remained intent. Then he shook his head. 'I can't. I'm not on a green pass. You have to be on a green pass to go off the grounds.'

'You're not on any kind of pass, Kevin. But it wouldn't matter anyway. You'd be with me. They'd let you come, if I took you.'

I could see the fear bright in his eyes, but he was not for telling me about it. His fears had begun to embarrass him of late. I think it was probably Jeff whom he wanted to hide them from. Kevin and I were old buddies but Jeff he still wanted to impress. In a way that was why I wanted to take him out myself, alone.

'It's too cold out,' Kevin said and leaned back over the map.

'No, it's not. It's a beautiful night. I was just out in it when I came over.'

'It's too far to go.'

'It's only a block and a half. Maybe two blocks.' I put my putty knife down. 'Come on. This'll wait for us.'

'It's too dark out there.'

'There's streetlights.'

'But it's probably slippery.'

'Yes, probably. But we'll make it all right.'

Nervously, he glanced up. 'I don't have a coat. I don't have any boots.'

'I'm sure the staff will find you something.' I was on my feet.

Kevin just sat. His shoulders started to sag dismally. I knew he was running short of excuses. 'You know what?' he said softly and stared at his hands.

'What's that?'

'I haven't been going out a whole lot lately.'

'I know that.'

'I don't want to go.'

'I know that too.'

'Then let's not, okay, Tor?'

I shook my head. Kevin's eyes wandered over our work on the floor. Absently, he scraped a bit of dried papier-mâché away from the edge of the board. 'I . . .' he started but never finished. A deep breath followed.

I knelt down across the map from him. 'Just trust me, Kev, all right? Gimme a chance, okay?'

Then there was silence. It dropped on us as if someone had been standing over us, as if we were on a marionette stage and the puppeteer let drop a down comforter over us. It came down suddenly but softly, smothering us sweetly.

I could not break out of it. Whether he could or not, I didn't know.

Gently I touched his hand. His fingers were cold. 'What's it feel like, Kev?' I asked. 'What's it make you feel like inside?'

He shrugged.

'How does the fear feel?' I couldn't imagine. I couldn't fathom what that much fear must have been like.

Giving a deep sigh, Kevin slipped his hand out from under mine and caught a falling tear. He was embarrassed by it. It was the first time he had cried in ages, since those first weeks. Too much had changed since then. Even with me he was embarrassed by the tears.

Again he shrugged. 'I dunno. I just get scared.'

'About what?'

'Well, like maybe something might happen.'

'Like what?'

'I dunno.'

We were still struggling with the silence over us. At least I was. It was like swimming in mud.

'I wonder sometimes,' Kevin began very slowly and his eyes studied the fabric of the carpet, 'I wonder sometimes why people hate other people. What do you do to make them hate you?' His eyes rose to mine. 'What do you do to make them stop?'

The gray of his eyes had paled. They were the color of winter water before it froze.

'Once,' he said, his voice hesitant and very soft, 'I had this book. My grandma gave it to me. About kittens. All these little kittens dressed up, doing things. I like kittens.' He looked up. 'Did you know that? That I like kittens? I do. And cats. Then . . .' He fell silent. His eyes fixed on some unseen spot in front of him, I knew he was looking inward into some inner place I could not see. He remained silent a long, long time. 'And then,' he continued very softly, 'when I came back I couldn't ever find the book again.'

Something had been left out of that story: I could not follow it. But he was communicating his feelings clearly enough. So it seemed inappropriate to ask for explanations.

He looked up at me. 'When someone sort of hates you,' he said, 'they do things to you. You never know when it's going to happen. You never know exactly what. But when someone hates you, you always know they'll do things.'

My God, I was thinking, I'd be scared to go out too.

Chapter Fifteen

We did not go to the Frosty-Freez that evening. However, the night after we did go. Still sharing with God the privilege of creating the North American continent, I had returned the following evening to help Kevin finish the project. This time Kevin knew it was coming. When I suggested I was thirsty, Kevin rose without responding and went to the door.

Beyond the small white room, I had to tell the aides what we were up to and get permission to take him off the grounds. Then we had to locate a jacket for Kevin because he didn't own one. Kevin went through it all mechanically and without words.

Outside it was bitterly cold for so late in the season. Yet it was a clear night, lit with the shattered brilliance of a billion stars. The Milky Way stretched out across the sky, a wide white pathway through the night. I pointed it out to Kevin but he kept his eyes to the ground. He did not fear attack from the sky; it was his least vulnerable direction. So he wasn't going to waste precious time looking there.

Our breath came out in huge white puffs. The cold air startled up the sensitive lining in my nose, giving a tiny spark of pain with each inhalation. I loved the night; I loved the winter. This was a perfect time to be out. We were completely alone, but with so many stars, one could not get lonely in the earthbound darkness.

'I've never been out in the night before,' Kevin said, his voice cautious sounding. 'At least not that I can remember.'

'It's beautiful at night. I think sometimes it's more beautiful than in the day. I love the night.'

'I don't,' he said. 'You can't see what's coming.'

The Frosty-Freez was a little hole in the wall with a serving counter, six or seven booths with overstuffed, vinyl-covered seats and pots of faded plastic flowers. The windows were steamed up against the cold night, and the humid, greasy warmth greeted us like a fat auntie's kiss.

There were a few other people in the place, teenagers mostly, hanging around the jukebox. However, it wasn't crowded by any means, and it was easy to go to the far end of the row of booths and slip into one where we weren't much noticed. I took out a menu.

Kevin was subdued. While there were no major manifestations of his fear outwardly, it obviously nagged at him, because he kept returning to it over and over in conversation.

'I never been out. It's been almost four years since I went outside. I never been out since the year I first came to Garson

Gayer. Three years, six months, two weeks and a day. That's how long I stayed inside.'

'Are you okay?' I asked.

Slowly, he nodded.

'So what do you want? Hot chocolate?'

'No, nothing. I can't eat. I feel like I want to throw up.'

'Well, I'm having hot chocolate. I'll be right back.' And I rose to go to the counter and order. When I came back to the booth with my cup, Kevin had disappeared.

'Kevin?' I looked around. 'Kev?'

A tug on the leg of my jeans. I leaned over.

Kevin had slid under the table.

'*Kevin*! What are you doing under there? Come on. Come up and sit on the seat.'

'I can't!' he replied plaintively.

Oh dear. I felt myself redden. Quickly I glanced around to see if anyone had noticed that my companion had decided to sit under the table. No one seemed to.

The least objectionable thing appeared to be to simply sit down at the table with my hot chocolate and wait for Kevin to come out. If he weren't so big, I might have taken a more charitable view of our predicament but as it was, I had to admit to being mightily embarrassed and in no way wanted to draw attention to what was going on. So it seemed best, if possible, to wait him out.

I hunched over my cup. Neither of us said anything, not that conversation would have been easy on two levels like that. I could hear Kevin rustling around down there but he stayed clear of my legs. The fixed seats of the booth made a small but effective place to hide.

It was seven-thirty when we arrived. As I sat, sipping the chocolate as slowly as possible, I watched the minute hand creep around to eight o'clock and then toward eight-thirty. The young man behind the counter came over and asked if he could get me anything else. I asked when they closed. Eleven, he said. I agreed to have another cup of hot chocolate.

The faces changed. The young kids hanging around the juke-box gave way to couples, still in their teens but older. More quarters clinked into the jukebox. I heard one song by ABBA eight times.

'Kev, how you doing down there?' I whispered, saying it over the rim of my fourth cup of hot chocolate. I had an order of French fries too, to soak up all that liquid.

He moved but did not answer. I knew he was crying. We had been there almost two hours, he cramped into that tiny space under the table and me, trying to look nonchalant as I sat alone, waiting and waiting.

What was I going to do? Should I call Jeff? Or one of the aides? Perhaps I just ought to get down there and haul him out myself.

I think my biggest worry was humiliating him. Kevin worked extremely hard at preserving what little self-respect he had managed to grasp. He had quite a bit of dignity for a kid in his circumstances. And it had taken a hell of a lot of courage to do what he had done so far this evening. Even sitting under a table in the Frosty-Freez was a huge step forward. So I didn't want to humiliate him by creating a scene, if I could help it. Undoubtedly, he was embarrassed enough on his own without my help.

Yet, what were we going to do? It was already 9:30 and there was only an hour and a half to go. My own embarrassment over the situation had long since passed. All I felt now was desperation that we should be able to resolve this with the minimum amount of fuss possible.

'Kev? You about got yourself together?' I asked. I brought my foot out to fake tying a shoelace so I could talk to him more easily. 'They close here at eleven. We got to go before then.'

I had a Dr Pepper this time and another order of fries. French fries were the easiest thing to stretch out over a long period of time. I was half sick from all the junk but I felt obliged to keep eating something. The boy behind the counter continued glancing in my direction and the only thing that put him off was if I kept ordering and eating.

But it was getting to be too much. By 10:15 I leaned over again. 'Kev, I'm going to leave for a few minutes, okay? I've been drinking stuff all night. I need to use the bathroom. I'll be right back.'

That wasn't a complete lie. I did need to. But I needed a phone too.

'Jeff?' I whispered. I didn't want Kevin to hear me. I didn't want the kid behind the counter to hear me either. 'What am I going to do, Jeff?'

He didn't know either and thank God, he didn't laugh. It was blessed just to hear his voice. Actually, that was all I really needed, someone to share my predicament with, because when I went back to the booth, I still had no idea other than waiting Kevin out. But at least I wasn't alone in it anymore.

Someone else knew. Someone else thought I was doing the best thing. So I felt better.

'Kevin, we got fifteen minutes. In fifteen minutes that guy over there is going to shut this place up, and if you aren't out of there by then, I'm going to have to tell him and it's going to be awful. Do you hear? We got fifteen minutes.'

The sound of a shifting body came from under the table.

'Kevin, do you *hear* me? You've got to come out from under that table. Do you hear?'

Silence.

I shifted my foot around until I located him. I sharply nudged whatever part of his body I had found. 'Do you hear me?'

'Yes,' came a hoarse whisper.

'Good. Okay, listen, I'm going to get up. I'm going over to the jukebox and put a song on, and if you want to get out from there, this will be a good time to do it. No one will see you.'

I rose, went over to the machine and read all the songs listed. I didn't like any of them very much. Finally, I chose something loud and raucous by Elvis Presley to cover up Kevin's coming out noises.

When I returned, Kevin still wasn't out.

'I thought you were getting up,' I whispered. 'Now, Kevin, you got to.'

'I will. Gimme another chance.'

'Do you want me to go away again?'

'Yes.'

So again I rose. I went back to the jukebox. We were the only people in there now except of course for the young man behind the counter. He was definitely giving me odd looks by this point. I had no idea if he understood what was going on. Probably not. Without a complete script none of this made much sense, no matter how you looked at it. Even if he had never noticed Kevin's existence at all, my behavior had been strange enough on its own.

I stayed at the jukebox several minutes and chose another song.

'We're closing soon,' the boy called to me. I nodded.

Back at the booth I found Kevin. Red-eyed and puffy cheeked, he sat with his head clasped between his hands. Relief washed over me and I wanted to hug him. I couldn't because of the table between us, so I just touched his face.

He was still crying.

'Come on, let's go,' I said.

'I wet my pants,' he bawled.

'That doesn't matter. Come on. Let's get out of here. Fast. Let's go.' I got up. Reaching across the table, I grabbed his arm. With a tug, I dislodged him from the booth and we galloped out of the door of the Frosty-Freez and down the street.

Kevin continued to sob. All the way back to the home, he bawled, mostly over his wet pants, I suspect.

'Well, we survived that, didn't we?' I said to him as we waited for the security guard to let us into Garson Gayer. 'Barely, but we did, huh?'

He nodded through his tears.

The night shift, whom I had never met, had questions in their faces as we went past but they didn't ask them.

Inside Kevin's room I pulled his pajamas out from under his pillow and tossed them to him. 'Here. Get these on. And no one will ever know about your pants, will they? I'll go stand outside the door. Hurry, now. Change. I'll be back.'

Kevin was under the covers when I returned. His clothes had disappeared into the laundry bag. I perched on the edge of his bed.

'So, what do you think? We did it, didn't we? We got you outside.'

'It was horrible.'

'Well, yes, it wasn't exactly flawless, was it? But we did it. You can't expect perfection. I mean, three and a half years is a long time.'

Kevin nodded.

'But we did do it.'

'That guy probably thought we were nuts.'

'Yeah, probably,' I said and smiled at him. 'Can you imagine what he must be thinking? You know, I had four cups of hot chocolate, two glasses of Dr Pepper and three orders of French fries? I was running out of money and had to use my parking change. It's all nickels and dimes and pennies.'

Kevin nodded.

'And I kept having to listen to that song by ABBA. You know, I counted it fourteen times altogether. I think I got the words forever in my brain.'

'So do I,' said Kevin. 'I have a dreeeeeeeam, a song to siiiiing,' he burst out in shaky falsetto.

I giggled. 'And after me sitting there for three hours all by myself and no one comes in and then suddenly we go dashing out together, when he probably never even knew you were there. He probably really wonders where you came from. We could make a movie about this. It'd be really funny.'

That made Kevin smile too. 'Yeah. You and me could star. We could call it the *Mystery at the Frosty-Freez*. Or no, we could make it a spy movie. That guy probably thought you were a spy or something, the way you were hanging around. And the way I came out of nowhere.'

'Yeah, probably.'

'We'll have to go there again,' Kevin said, 'and really confuse him.'

'I don't know. Better not. I didn't have much money left. After all that, I only left him an eight-cent tip.'

'That's okay,' Kevin said. 'I left him a puddle.'

And we both fell about laughing.

Chapter Sixteen

While Kevin moved ahead with leaps and bounds, one person in my life was going, if anywhere, backward. That was Charity.

I knew things hadn't been going well for her. While there had been no crises, so to speak, her whole life was sort of a slow-boiling catastrophe. Charity's family was a huge, indistinct group that expanded and contracted like a sleeping animal. An uncle or an aunt or a passel of cousins would move in one night, a grandmother or a sister would be gone the next. There were about four or five branches to Charity's family from what I could make out, two in town and two or three out on the reservation. The main bulk of the members seemed to move regularly from one residence to another. So I never knew exactly who was who when I went to the door. Different people were forever answering it, but they all knew me. I relieved them of Charity for a few hours.

Within this sprawling clan festered many problems, alcoholism, brawling and, I suspect, prostitution, involving Charity's mother, were the most notable. But there were good things too. They had a tremendous sense of kinship and a lovely oral tradition of stories. Her grandfather on her mother's side, whom I never met, seemed to have a wealth of information about the old ways, which he regularly passed on to Charity and the other grandchildren.

The most influential person in Charity's life appeared to be her mother. Her name was Michaela and she was very young, quite a bit younger than I, I thought. She had a dark, wild-eyed look about her and a nervous mannerism of jerking her shoulders. She seemed a tortured soul fluctuating between violent outbursts and withdrawn piety. She had had Charity baptized into three different religions and took her regularly to two church services on Sunday. Yet Michaela locked herself into different parts of the small house and often drank herself into unconsciousness. And of course, as Charity had pointed out, Michaela worked every night except Mondays.

Charity seemed to cope with the problems in her home life in quite creative fashion. When I had first met her, she had seemed such a down-to-earth sort of kid. It came as a rude shock to me to discover that nearly everything she had ever told me about herself was false. She had no sister Sandy. Indeed, she had no sisters at all. She was not the youngest but the oldest. She had four small brothers. For Charity the world was never good enough as it stood, so she embroidered on it. The lies were usually harmless enough, although exasperating because I *never* knew what was actually true and what was not. But for Charity they were all true. What she could not have in fact, she gave to herself in her heart.

Her stories *were* the way things were for her. And she'd deck anyone who dared to disagree.

I knew Charity was having problems at home. And I tried to do something about it. I made countless phone calls to the organizer of the Big Brothers/Big Sisters program and then to social services. But it was one of those hopeless affairs where one could not treat the problem until it got too big to treat. So I was going day to day, week to week, with Charity blithely taking over my life, like someone from *Invasion of the Body Snatchers*. It was an old song and dance, this one, one I thought I had finished dancing when I had walked out of the classroom, one of the few things about teaching I had never regretted leaving behind.

In bleaker moments I even considered dropping out of the Brothers/Sisters program. I especially thought that at 6 A.M. on a weekend morning when Charity was banging on the door for breakfast, or in the middle of the night when she had ostensibly run away from home to my house for the millionth time. But I knew I never would drop out. I knew she had no other recourse and that I, what little comfort I was, was all that held soul and body together in some instances. I couldn't drop out. I knew I couldn't. I was too soft in the head. Besides, she had such creative catastrophes.

The phone rang at the office one morning mid-March.

'Hello, Mrs Hayden?' a man's voice asked. 'This is Officer Cooper down at the police station. We have your daughter down here at the Seventh Street Station.'

My jaw dropped. Before I could tell him I had no daughter the telephone changed hands.

'Listen, Mom–'

'*Charity*! What *are* you up to? What the heck is going on?'

'Listen, Mom, I'm kind of down here at the police sta–'

'*Charity*!'

'Well, could you sort of come down?'

'What did you tell them I was your mother for, Charity?'

'Well, they said for me to call my parents.' There was a long pause. Charity would never have called her own mother. For one thing, they had no phonc. For another thing, fox that she was, Charity knew I wouldn't lay a hand on her. Not the way her mother would.

'Listen, Charity, they're not going to believe you when I walk in there. They're going to take one look at me and know I'm not your mother. It's pretty obvious.'

'Oh but, Mom,' she pleaded, 'I already told the nice man how wonderful you are, how you and Daddy gone out and adopted this poor little Indian kid. I know I'm a lot of trouble to you but you got such a good heart.'

'*Charity*!'

The policeman came on the line. He was a kind-sounding man with a patience in his voice that caused me to suspect he hadn't been totally taken in. I didn't confirm or deny anything. Instead, I asked why she was down there in the first place.

'Well, ma'am,' he said politely, 'she was trying to derail trains.'

Only Charity.

'Well, I *wasn't*, Torey. Honest, I *wasn't*! I was just trying to see what they looked like. You know. If you put stuff on the track it gets all ironed out when a train goes over it. And I just wanted to see what it looks like. That's all.'

We were in the car going I didn't know where exactly. I had had to do more than a little fancy talking and show my clinic ID and everything but my passport to get her released to me without phoning her real mother. Now I had her and I didn't know what I was going to do with her.

'Why ever were you out there in the first place? It's a school day. Why aren't you in school like you ought to be? Then you wouldn't be getting in trouble for putting things on the tracks.'

She shrugged.

'Don't shrug at me. Answer me. This is serious business, Charity.'

'Are you mad at me?'

'In a word, yes. This isn't funny. That officer was right, you know, you could have really hurt someone doing that. You could have made a train go off the track. It could have caused a lot of damage. And maybe someone would have been hurt or even killed, just because of the silly thing you were doing.'

'But I wasn't *trying* to make them run off the tracks.'

'That's not the point, Charity. The point is, whatever you were doing down at the train yard, you weren't supposed to be doing it. You were supposed to have been in school, plain and simple.'

I didn't know what to do with her. I was driving toward her school but I knew Charity well enough to realize she wasn't going to be very impressed with the seriousness of this sort of behavior if I just drove her back to school and let her out. She'd be out flattening things on the track by afternoon. On the other hand, I did not want to drive her to her house. What would her mother do? Beat her for it? Ignore it? Most likely, there would be a couple of good swats for causing trouble and Charity would be turned loose again while Michaela would sink into bleak depression over the incident and drink herself senseless. That was, of course, supposing anyone was home.

I was in a terrible position. I had no real rights, no legal responsibility, nothing to put me in a position of power over Charity's life. It was ten times worse than my powerlessness as a teacher had ever been. No matter what I did now, whether it be talking to her mother, seeing her teacher, contacting the social worker or the welfare people, I could do nothing vital myself. I was just a voice in the wilderness. Without legal rights, I was like a ghost, there in spirit and no more.

'Look, Char, have you had breakfast?'

She shook her head.

I turned into a McDonald's. 'Well, let's stop and eat and see if we can't sort some things out.'

Charity sat hunched over her Egg McMuffin. The fight had gone out of her. I think she realized I was serious, *really* serious, and things looked a little black to her. Her shoulders sagged, her head was down.

'So you want to tell me about it?' I asked. 'How come you weren't in school?'

She shrugged.

Silence. I sat watching her; she sat watching her Egg McMuffin. I let the silence play around us. One advantage of working with mutes so long was learning to be comfortable with such a powerful weapon as silence.

'I don't like school,' she replied at last. 'I don't like having to ride on the bus.'

'How come?'

'The other kids make fun of me.'

'Over what?' I asked.

She shrugged again. 'Over just stuff.'

'What kind of stuff, Charity?'

'Just stuff.'

Again the silence. The restaurant wasn't very busy. It was a Wednesday, and only a few truck drivers and some moms and their kiddies were there. I watched them. Charity played with her food, pulling crumbs off the muffin and putting them in her mouth one at a time.

'They call me "Fatty,"' she said in a low voice.

'I see. And that makes you angry with them.'

She nodded. 'I'm not *really* fat. I just got big bones.'

Silence. I had finished my English muffin and orange juice, so I only sat.

'The kids call you names and that upsets you. So you don't want to ride the bus. Is that it?'

She shrugged again. I felt like nailing her shoulders down so she'd quit doing that. 'I hate Yolanda too.'

'Who's she?'

'The bus monitor. She gets mad at me all the time and it's not my fault. The kids call me names and then she gets mad at me.'

'Oh, I see. You feel it isn't fair that she should get angry with you when the other kids are picking on you too?'

'Yes. And so I told her last night I was going to get Sandy to come beat her up. Sandy's twelve and I said she was my big sister and she was going to beat stupid old Yolanda up. I said Sandy'd punch her in the mouth.'

'You told her this last night?'

Charity nodded. She fiddled a little more with the Egg McMuffin, which was largely uneaten. 'And she said I was stupid. She said I don't have a big sister.'

'Mmm. I see.'

'But I *do*.'

'I think you might want to have a big sister.'

Charity looked up. For the first time there were tears in her eyes. 'I *do* have a big sister! I do. And if you don't shut up, I'll have her come down here and beat you up too.'

'Char, calm down. There's nothing to yell about.'

'I do *too* have a big sister! You say that. You say I do too have a big sister!' Her voice had risen and people at other tables were pretending not to look.

'She'll beat you up, Torey Hayden. She will. I'll tell her about you and she will. She'll come right down here and punch you in the face.' Charity was half crying and half screaming at me now. People were no longer pretending they weren't looking at us. Now they just turned their heads and stared. Charity continued to bellow.

'Come on,' I said and stood up.

Charity screamed.

Coming around to her side of the table, I put my hands under her to lift her up. It was a job; she was no feather-weight. Protesting violently, she screamed and wiggled and fought my attempt to get her out of the restaurant. Halfway to the door, she sank her teeth into my hand. I yelped myself and couldn't make her let go. At least it gave me some way to drag her through the door.

I shoved her in one side of the car and went around to the other to get in. Charity was beside herself. I think maybe it was no more than an accumulation of things.

For a few moments we just sat in the privacy of the car. Charity continued to shriek. I sat, wiping blood off my hand where she had bitten me and thinking how truly unpleasant my restaurant experiences had been recently, between her and Kevin.

'Come here,' I said at last. The gearshift separated us, and when she didn't respond, I had to lean over and pull her across the barrier onto my lap. I had never held Charity before. She wasn't the sort of child one held, which I think may have been part of the problem. By this time she was only crying, and when I brought her into my arms, she clutched my shirt to her face and sobbed. I held her close, all of her, the sticky toast crumbs, the straggly braids, the grimy sweater, all of her.

'So, what's the matter, lovey?' I asked.

'I dunno.'

'Just things?'

She nodded and snuffled against my shirt.

'Sometimes it is that way. Things get hard.'

'Do you still like me?' she asked and looked up through tears.

'I still like you.'

'You still want to be my big sister?'

'Yes, I do.'

'Even though I'm bad?'

'We all do bad things sometimes. That's the way it is.'

She snuffled again. Pulling my arms physically closer to her, she snuggled against me.

'You know something?' she said.

'What's that?'

'Diana, that's my other Big Sister, she didn't like me very well. She stopped being my sister. She asked them for someone else and so she got to be Rosa's Big Sister instead. She didn't like me.'

There was a pause. Charity mopped up a little more. 'And neither did Sandy. Or Cheryl. I *did* really, truly have Big Sisters. They just all stopped, except you.'

I didn't speak.

'Are you gonna stop?'

'No. I said I wouldn't, didn't I?'

She sighed and then crawled off my lap and over into her own seat. 'That's what they all said.'

I took her back to school. Then I went back to the office and cleaned up. When she had bitten me, it had torn the skin in a neat little half-moon and I had bled all over everything. At the time it had been the least of my worries, but when I got back to work, I realized I wasn't very presentable. So in the rest room I sponged blood out of my shirt and applied Band-Aids. But they wouldn't stick. It was a too-mobile part of my hand. So I dried the area carefully and decided to forget it.

What a laugh that was.

By evening I felt hot and achy.

By the next morning I was running a 102° temperature. I was in bed for a week and had to get a tetanus shot.

Chapter Seventeen

The months turned. Winter had given way completely to spring. Easter came and went. The buds on the lilacs were starting to swell.

So much had changed since early winter when Jeff had joined Kevin and me. There were still the occasional moments when Kevin balked at something or gave evidence of his few remaining fears, but in general, he was so vastly improved as to not be recognizable as the same boy who hid under tables all those months before.

We went out of the Garson Gayer grounds regularly now. Jeff and I would even occasionally take him out on a weekend to go to the places he especially enjoyed. The zoo was popular because Kevin loved the seals. He saved his meager pocket money to buy packet after packet of fish to feed them. But his favorite destination of all was the amusement park. This puzzled me somewhat because Kevin remained too fearful of most of the rides to go on them, and the cost of the entrance ticket always seemed an extravagance to me because the park was one of those where, after you paid the cover charge, the first ten rides were free. Kevin never did anything there except walk around. He almost never had extra money to buy cotton candy or caramel apples unless Jeff or I gave it to him. And there weren't many other things to do except the rides. But the park remained his favorite place to go. The only explanation I could settle on was that both Jeff and I liked many of the rides, and Kevin would carefully dole out to us his own tickets to go on the rides he thought we liked best. Perhaps that was it, the only time Kevin could genuinely do something for us.

The time was coming when Kevin would have to be moved from Garson Gayer. He would be seventeen in September, two years older than the home's legal age limit. There really was no way that Dana could put off transferring him soon.

The prospects, however, looked far different than they had in September. The state hospital was seldom ever mentioned anymore. Free of most of his fears, talking, relating well, Kevin stood a much better chance of living in a less restrictive environment. Even his appearance had improved remarkably. With treatment, his acne had gotten better. The new haircut, the up-to-date clothes and a new pair of glasses gave him the casual appearance of most teenage boys. He wouldn't stand out now, not much.

Dana searched vigorously for a foster home for Kevin, or failing that, a group home where he could be exposed to other, more nearly normal boys his own age.

Kevin was well aware of this new step. He cherished it like a gem in a treasure chest and much of his time was spent speculating about his future.

Therefore, when the call came in mid-May none of us was too surprised. Dana met Jeff and me at the door on Friday morning as we arrived. Her face was alight. Dana really was a beautiful woman when she smiled like that, and she infected both Jeff and me with her pleasure before we knew the reason for it.

A group home in Bellefountaine, an outlying community, had accepted Kevin for placement. It was a home for seven boys that had an excellent reputation for work with difficult kids. Kevin would go there at the end of the month.

It was a placement I had not dared hope would come true. The home was a small working farm on the outskirts of Bellefountaine. They had sixty acres of market gardens as well as cows and sheep and horses and pigs. After seven years of incarceration, Kevin would at last be free.

Kevin, of course, was delirious with joy. He leapt up on the table and danced for joy when we went into the small white room. 'I'm free,' he shouted at the top of his lungs, 'I've got a home; I'm free.'

There would be a lot of changes in his life. Both Jeff and I had been exploring this fact with Kevin in preparation for whatever might take place. The end was coming for us, for our sessions. Now that he was going as far away as Bellefountaine there would be no way either Jeff or I could continue to see him after he left Garson Gayer. Whatever his future needs, he wouldn't be with one of us.

As we talked about it, I could see the time really had come for Kevin. He expressed regret that we were breaking up; he worried that we might forget to write. But they were only fleeting concerns. His heart and soul were in the future. Jeff and I belonged to the past.

On the very last session on the twenty-seventh of May, Jeff, Kevin and I had a bit of a private party in the small white room. Jeff brought his cassette player and some tapes and his guitar. I brought some goodies to eat and we celebrated together.

Toward the very end of the hour, Kevin was lying on the floor putting cake into his mouth crumb by crumb. Jeff sat on the table, his legs swinging. We were kids, really, all three of us. That thought struck me abruptly as I sat on the floor beside Jeff's swinging legs. In a way I think that was what had brought us together and kept us together long after Kevin ceased needing a fully-trained psychiatrist and a psychologist. Jeff and I were only kids ourselves, a couple of whiz kids in a grownups' world. But Kevin had given us an excuse to play again ourselves, while teaching him to play. It had felt good.

Then as we were sitting there, enjoying the last bits of the party food, a waltz started to play on one of Jeff's rather uniquely created cassettes. *Tales from the Vienna Woods.*

Jeff hopped to his feet. Stretching a hand out to me, he bowed. 'May I have this dance, madam?'

I giggled from embarrassment. 'I can't dance.'

'Yes, you can. With me you can. Come on, the music doth pass us by.'

'Honest, Jeff. I'm terrible.' But I got dragged to my feet anyway.

Jeff put his arms around me and waltzed me off around the room to the strains of Strauss. His steps were sure, his

movements decisive. Mesmerized out of a cramped, bare
room in an institution, I saw the white latex melt away as I
watched Jeff's face. He was smiling, his eyes laughing. I was
in the Stardust Ballroom. I was in the cool, verdant woods
of Vienna.

'Look behind you,' Jeff whispered and turned us so I could
see.

Kevin had risen too. His arms outstretched to hold an
invisible partner, he had closed his eyes. Head back, he
twirled around and around and around the small room. In a
strange way he was very graceful. It was an eerie grace.

When the music stopped and Jeff and I had finished, Kevin
kept on for a few bars more, waltzing around the room to his
memory. Even when he slowed and stopped, his body
swayed. He came up to us.

'Teach me how to do that, Jeff. Put it on again and teach
me, okay? So I can do it right?'

Jeff ran the recorder back.

'Here, it's easy. Just like this.' He put his arms around Kevin
and showed him the steps before waltzing him off around
the room.

They were an unlikely couple, the brilliant young doctor
and the animal boy. Kevin was almost as tall as Jeff but was
so much thinner and more slightly built. Jeff was very gentle with him, pushing him in the way he should go in such a
way that his mistakes did not show. On Kevin's face there
was a profound and enigmatic expression.

I found myself on the edge of tears as I watched them.
There was something beautiful about them and the music
and the springtime brilliance streaming through the window.

It was a terrible beauty that woke something deep and unspoken inside me. I think it was touching all of us, this uncanny thing.

When the music stopped, Kevin turned to me. 'Will you dance with me now, Teacher?' he asked.

I regarded him.

He smiled.

'I'm not as good as Jeff,' I said.

The waltz started again and I felt Kevin's arms around me. The dance was instinctive in him as it had never been in me. He took me confidently and danced with me. Perhaps it was not the waltz. I suspect it wasn't. Kevin made his own dance. The dance of the phoenix.

Part II

Chapter Eighteen

I heard about Kevin only through Dana. He left Garson Gayer the first day of June and moved to Bellefountaine. In mid-June he went to a special-education summer camp for two weeks. Apparently he was doing well.

Then I heard no more. That was the way it usually was with my kids. It was something one grew used to, that final parting and then the silence. It seemed incongruous at first, after sharing such intense and intimate moments of each other's lives, but it was a natural facet of the job.

For the first two months of summer I carried on as usual at the clinic, working with the kids and teaching a summer-school course at the local college. My time seemed suddenly very free.

Over the Fourth of July weekend I took Charity camping with me and some of my friends and their children. We went clear up into the Rockies, driving as far through the trees on the mountainside as the Jeep would take us and then packing in almost three miles farther beyond the end of the road.

Charity complained the entire three miles. She wasn't used to walking that far, and even though I had found a pair of decent hiking boots for her, she said her feet hurt and her back hurt and she was tired. It was a bit of a bother as my friends' twin sons who were five and their little girl who was three all carried their own sleeping bags and rucksacks and even the dog carried his food. But Charity didn't care if she was almost nine and carrying only a pack full of clothes. She was tired and hot and thought the things were too heavy. But since we weren't in any hurry, when Charity complained of being tired, we stopped. When her back hurt, I took her pack. And in the end, we made it.

It was a lovely weekend. Charity came alive in the mountains. I taught her to swim in the small, icy pools under the waterfalls. Charity adored that. We had neglected to pack bathing suits, so she started out swimming in her holey, grimy underpants. However, in a short time she had both pairs wet and none dry and so she dropped her inhibitions altogether and cavorted through the water bare. It was the way it should have been, I thought, as I sat on the rocks by the side of the stream and watched her. I had unbraided Charity's long thick hair and it flowed about her like a black cloak. The pudginess which made her fat in polyester was robustness against the wraithlike lodgepole pines that came right down to the pool's edge. She was beautiful there, a native to the forest and the water, at once one with the world about her.

She learned to fish too and loved that best of all. She had a hunter's instinct. Searching out the best 'holes,' watching silently on the banks to see fish moving in the depths below became an hours-long occupation for her.

And there were also the normal chores of camping. Fuel had to be found, fires started. Tents had to be straightened each morning. Suppers of roast potatoes and hot dogs cooked, smoke wafting up through the pines. Afterward we sat around the campfire in the growing dusk telling stories. A far-off forest fire deepened the air around us and made it pungent with a smell which simultaneously evoked warmth and death.

We made strange conglomerations out of bananas, marshmallows and chocolate bars and wrapped them up in foil to bake in the embers. We told such stories. We all did. Even Maggie, the three-year-old, had a story. So did I. And so did Charity. I suppose because she was so good at creating her own tales, I ought to have known she'd be a storyteller, but I hadn't. No one among us was more captivated than I when she started in. She was sitting on the far side of the campfire, almost apart from the rest of us. The flames did not illuminate her face as they did ours. It gave mystery to the small, almost disembodied voice that told us of The Unknown One, who was Son of Two Men. We heard of camps and lodges long dead, even in memory, of gods who had no more worshipers, of a people now faded as mist into darkness.

There were long pauses in Charity's story. Not thinking pauses so much as listening pauses. She would cock her head and listen to the night sounds and then continue her tale. At one point, with her voice quiet as the wind through the pines, she lapsed into her native tongue. It didn't matter really. The soft, strange words carried the meaning of the story just as well.

Then we were alone, Charity and I, snuggled warm in our sleeping bags. The air was summer warm, a breezy, breath-soft sort of night, and the stars were veiled behind distant smoke. I left the flap of the tent open so that we could see the night.

We had camped up on a ridge between two mountains. The taller was to our left, an old extinct volcano named Hollowtop. From where we lay in the tent, the huge massif of the mountain was silhouetted against the hazy tapestry of stars.

Long after all was quiet in the camp and I had drifted asleep, I heard Charity call out cautiously. 'Torey?'

'Mmm?'

'Where are we?'

I rolled over sleepily. 'In the tent. We're camping, re-member?'

'Oh yeah,' she replied, a little troubled.

'Are you frightened, Charity?'

'Oh no. Not me.'

Silence.

'Are there any bears up here, Torey?' she inquired politely.

'No,' I answered. 'I shouldn't think there are. They'd be other places.'

'Do you know that for sure?'

'Yes.'

'There might be bears.'

'No.'

'How do you know?'

'Because I know bears, Charity. And none would be here.'

'What if there were?'

'I'd keep them all away from you, Char. I'd keep you very safe. Now go back to sleep.'

'Torey? How'd you keep me safe? Would you fight 'em?'

'I'd fight 'em, Char. And I'd win. Now go to sleep.'

Silence.

'Torey?'

'Ye-es.'

'Are there any lions, Torey?'

'No. There are absolutely, positively no lions. None at all here. Now go back to sleep and don't worry about it.'

'What about mountain lions? There might be mountain lions.'

'No. No mountain lions. I'd hear them, if there were. And I don't. So we're quite safe. Now go to sleep.' I closed my eyes. Charity moved her sleeping bag closer to mine and I made a little hollow where she could cuddle.

The night-time stillness came down again and I thought she had fallen back asleep.

'Torey?' in the tiniest voice.

'Yes, Charity.'

'Well, my mom said I wasn't to sleep with you unless you asked me to. But if you did ask me, well, she said I could, you know.'

'I see.'

'I thought you'd want to know that. Just in case you did want me to sleep with you.'

'Are you scared?'

'No. No. I just thought you might be cold or something and didn't like to ask. But if you did want me to, I wouldn't mind.'

Sleepily I sat up. I smiled at her. 'Yes, I wanted you to sleep with me all along.'

She broke into a most glorious smile. 'I thought you did!'

Then I took a month off and went to Wales.

The cool, misty mountains in the north of that small country had become a home to my heart. I never knew quite why; I only knew the yearning, the *hiraeth*, as the Welsh called it in their own language. So in late July I packed my mountain boots and my rucksack and left the clinic and the city and the hot Western summer behind. I spent weeks walking through the wet, wild places, across the windy moors and over the Pass of the Arrows, where King Arthur met defeat. Nights were spent in small stone cottages of friends or around the coal fire in the pub while mists rolled up from the Irish Sea. They are called simply The High Places by their own people. And one local poet said that the Welsh left their mountains only once because they could never bear the pain of leaving them again.

Chapter Nineteen

My head was still somewhere over the Atlantic Ocean when the phone rang. I lifted my head from the pillow and was totally disoriented. It was daylight. Morning? Afternoon? Yesterday? Today? Tomorrow? I still had not managed to answer that question satisfactorily by the time I had stumbled to the telephone.

It was Jeff. I was in no mood for his company.

'My God, Jeff, I just got back. What are you calling at this time of day for anyway? What time is it?'

'8:30.'

'Oh. In the evening? The morning?'

'In the morning. I'm at the office.'

I was squinting at the kitchen clock. Yes, it was 8:30. 'I'm not due in today, Jeff. It's still my vacation. I'm not coming in until Monday.'

'I know it.'

'Then what on earth do you want?'

'Well,' he said, and there was a sigh. 'Do you remember Kevin Richter? From Garson Gayer?'

'Of course I remember him.'

'He's in the psychiatric unit at Mortenson Hospital.'

I came fully awake. In a way I wish I hadn't. I wished I were still in Wales and this was all just a dream.

On a hot August night Kevin had apparently become involved in a fracas out in Bellefountaine with a couple of other boys and with a woman counselor. It wasn't clear exactly what had happened, according to Jeff, but Kevin seemed to have attacked the woman in the course of an argument. He broke her arm and dislocated her shoulder. The police were called. Kevin was summarily removed from the home and taken down to the juvenile center at the courthouse.

Geez, I said. Just wait, Jeff replied, that's only the first of it.

Kevin was retained at juvenile hall for three or four days while they tried to decide what to do with him. Then he broke out. Loose for two days in the city, he had broken into the clinic the previous night.

The clinic? I echoed. Yeah, Jeff said. Our office. What the hell did he want to break into our office for? I asked.

Easy. He was looking for his knife, for the blue metal bed-stead knife he had given me to keep for him so many months before. Did I remember that? Jeff asked. How could I forget it. Apparently, Kevin had only one goal in mind when he escaped from juvenile hall. To kill his stepfather. He knew I had the knife, although he didn't know I had been on vacation. A boy matching his description had been around the clinic during the day, pestering Shirley, the receptionist, to see me. When she had told him I wasn't due back yet, from Wales, he had left. Then after dark, he had broken in.

They caught him, the police did, him and his knife, which he had found in my desk drawer. Now he was in the high-security unit at Mortenson.

Understandably, Jeff and a whole lot of other people were quite keen for me to come in to work. You ought to see what our office looks like, Jeff said. You just wait. And wait until the people from Mortenson get hold of you. They're dying to talk to you.

I just bet they were.

I went into the bathroom, ran a basin full of water and had a good scrub. As I pulled the washcloth down over my face, I saw myself in the mirror. I literally had not been back twenty-four hours and was exhausted. It showed in my face and no amount of soap and water could wash it away.

I arrived to find our office a declared disaster area. All the drawers had been pulled out of both our desks and the contents strewn about the floor. The bookshelves had been emptied. Paper was everywhere.

Jeff sat in his office chair in the middle of it all. He looked like I felt, devastated.

'I suppose it's what we should have expected,' he said forlornly as I picked my way across the room and sat down in my chair. 'There had to be more to that kid, didn't there? It couldn't have been as easy as it was, could it? Not after all those years.'

'I had been kind of hoping it had been,' I replied.

'Yes, So had I. But …' Jeff swiveled his chair back and forth aimlessly. 'I guess I have to face the fact that the kid never really ever told me much. Not really. To be perfectly frank, I don't think he ever told me anything.'

'What do you mean?' I looked over at him.

Jeff shrugged. 'You know. You know as well as I do. He just never *said* anything. It was all surface stuff. It's just that …' Jeff paused. 'It's just that I got so sick of you. You always sitting there, saying "My gut says this." "My gut says that."' He smiled drily. 'I knew you were right all along. I knew the stupid kid wasn't telling me a damned thing, that it was all just some sort of class act of his. But I got so blooming sick of hearing about you and your gut …'

I grimaced.

Jeff shrugged again. 'But I got nothing from him. And after a while you begin to believe in nothing.'

'I'd believed,' I said softly. 'I think I really did believe that he was getting better. I thought we'd fixed him.'

I felt like crying. I hadn't wanted Jeff to say something like that to me. I hadn't wanted to know the actual problem had been the communication between him and me. Most of all, I hadn't wanted to be right.

'Well, yes,' said Jeff gently, 'I guess maybe I believed him too.' He smiled at me. 'Don't blame yourself for it.'

'But he *was* getting better. He did improve, didn't he? What more was there? I guess I thought maybe that was enough.'

'I guess we both did,' Jeff replied.

'But he *was* improving, Jeff. He *did* get better. Even this, Jeff, is better than what he was under his table. At least I think maybe it is. I don't know. What more is there? I have no answers. I was good at the questions but I never had any answers.'

'No,' he said. 'We never had any answers. In a way we never even had all the questions. We really don't have anything.'

The hospital wanted me up there. They recognized, I suspect, the strange, twisted part I was playing in this. Moreover, Kevin had ceased talking. He hadn't said a single word to anyone other than the police. So after an hour with Jeff in the office, picking up the ruins of our desk drawers, I got back into the car and drove across the city to Mortenson Hospital.

It was a huge hospital, one that I did not know because it had no affiliation with the clinic. It was built up on a rocky outcropping overlooking the city, and part of the hospital was as many as ten stories high while other parts, because of the hill, were only seven or eight stories. It was a gigantic complex, sprawling over the rocky ledges above the river like a great sleeping beast.

While the hospital catered mainly to medical patients, it contained the county's largest long-term psychiatric unit. It also had the only unit equipped to hold the criminally disturbed. The entire fifth floor was devoted to psychiatry, and getting into the unit was an experience in itself. One had to take a public elevator to the fourth floor then locate the private elevator, which went only to the fifth. To use the private elevator, one had to be accompanied or be issued a key. On the fifth floor, the elevator opened into a reception area. One's appointment was confirmed and a large set of metal double doors were opened electronically by the receptionist. Inside these there was a second set of double doors. There one buzzed the unit and a staff member came and unlocked one of the doors.

I had been in a number of hospital psychiatric wards before, including the ones at the University of Minnesota where I had worked, and I had never come across a security system as imposing as this one. After I got used to it, I could get through the entire setup in about four minutes, if the elevators cooperated. But that first day I got lost repeatedly and confused and grilled by untold numbers of white-suited people before I finally made it, almost twenty minutes after coming through the front door.

Kevin was in his room. It was a long, narrow room with a largish window at the far end and a bed and chest of drawers, which reduced the width of it even more. There was a chair, too, a small plastic sucking type. Kevin's gangly frame was sprawled over it.

He regarded me as the nurse led me in. He didn't look especially surprised to see me. Perhaps he had known all along that his actions would bring me back in one way or another.

He'd grown since I'd last seen him. He must have reached six feet sometime during the summer. His hair was quite a bit longer. It still kept roughly the style Jeff's barber had given it in the spring but it was shaggy now. The rumpled length gave him a sort of wild look, not unappealing, but different. In a way he was even rather attractive. His skin was dramatically improved. Either the summer sun had helped or the antibiotics had finally taken hold. He was seventeen now and he definitely had the look of manhood about him. It had been a long, long year since last September.

I asked the nurse to leave us. When she did, I shut the door behind her quietly but firmly. Then I returned to where Kevin was sitting. There was no other chair in the tiny, narrow room so I sat on the bed.

We regarded one another in silence.

'So?' I said at last.

Kevin looked down at his hands and shrugged.

'What the hell happened?' I asked.

Another shrug.

Silence. It was a wicked silence, grabbing me around the throat and not letting go. I kept having to swallow.

And deep inside I was angry. I could feel it and identify it as anger. 'Whatever were you thinking of, Kevin? What did you do out there? What happened at Bellefountaine? And what the hell did you think you were doing with the knife?'

No answer.

Silence. And again silence. Just like all my other feelings, the anger sat in my gut. It boiled. Putting my hand over my stomach, I could feel it, pulsating heavily to the rhythm of my heart.

'You want to be your father's son? Is that what you want? You want to prove to everyone that you're just as brutal a man as your stepfather is? He's getting inside you, Kevin, and if he does, you'll never kill him because you'll be carrying him around with you. You'll never be rid of him. Is that what you want? To be like him?'

Kevin sighed.

'There's a better path for you. There's a better way than that one. Don't go out and prove that everything he said about you is true.'

There was no change in Kevin's expression. In fact, there almost was no expression. He only sat in his chair, twiddling his fingers back and forth. He would not look at me.

'So what the hell did you think you were doing?' I asked. 'What got into you?'

His shoulders sagged slightly. He took a deep breath. 'You know Murphy's Law?' he said softly, 'the one about if anything can go wrong, it will?'

I nodded.

'Well,' he said, 'I reckon I must be Murphy's boy.'

Chapter Twenty

And so, we started over again.

Kevin crashed into depression within days of arriving at Mortenson. I don't know what caused the depression. Perhaps having lost the opportunity to kill his stepfather— that central goal in his life—left him empty and without focus. Perhaps it was just another way of avoiding the war within himself that we on the outside could not yet fully see. It could have been any number of things, but whatever it was, he plunged headlong past us into it and left us with less to work with than we had had before.

The logistics of starting over were wretched. What the hospital wanted from me was my ability to make Kevin talk again, because at that moment, apparently he talked to no one except me. However, they didn't want me for therapy.

They had their own therapists, and Kevin now had a psychiatrist, as well, the man who had admitted him from the emergency room when the police brought him in. Therefore, it was obvious they would not allow Jeff to come at all. Policies regarding actual psychiatrists were rigid.

The hospital did not want to pay the clinic for my release. Under what sort of contract could they obtain my services? Could I guarantee the length of time I would be involved? Could I guarantee my work, if they paid the clinic in advance? God, it sounded like I was repairing motor cars or something. And what about my unorthodox preference for seeing the patient more than once a week? Would that cost proportionately more? Would they have to pay me for every visit? Or could they just pay, say, for a block of time, like two weeks? Money, money, money. All was money.

I wanted Jeff. And Jeff wanted to come. But there was no way. He was overqualified. They could not ignore the fact that he was a bona fide psychiatrist, despite his willingness to attest that he was working under me, the psychologist, on this case. Back and forth we went over the issue. How much would he cost? The clinic would have to release him, even if the hospital would not pay for him. Understandably, that upset the clinic and made them unwilling. And because the hospital was paying the clinic for my services and not paying me, myself, I could not give over part of my income to cover Jeff. It was a nightmare in 3-D.

In the end we cheated a bit. My integrity was not such that it disallowed a little fiddling. They didn't actually know what Jeff looked like over the hospital, so we gave in to them about not having him as co-therapist and dropped the issue.

Jeff was then reduced to the ignominious role of 'research assistant' with my elective mutism project and came in to see Kevin as my 'aide.' Because the clinic did not feel it could afford to release him, Jeff had agreed to come in on his own time after work. And bless him, when I offered to pay him meagerly from the funds of my research grant, he just shrugged and smiled and said not to worry about it.

It was all through this tangle of finances, when I spent so much time with Dr Rosenthal and the clinic bookkeeper, that I began to perceive one of the major differences between what I did in education and what I was doing now. There is something basically disgusting about being paid to care about someone and being able to decide on the basis of money, if one will or will not become or remain involved in someone else's life. While teaching, I had been paid only to transfer knowledge. The caring I did for the kids had been all my own. But all of this work now at the clinic seemed a little whorish to me.

The first few weeks were agony. Kevin was terribly depressed. He had plunged us all back into the old quagmire of selective speech because, while he willingly spoke to Jeff and me, he spoke to no one else, and nothing we did or said could persuade him to do otherwise. It was a saving grace, I suppose, because if he had talked to others, undoubtedly Jeff and I would have been booted out.

However, even we weren't greatly blessed. He spoke only when he chose and that grew to be less and less frequently. I never knew for sure when I arrived if he was going to do anything with us, if he was going to sit with us and talk or if he was going to spend the entire time hidden under his bedclothes, blanket over his head, and refuse to even look at us. We had had to schedule our sessions in the vicinity of five o'clock, because of Jeff's situation, and that seemed to be everyone's absolute worst time of day. I was usually tired and hungry and not at my most understanding. Jeff was more hyperactive than normal then. And as for Kevin, well, nothing seemed to improve him much.

One evening when I was sitting in the dusky September darkness because we hadn't turned the lights on, I recalled only a year ago when I had first encountered Kevin rocking under his table. As I sat in the semidarkness and listened to Kevin's and Jeff's soft breathing, I remembered how Kevin used to line the chairs up and cower in the gloom and how in the beginning I had had to crawl under the table with him too. With sharp abruptness I longed for those first days again. Tables and chairs had never been able to form the kind of barrier that Kevin had built around himself now.

The weeks went by. I cannot even remember them now, as to how they passed. Nothing happened; nothing changed. Kevin remained sunk in his depression, medicated beyond coherence, locked in some internal prison. I didn't know what to do to get him out. No one did, neither Jeff nor I nor the hospital staff nor the consulting psychiatrist. So we simply lay siege and waited.

Jeff and I started having dinner together afterward, mostly as a catharsis for having sat in silence for the hour before, but also partly as a bribe to keep us doing it. At least if we had something to look forward to, it didn't seem too hopeless. We began first by eating at the fast-food places around

Mortenson, and then Jeff started coming over to my house for supper when we got tired of greasy food and wanted more time to just sit and talk. I don't think we meant to take over one another's lives. It just sort of happened. Kevin's depression was catching.

Then we split the sessions up, me with three and Jeff with two, because he just couldn't balance it out with his work and his on-call roster at the other hospital. That eased the burden, but we found we had to continue our suppers together. Sanity sessions were what Jeff called them. He was probably right.

There was a window in the room, down at the far end. The view was panoramic, looking down from the rocky aerie where the hospital sat. The city stretched into the distance, and below the river moved angrily in eddies and rapids through a narrow canyon it had carved into the heart of the stony land. On the far side, houses and office buildings crawled up the tangled slopes, their angles softened by autumn-colored trees.

Kevin began to live at that window as the weeks passed. Every time when I arrived, he would be standing there, hands behind his back, eyes fixed on some unseen point beyond the glass. That window became the thing around which our whole lives revolved. Kevin was able to stand there and talk to me without having to actually look at me. Often, he was able to stand without talking either. I was not much competition, I think, for the things he was looking at.

'I wonder what's happened to my sisters,' he said to me one afternoon when the sun had set and still he stood, a silhouette against the brightening city lights beyond the glass. I hadn't heard him speak of his family in a long, long time.

'I don't know,' I replied.

'I wonder. I think about them sometimes. You know how long it's been since I seen them?' He turned briefly to look at me. When I shook my head, he turned back. 'A long time. Six years. Well, almost six years. Five years, eight months and about a week and a half.' He fell silent a moment in calculation. 'Eight months, one week and three days. You know how I know that?'

'How?'

'I remember. I remember and I don't forget. I got a very good memory.'

'I can tell.'

'But that's a long time in a little kid's life. My sisters were just little when I saw them last. I wonder how they are.'

I said nothing.

'My stepdad, he'd come home drunk. He used to get my sister Carol out of bed sometimes. You know, I think he did things to her sometimes. You know. Dirty things. She never said he did, but I think he did. Carol'd be embarrassed to say those things, even to me. But I think I knew anyway. I was always watching. And once he got Barbara out of bed too. But mostly it was Carol. She was oldest.'

He paused.

'They had to take Carol to the hospital once. After he'd gotten her out of bed.'

Kevin turned to me. The dusk had just settled and I could barely distinguish his features when he had his back to the window, blocking the lights of the city. 'I wonder how my sisters are now. I haven't seen them since ... well, since all that time ago. Ever since my mother stopped coming. That's a long time. A lot can happen in that time.'

He returned to the window. 'You know what, Torey? I worry about them sometimes. I'm laying here and I get to thinking. Maybe my stepdad's still doing things to them. Maybe he's even doing it to the baby now, only she wouldn't be such a baby anymore. But maybe he is. Maybe they weren't so lucky as me and got out.'

Some luck, I thought.

'I'm sure they're okay, Kev. Social services would be watching. After your going away, social services would watch your stepdad.'

He shook his head. 'No. Not really.' Slowly he let out a long breath of air. 'They never really care. If you get beat up just a little, they turn their heads and pretend they don't notice. If you get mucked about with just a little, they never really pay attention. There's too many big things they got to worry about. But what they don't know is that it isn't the big things that get you in the end. It's the little things. Someone whacks you once every night of your life just for being alive, that hurts a lot worse than being knocked half-dead once.'

I nodded and retreated back to the bed, where I sat down. My heart ached. It was a dreary, disconsolate pain in my chest, weighing down like a wet towel inside me.

He turned again and looked at me. 'How can you care about a world like this? I don't really want to even be part of it. I'm crazy. And I think being crazy probably isn't so bad. I mean, if worse comes to worst, all they do is pump you full of stuff and you don't feel anything. But Carol wasn't as lucky as me. She didn't go crazy first. I think maybe she ought to have. I think there's lots worse things than crazy.'

Chapter Twenty-one

Kevin certainly seemed to have settled that matter in his own mind. Whatever had happened to him over the summer during his brief flirt with the outer world, he had returned, deciding normalcy was not for him. He was crazy; he was completely resigned to staying that way. And perhaps it was that resolve that caused his incredible depression. I imagine concluding that the life he was currently living was the best available to him would be pretty shattering news.

I found this attitude no small thing to deal with, particularly in light of the hospital situation he was in, where drugs to dope him into incoherence were distributed every four hours. Just as bad was the token system all the patients were on. They earned points for appropriate behaviors and these points determined all aspects of their day, including going to therapy sessions, attending the on-unit school programs and gaining passes to go off the hospital grounds. It was a perfect setup for someone convinced he wanted to stay crazy.

Kevin refused to cooperate at every turn. If he did not feel like getting up in the morning, he did not get up. And he lost points. If he did not want to wash, he didn't wash. More points gone. If he did not want to go to the schoolroom, he did not go. Each thing lost him more and more points or at least did not give him the opportunity to earn more, but Kevin was so unmotivated that none of the privileges he was losing was worth enough to make him try. The bottom line was seclusion, either in the patient's room or ultimately in the seclusion cell. Kevin, after a few weeks, became almost permanently confined to his tiny room. He loved it. What they ought to have done was boarded up his window.

Understandably, the hospital staff was in a frenzy over him. He was so passively uncooperative that they were ill equipped to deal with it. He did not rage or scream or do anything aggressive, which merited time out in the locked seclusion cell, although when they came to the end of their ropes with him, they occasionally put him in for a spell anyway, to see if it might motivate him out of his lethargy. It didn't. The psychiatrist upped his dose of antidepressants. No change. The staff decided to try the opposite of their normal routine. Kevin was not allowed to enter his room unless he earned the privilege, but the only place to keep him was in the TV room or the games room and they were hardly nonreinforcing. Or in the hallway where he would sit on the floor outside his room, his cloak of silence wrapped around him, and stare at the staff and visitors as they went by, his long legs sticking out across the corridor to trip unsuspecting passersby.

My greatest difficulty grew to be simply seeing him. I couldn't half the time. He got put on a system where he had to earn points to have Jeff or me come, and often as not, he wouldn't earn them. Kevin maintained a slightly closer relationship with Jeff, and occasionally he did appear to make a token effort to get Jeff up there on Jeff's two nights, but even these he lost frequently.

It was like swimming in molasses – a lot of effort and very little progress. Jeff was more troubled by the situation than I was because he objected not only to our stalemated position but also to the types and quantities of medication Kevin was on. I entirely agreed with him but, because I normally couldn't do much about things like medication, it didn't eat at me. But for Jeff, who was used to being able to prescribe medication himself, it was agony to live with somebody else's program when he thought it inappropriate, just because his ignominious status didn't allow him to say anything.

I almost threw in the towel. Several times I consciously decided it would be better for all concerned to give up on Kevin. I mean, after all, what did we have here? A kid who had been severely deprived and abused in childhood, who had spent most of his life in institutions, who demonstrated violent and aggressive behaviors, and perhaps most importantly, a kid whom nobody wanted. There was absolutely no one on the outside who cared one way or the other if Kevin improved. Just me. And Jeff. And we weren't much. There'd been a whole lot of kids in my career with a great deal better prognoses than Kevin had and they hadn't made it. Not a lot of kids did. Why did I bother to think this one might? Why did I keep endlessly chucking time and energy down the sewer? He sure never gave any signs of real promise.

It got so easy to think of giving up. And I knew what they were, those thoughts. I had had them so often before. They were the mind's way of preparing itself, the process of mentally letting go, so that when the inevitable happened and I had to give up, I could accept it. Even before I had decided, my subconscious was clearing the deck.

God. The thoughts preyed on me. Especially when I had bothered to make a trip clear over to Mortenson and was turned away at the last minute because Kevin had lost points. Or when I had missed him for four or five sessions running and my life began to move on nicely without that 4:30 trip. Or when we sat face to face—or rather, face to back, because he'd always have his back to me while he stared out of the window—and I'd not talk and not do anything and just sit there feeling the minutes of my life trickling away while this kid did nothing. It was so incredibly easy to consider giving up. I even tried it tentatively a couple of times. I was supposed to come and I didn't. I phoned with false excuses. A lot different this, than months before when Kevin had become so distraught because I had missed one day. We skipped so often now that I never knew if he missed me or not. If he did, he never said.

But I didn't give up. I don't know why. There were a whole lot more reasons why I should have. But I didn't. I never quite ever got around to doing it. I meant to, but I didn't. I kept on.

Kevin, however, seemed to have given up long ago. He got worse and worse and worse. It got harder and harder to see him and harder to do anything with him when I did see him. I wanted to be understanding. In the office with Jeff or at night when we were eating, I'd keep coming up with intellectual reasons for what Kevin was doing to himself and why. But when I was in the room with him, frustration overpowered me. My own insecurities would surface eventually. Maybe he didn't like me. Maybe he was angry with me. Maybe he thought I'd let him down or not done enough. Maybe he just thought I was stupid. But mostly I just grew angry. As the days continued to string out and September became October, I became angrier and angrier with him, resenting him and the time I gave to him. We became in the end like troubled lovers, unable to live with one another and yet unable to live without each other either.

I came after several days of being absent because Kevin had not earned sufficient points to see me. He had missed Jeff as well that week. In the end I suspect it was the hospital staff who capitulated and let me in because, when I reviewed his chart, there was no evidence Kevin had done anything more to earn my presence that day than any other.

The weather outside was fierce. It was late October and the cadaveric feel of November was in the wind. Daylight saving time still smuggled us an extra hour at evening but it really wasn't enough. I arrived late that afternoon, and the day was bound into darkness.

Kevin stood before the window, as usual. He did not bother to acknowledge my arrival. There were no lights on in his room, and he peered out into the half-gloom, his silhouette blending into the grayness beyond the window.

I flipped the light switch on.

No response.

'Kev, it's me.'

No response.

'What do you see out that window?' I asked.

No response.

'Kevin?'

I studied his form. His hands were behind his back, one clasping the wrist of the other. I set my box down.

'Kevin.' The seconds slid by.

'Kevin!'

No movement. No nothing, as if he hadn't heard me.

The anger over all these wasted weeks began to froth up inside me. 'Kevin,' I said, 'turn around.'

When he did not respond I approached him. 'I said, turn around, Kevin.'

Nothing.

'I said turn around, Kevin. When I say turn around, I *mean* turn around.' I grabbed his shoulder. While he did not turn to acknowledge me, he resisted my grip, his muscles going rock hard under my fingers. Yet, he wasn't a match for me. When I gave him a shove, it turned him.

'Damn you, Kevin, turn around when I'm talking to you. I'm sick of this. I'm sick to death of sitting here in this stupid room and having you ignore me. So turn around and stay turned.'

He glared at me.

'What the hell do you think you're doing, Kevin? Acting like this? Do you want to stay in this place?'

'I don't care.'

'What's the matter with you? You're wasting your whole life in here.'

'So what?' He shrugged and turned back to the window. 'I couldn't care less.'

With force, I grabbed his shoulder and yanked him around to face me. The power of it set him off balance and he fell back against the window. He remained there, regarding me. I could not read his feelings.

Silence. We sized one another up.

'What have you got in this life, Kevin? Are you going to just lie down and die? Are you going to confirm everything your stepfather said about you? Are you just going to give up?'

'I don't care. Go away. Just leave me alone, would you?'

'You've got to care, Kevin.'

'Why?'

'Because. Because this is all you've got, Kevin, and the only way to make it better is to change it. Nothing else will, no dreams, no fantasies, no fairy godmothers. You've got to do it. Nothing else will.'

'I don't care.'

'You've *got* to care,' I cried.

'Why?'

'*I* care!'

'Why? Who ever asked you to care? Who asked you to come butting into my life anyway?'

'You did, as I recall.'

'I did not. I never did. I never asked them back at Garson Gayer to go get you. And I never asked you to come back this time. And I sure never asked you to stay.'

That was a rather hard thing to rebut.

'So how come you're here then? What have you got to be mad about, when you never were asked here in the first place? How come you keep coming back when I don't want you?'

There must have been a good answer to that. 'Because,' I said. It sounded like an answer to me.

'Because why? Because someone pays you? Because you make your living off other people's suffering?'

'No.'

'Because why then? Because you think you can help me? Are you coming because you think if you bleed on me enough, you're going to save me from myself or something?'

I shook my head.

'Then *why?* What *do* you care for? It isn't any of your business.'

'Because that's just the way I am. Just like you're the way you are.'

'Then it's a pretty stupid way to be. You're pretty dumb, that's all I can say. Dumber even than I thought.'

'I never said I wasn't.'

Dead silence. We glared at one another.

'To be perfectly honest,' he said, 'I hate you.' His voice was soft and matter-of-fact. 'You come in here where no person has a right to be and you pry where no person has a right to pry. You made me hope I could be like everybody else. You made me think I deserved to be. When we both knew I'm not and I don't.

'Who are you anyway, to think you know anything? You've never been me. You just sit there and you pretend to know. But nothing's ever happened to you like's happened to me. All you've ever done is read about it in books. I lived it. So who do you think you are to believe you can help me?'

I hurt. Quite unexpectedly he had taken what was supposed to be my argument and had turned it against me. And he had hurt my feelings doing it. I found myself remarkably close to tears. Desperate not to cry, I spent a couple of exceedingly uncomfortable minutes.

Kevin looked me over. His gaze was hard, and I knew what he had said about hate was in its way very true.

'Look,' I said, 'I may not be much. And yes, I get paid for coming up here and maybe that makes me some sort of emotional prostitute to you, but I am here, aren't I? Of all the possible people in your life who could be here, Kevin, I'm the one who is. If you don't want me, then I'll go. If that's what you want, then that's what I want too.'

He said nothing.

'Shall I go?'

No answer. He still studied me.

'Is that what you want?'

Silence.

The world sat on me. I felt tired and unhappy and out-of-sorts. 'Listen,' I said, 'I'm going.' I turned and went to the bed. I lifted the lid off my box. Kevin remained at the window but he watched me.

'You want these?' I lifted the sketchpads out of the box.

He shook his head.

'I got them for you. They're no good to me. I can't draw. You sure you don't want them?'

'No.'

'The pencils?' I held up the box of colored pencils.

Again he shook his head.

I pitched the whole works into the wastebasket. 'You don't want anything, do you?'

Kevin shrugged.

I then picked up my jacket and put it on. I closed the box. 'I don't know what you wanted from me, Kevin. I can't change things for you. I can't go into your head like some surgeon and take out all the rotting parts. I can't take away from you all the bad things that have happened to you. I can't do any of that. No one can. There isn't a psychologist or a psychiatrist or a witch doctor or a wizard who can. It's all up to you. The most I can do is be with you. I can come along. I can keep you company. But the journey itself is yours.'

He looked away from me. I zipped my jacket and turned to leave.

'You could have called me Bryan,' he said softly.

'What?'

'I said, you could have called me Bryan. If you'd really cared.'

I was very nearly to the door when I paused. I turned back to look at him. He was still leaning against the window, hands in his pockets, shoulders drawn up. His eyes were on his shoes and not on me.

'Would that have made a difference, Kevin?'

It was he who was now about to cry. Still upset myself, my instinct was to get out of there. My anger ran deep. Yet I knew if I walked out the door I would be leaving for good. Kevin would never ask for me back. Even if I left him a face-saving way, I knew he wouldn't. I remained immobile at the door.

The silence grew long and thin and brittle between us.

Kevin swallowed to keep the tears back but in the end he was unable to. Head down, shoulders up, he stood with his eyes squeezed tightly shut. Then slowly, he began to slide down the window and the wall to collapse into a small heap on the floor. Burying his face in his arms, he wept in great, inelegant sobs.

I stood. I did not go to him because this was not the moment to do it. These were not that sort of tears. So I only stood, too warm in my jacket. Beyond us, behind me, were the sounds of supper arriving on the ward. I could smell the homey odors of beef and potatoes, mixing with the everlasting hospital antiseptic.

I came over and squatted down beside Kevin. His tears were hard but short-lived. Within moments he surfaced for air. Cradling his head in his arms, he looked at me.

I smiled, sadly, for the things we had lost, for the innocence, whatever innocence there had been between us. Then I reached across the gulf between us and hugged him. It seemed a long time coming, that hug, and we clung to one another like survivors of a disaster.

'If only I could have been Bryan,' he said at last, when we broke apart. 'If only I could have been Bryan. Even to you I wasn't. Even you couldn't see him.' Kevin studied my face a short moment before looking away. 'That's what's wrong with the world, you know. So many of us shouldn't have ever been.'

He paused and sighed.

'We're like ghosts,' he said, 'like mirror-ghosts, really. Instead of spirits without bodies, we're bodies without spirits. Empty shells with the wrong persons trapped inside. Or with no one inside at all. Mirror-ghosts. Half a million, half a billion, geez, half a world probably, of mirror-ghosts. Just bodies taking up space, walking around empty.'

He brought a finger up and wiped away the last traces of tears from his eyes.

'If only I could have been Bryan, if I could have really been Bryan. But I'm not. I'm just a mirror-ghost too.'

Chapter Twenty-two

The one person keeping body and soul together for me was Jeff. Despite our working different sessions, he still usually came over to my house for a meal in the evenings. The only change was that now he often brought his roommate along too. Neither of them was too keen on cooking, it seemed, and I was glad enough for company after Kevin that I didn't object too much to doing it.

Jeff's roommate was a big, strapping German named Hans who taught the language at the local college and played semi-professional hockey. I liked Hans immensely from the first time I met him. He had the polished, urbane, intellectual style so common to European men and yet was full of humor. And exceptionally tolerant of Charity, who had decided he was the best thing since sliced bread. Hans was also very handy around the house, and for the first time in years all my drains ran, no hinges squeaked and there were honest-to-goodness shelves replacing my brick-and-board concoctions.

Jeff was the only person I knew who could persistently invite himself to dinner and make you feel it was your privilege. Hans felt guilty about it, I think, and hence, all the handyman behavior, but Jeff remained unabashed. However, he honestly was saving my sanity in those tremendously difficult weeks with Kevin. He and I would stand out in the kitchen peeling potatoes and talking, while Hans entertained Charity, if she was over, or puttered about the house. After dinner we would all do dishes, me washing, Jeff drying and Hans forever flicking the dish towel at Charity, who would shriek with delight and bait him into doing it again. Jeff was a fanatic for board games, so if he did not have duty, we would sit around afterward, losing ourselves in Scrabble or Clue or Sorry! Hans loved backgammon but in the end gave up ever teaching Jeff or me to play it. It was too high-brow for my tastes, and Jeff preferred the elemental malice of wiping me out at Monopoly.

But amidst our laughter, Jeff and I spent a god-awful amount of time trying to understand Kevin. The difficulty with that was that in the process, we had to devote a certain amount of time to trying to understand each other and ourselves. We were quite different people, Jeff and I, and while that brought a wider perspective to the problem, it also brought disagreement between us.

The most serious problem I had and had had throughout my ventures into all sides of treatment of the mentally ill was that I was an atheist amongst the pious. I could *not* bring myself to honestly believe in any of the theories of psychology or psychiatry, whether they were Freud's, Skinner's, mine or anyone else's. They were all guesses and no more. And thus, to me, the schools of thought and the followings that had grown up around each theorist's ideas, while interesting, all seemed of the same fabric as the emperor's new clothes.

Certainly, I enjoyed a rousing session of theorizing as much as the next person. There was nothing so exciting to me as the thought that that *might* be the reason for a certain behavior or action. But I could never carry it beyond that intellectual-curiosity stage. I wished I did know but I didn't and I couldn't make myself believe I did. This quickly branded me as a heretic.

And it drove Jeff wild. While he was not among the hard-liners in psychiatry, like Dr Rosenthal, he was a firm believer. He fretted about transference and the fact that working the way he was with Kevin, he could not properly distance himself. But what bothered him even more was my part in it, that he could not convert me to what he considered to be basic truths about the human mind. He would have preferred, I think, for me even to hold completely polarized views to his, but that I held none at all troubled him. Of course, I wasn't much better. I couldn't see how he *could* believe. He was so intelligent; how could someone with all those brains actually think we *had* answers when we so obviously didn't. If Freud were right, I'd rant, why didn't he have a hundred per cent success rate? The same percentage of people are helped with psychoanalysis as are helped with laying on of hands. Explain that, Jeff.

* * *

I slumped onto the living room couch without even bothering to take off my jacket. Jeff and Hans were already there, and Jeff, in one of his rare philanthropic moods, had brought supper in the form of half a dozen Big Macs, fries and Cokes. Charity was ecstatic. The whole house stank of hamburgers. On the coffee table, Jeff had the innards of two Big Macs strewn out while he made sure he wasn't going to be poisoned by any stray dill pickles. When I flopped down, Jeff spun a Styrofoam hamburger container top full of dill pickles in my direction. It whirred through the air like a flying saucer.

The raging argument I had had with Kevin was still on my mind and I needed Jeff's solace. He leaned back in a chair and nursed a large cup of pop as he listened.

To Jeff's way of thinking, Kevin was dredging up all sorts of things from his childhood; hatred, fixations, oedipal feelings, thwarted desires, and transferring them all onto me. The way I worked did not allow the distance from the patient that Jeff's training had said was necessary, and because I did not remain cool and uninterfering in Kevin's life, Jeff was uncertain if Kevin could sufficiently work out his problems. I did the things Jeff had been taught not to do. He believed they were wrong, or at least if not wrong, then not right. I, of course, saw no evidence that they were either one. And because I was as successful at my work as anyone else on the clinic staff, I knew I plunged Jeff into all sorts of intellectual dilemmas.

Jeff shook his head as he listened to me. 'How the hell do you work? Do you have any theory at all that you function from?'

I contemplated a dill pickle for a moment. 'Yeah, I guess. The theory of probability.'

'What's that mean?'

'That if I keep trying long enough, sooner or later, the probability that the odds will be in my favor has to occur.'

Again, he shook his head. I knew he wasn't thrilled with what I'd done with Kevin this night, with my getting angry with him and making him cry. I knew he thought I was some sort of aerialist, swinging dangerously between points and never firmly grounding myself anywhere. He picked up the Coke cup and fished a piece of ice out of it. He stared into the cup, shook his head again and sighed.

'For me, Jeff,' I said, 'it's more like doing a jigsaw puzzle without the picture on the box to follow. You have a thousand little pieces to try and fit together and only so much time. I don't know what the picture looks like, so I forget the picture and I just try to get as many of the pieces together as I can. To me all your theories are like sitting around trying to decide what the picture on the box must look like and then searching for the pieces to make up that picture. Maybe that works for some people. But for me it doesn't seem like the most effective way to go about it. I just try. I fit a couple of wrong pieces together sometimes, but that happens no matter how you go about it. All I want to do is get it together and get it together as fast as I can, because for the kids, every day is a day lost. It is for everybody.'

Jeff frowned. 'But you've got to know *why*, Torey. You've got to *understand* what you're doing.'

'And you do? Jeff, no one understands. It's all guesses. The theories are for *us*, Jeff, to make *us* feel better, to keep us from feeling stupid because we can't understand, to make us feel less insecure about that incredible unknown place between our ears. And probably just because theories are fascinating things to think about. But they're all academic, every single one of them, and it's sheer intellectual naïveté to think we do understand. Worse, it makes us lose sight of why we're actually doing what we're doing. The purpose of doing jigsaw puzzles is not to appreciate the artwork of the finished picture. It's to get the pieces together.'

Jeff was silent. With one finger he etched away the wax on the outside of the Coke container. 'Shit,' he said at last, his voice soft, and then he fell quiet again, staring moodily into the cup. 'You're not right, you know. I don't believe you. The Hayden 1000-Piece View of the Universe. I don't believe you.' He paused and let out a long breath of air. 'But shit. What do I believe? What do I understand? It's pointless, isn't it. I mean, if you really stop to think about it. It's pointless, what we're doing. Because in fact, we really don't know a thing.'

But for all our differences, together Jeff and I made the greatest team. And I grew to cherish those evenings when he was over, when we were uninterrupted by the phones and the chaos of the clinic and we could just talk. He was an incredible person to stretch a mind with. We could talk together for hours, building our own brave new world.

I never really stopped to consider how Charity or anyone else, for that matter, might interpret these evenings. My social life had not exactly been on fire previously, and so there was plenty of time to enjoy sitting around talking or playing board games. Jeff was over as often as three times a week, and often Hans was as well, although it was clearly Jeff and I that had the compelling need for one another's company. Yet it was on a purely intellectual level. Even Hans gave up on us eventually to watch TV. He called it 'mental netball,' what Jeff and I were doing, and he couldn't believe we'd keep at it so long and so often. But I never stopped to think how others might see it. It was all innocent fun. However, I discovered, innocence, like beauty, is in the eye of the beholder.

We were finishing up the dishes one evening when Charity went into the other room and got her coat. 'I got to go home now,' she said.

'You do?' I replied. Normally she didn't leave until I turned her out. 'How come?'

'My mom told me to.'

'She wants you home early tonight?' I asked.

'Oh no,' said Charity. 'No, my mom said I shouldn't ought to disturb you so late, since you got to work in the morning.'

'But it's only 6:30, Charity.'

'Yeah, but my mom said you must get awful tired.'

'What do you mean? Why would your mom say that?'

Charity smiled sweetly. 'Well, see, I told my mom you were a *real* woman,' she said with pride.

'*You what?*'

'Well, my mom, she only gots one boyfriend. But I told her it took *two* men to keep you satisfied.' Another angelic smile. 'So my mom said I better come home early.'

'Kev,' I said one afternoon, 'I got something I have to ask you and you got to tell me.'

Kevin turned from the window to look at me.

'What happened out at Bellefountaine?'

Silence. He returned to staring out into the dusk.

'Kevin, you got to tell me. I can't help you unless you help me. To change things, Kev, I got to know more.'

Still silence.

'I don't want your help especially,' he said softly. It was not spoken in defiance, just a statement.

'I know you don't.'

More silence. It was very complete. The doors were thick and so the room was not fringed with outside noises. There was nothing but Kevin and me, and I was too far away from him to even hear him breathe.

'Things have gotten out of control, Kevin. You're stuck here in this place. You're feeling awful all the time. It makes me want to quit and I know that's not the best thing for either of us. So we need to get back into control again. We can. But you got to help me a little. Okay?'

He did not answer.

'Okay, Kev?'

'Nothing happened out there.'

'But you're in here now. Why?'

I saw him clench his fist, bring it up and lay it against the glass of the window. 'Because I busted that woman's arm.'

'Why?'

He shrugged.

'Why did you do it, Kevin?'

'I just got angry, that's all.'

'But why?'

'I dunno. I just did.'

'But why did you get angry? What happened? What did she do?'

'Nothing. I just got angry with her. I just did, that's all.'

'People don't just get angry, that's all, Kevin. Not for no reason, they don't.'

'I did.' He leaned forward, pressing his face against the glass. He was studying something beyond my view. 'Look. Look, they're cleaning out that empty lot over there. They're taking off the garbage that was there.'

'Kevin, come away from that window.'

He did not move.

'Kevin, come here. Come away from that window and come over here.'

For a long moment I thought he wouldn't. He never moved from that window. It was like a mistress and I wasn't much in comparison.

But slowly he turned. He came over to the bed where I was sitting.

'Sit down,' I said and indicated the end of the bed beside me.

He sat.

'So what happened, Kevin? You haven't told me.'

He shrugged.

'I hate to have to ask at all, but you haven't told me. And I'm stuck. I can't figure out where to go next or what to do because you don't tell me where you've been. I hate to make you feel bad. I hate to ask but I need to.'

Something about him was unsettling. I couldn't tell what, if it was the way he held his body or his expression or some aura about him, but whatever it was, it ran through me. It was a deep, subterranean sensation, like heavy notes on a piano played very loudly so that they vibrate the soft inner organs. Like the opening of Beethoven's Ninth.

'I don't know what happened,' he said again. 'Honest, Torey, I don't. I liked her. I really did. Her name was Margaret and she was really nice to me.'

'What sorts of things happened in the home that night?'

'We were sitting watching TV. I got up to go to bed. And then these other guys started arguing. So I got out of bed again and went to see what was happening.'

'Were the boys arguing with Margaret?'

'No. Just with themselves. And Margaret was standing there. So I broke her arm.'

'You broke Margaret's arm? Margaret was standing there and the boys were fighting and you came down from your bed and broke her arm? Why? Did it make you angry that they were fighting or something? Why did you break Margaret's arm then, and not one of the boys'?'

Kevin shook his head. 'I don't remember.'

'You said before that you were angry. How come?'

Kevin paused. 'I don't know. I just got mad at her. And the next thing I knew, I broke her arm. I threw her against the wall.'

I did not speak. The silence slipped in around us like the tide coming in.

'Remember that time at Garson Gayer?' Kevin asked. 'That time in our room when you and me were doing that rocket poster?'

'Yes.'

'And I got so upset.'

'Yes, I remember that.'

'I could have broke your arm then.'

'Yes, you could have.'

'But I didn't though,' he said. 'They came and got me first.'

'Would you have, if they hadn't come so soon?'

He paused thoughtfully. Then he shook his head. 'I don't think so. That was different.'

'How so?'

Kevin did not answer immediately. In fact, he took so long in responding that I did not think he would.

'I wasn't angry at you. I was scared. If I'd have hurt you, I wouldn't have meant to.' He glanced at me briefly before hoisting himself off the bed and returning to the window. 'But I think I might have killed her if I'd had the chance.'

Chapter Twenty-three

Then very, very slowly Kevin begin to improve. He had been in the hospital ten weeks before even the slightest signs of growth started again and those weren't many. Perhaps he would get up when called one morning. Perhaps he would attend the school program or the therapy sessions or the meals without coercion. With excruciating slowness, he began earning his points, and at last Jeff or I could come every time without interruption.

What caused the improvement was not clear. Undoubtedly, it was a combination of things. There was, however, no new face to his personality. This gradual change for the better was not one of Kevin's chameleon shifts, and that gave Jeff and me some hope that the boy we now worked with was the real Kevin and that the improvement, agonizingly slow as it was, was genuine.

Jeff started to be more and more obsessed with Kevin's past. The records were so spotty. Certainly, for a kid who had spent so much of his life tangled up in the red tape of the welfare system, very little indeed was written about him. He seemed almost to be a kid without a past, despite the fact that both Jeff and I knew from our conversations with Kevin that he had had a childhood worth noting.

One morning I came into the office to find Jeff kneeling on the floor and dozens of little bits of paper spread out around him. Carefully, he was shifting the pieces back and forth from one place to another.

'What are you doing?' I asked. He was due to speak at a conference later in the morning and was all kitted out in a three-piece suit and tie. When I found him on his hands and knees on the floor with all that paper, I thought perhaps he had dropped some odd sort of material for his presentation.

Jeff rose up on his knees and surveyed the situation. 'Well, when I was in bed last night I got to thinking. Trying to figure out how all the pieces of Kevin's background go together. You know, your old jigsaw theory. But I just couldn't conceptualize it.' Then he looked up with a grin full of boyish pride. 'So I've *made* the jigsaw puzzle up.'

'You idiot,' I laughed. 'It was a figure of speech.'

'Well, I got to thinking, if I made a sort of time line … and put in order …' He studied the paper on the floor.

I walked around the snowfall and knelt down myself to see what Jeff had written on the bits of paper.

'See, here's his stepfather,' said Jeff. 'And there's Carol. I think Carol's mixed up in this. His relationship …'

I picked up another piece of paper.

'How many sisters does Kevin have?' Jeff asked. 'There's Carol…'

'And Barbara. He told me about Barbara.'

'Then who's Ellen?'

'Ellen? I never heard about Ellen. Besides, we got two and that's all his folder says there is. Just two sisters. And we know about Carol and Barbara.'

'But there's Ellen. He mentioned Ellen once. Do you suppose Carol's a brother? Carroll and not Carol at all?' Jeff suggested.

'No. He drew a picture of her for me once. And he says "she" when he's talking about her. We wouldn't have made that mistake.'

Jeff shifted a piece of paper around. 'Okay, so if this area is his early childhood, before he got carted off to a residential center, when do you reckon the abusive acts he talks about took place? There isn't really anything in his records on it, is there?'

I shook my head.

'You do think it's true, don't you?' Jeff looked up. 'You don't think he's fabricating a lot of this? I mean, he's such a clever so-and-so sometimes.'

'No. I've seen his back. Have you seen it? All those little scars. If they happened, the other stuff probably did too.'

'I'm going to ask you something, Tor, something that's been eating at me. But it sounds farfetched. Do you suppose he's making Carol up? That she's some sort of fantasy person? That things got so bad for him that he had to personify some of his feelings? Make up someone who cared for him?'

The same thought had crossed my mind too, but deep down I couldn't believe it. Yet, hadn't Charity told all those fantastic stories, and I'd swallowed half of them before I discovered the truth? And Kevin was so much subtler than Charity. 'I don't know,' I replied.

Again Jeff moved bits of paper. He regarded them, shifted another. Then he rose and sat in his desk chair so he could survey the whole arrangement. I leaned over and brushed the dirt off the knees of his trousers.

'His mother ...' Jeff said thoughtfully and leaned down for one scrap. 'I wonder where his mother got to. How long's she been off the scene?'

'Since Garson Gayer, I think. I'm not altogether sure.'

'*Shit!*' said Jeff suddenly and crumpled up the piece of paper he was holding. He pitched it across the room. 'Shit. Shit, shit, shit.' He looked at me, his forehead puckered in angry frustration. 'God damn it, Torey, how the hell are we supposed to do anything? Look at this. Look at this damned sideshow we're running. We don't know anything. How can anyone expect to help a kid when we don't even know who his mother is? The kid might as well not even exist for all we know about him. Damn it. We're like fortune-tellers. We might as well be reading tea leaves.' He kicked out at the papers and they fluttered up into the air.

I felt sorry for Jeff then, for his distress, which was mine as well. He was right, of course. But that didn't make it any better.

When I got to the hospital later in the day, I was accosted by one of the nurses. Kevin, she said, had stolen a coat.

A coat?

They knew he had to be the guilty party. He had been the only one in the vicinity at the time, and all the other kids had been cleared. The evidence all pointed to Kevin. Since he was still refusing to talk to anyone, would I take the matter up with him?

Horrible thoughts went through my head. Why on earth would Kevin take a coat? The only thing I could imagine was that old specter of his stepfather had come back to haunt him and he had decided to run off and kill him once and for all. The conversations between Kevin and me were slowly turning back to his family again, so that was the only thing in my mind. It was a dreadful thought.

But why steal a coat? That didn't make 100 percent good sense. Kevin did, after all, have a coat of his own. Right there in his room.

Hating to have to take up an argument that I initially was not part of, I begrudgingly went into Kevin's room. He was sitting on the edge of the dresser. It had been pushed closer to the window, and he sat there on it, with his feet on the windowsill.

'Kev,' I said, 'I hate to be the bearer of tales but I understand there's been some trouble up here.' I closed the door firmly behind me.

'Oh? I'm not having any trouble.'

'Over a coat.'

'Oh, *that* trouble,' he replied knowingly.

'Yep. That trouble. You want to clear it up for me? They seem to feel you're involved. Are you?'

'Me?'

I nodded.

'What would I want a coat for?' he asked.

'Well, that's what I told them. But they seem to still feel you may have taken it.'

'I didn't.'

'If you don't mind, I'll just have a look around the room for it then. Just to say I checked the matter out thoroughly. Okay?'

'I *didn't* take it, Torey. I wrote them a note. I said to them I didn't take it. And I didn't. Why are they making you come after me?'

'Do you mind if I look around?'

'I didn't take it! Yeah, go ahead. Look if you want to. Search me. Search my room. See if I took the stupid coat. What would I want a coat for anyway? I never go out.'

I was beginning to have a hunch he did take it. His voice was rising in pitch and something in his demeanor hinted at guilt. 'Yes, I was thinking those same things myself, but the question is, did you take it?'

'I didn't! How many times do I have tell you I didn't?'

I paused and looked over at him.

'I *didn't!*'

'Well, if you did, it would probably just be easier to go get the coat for me and not make me have to look for it. Then we could get on with other things.'

His face crumpled and I thought he was going to cry. 'I said I didn't. Why don't you believe me? I said I didn't.'

I pulled the orange plastic chair over and sat down. 'Sometimes these sorts of things happen. They shouldn't and it would be nicer if they didn't, but they do. People are that way. Everybody does this sort of thing occasionally.'

Kevin just sat, his face frozen in a grimace, not crying but not quite not crying either.

'Why don't you just get me the coat, okay? And I'll take it out to the nurses' desk and we'll be finished and done with it. All right, Kevin?'

The pause was lengthy. 'I didn't take it,' he said one more time under his breath and kicked at the dresser with one toe. When I said nothing and did not rise to search the room, he regarded me through his eyelashes. Then very slowly he rose from where he was sitting. His movements were heavy as if his limbs were unwilling to cooperate. Coming over to the bed, he lifted the mattress. There folded carefully between the mattress and the box spring was a duffel coat with toggle buttons and a hood. Kevin took it out gently and handed it to me. Then he returned to the window. I went and took the coat out to the nurses' desk.

'Kev?'

He knew what I was going to ask. 'I thought you said we were going to be finished with it, if I gave it to you. You weren't going to ask any questions.'

'I was just wondering . . . Just between you and me.'

'I thought you said.'

'I did say, I guess. And if you want, I won't ask any questions.'

'I do want.' With that he turned and came over to the bed and sat down on it.

Most of the session passed quietly. We did other things and talked on other topics. However, for both of us the coat remained a ghost haunting every conversation. Toward the end, just as I was packing up, Kevin relented.

He rose from the bed, paced the small room, kicked at the dresser leg and the chair leg before settling down in front of the window. Half his life must have been given over to that window.

'You know,' he said quietly, 'clothes make you feel like you are inside. Have you ever noticed that?'

'Yes.'

'It was weird. I saw that coat . . . I saw it and I thought, well, . . .' He paused. There was dust on the windowsill and he reached out to push it aside with one finger. 'That's sort of a Bryan coat. You know what I mean? That's the sort of coat a Bryan would wear, it's so neat looking.' He turned. 'I wasn't stealing it, Torey. I wasn't, honest. I just wanted to try it on. I just wanted to see what I'd look like in it.' He smiled pathetically. 'That was all, just to try it on. But I couldn't very well ask, could I?'

'Well, maybe,' I suggested.

'No.' He shook his head. 'No, I couldn't have. They wouldn't have understood. It was me asking. Bryan could've but not me. They didn't see Bryan. Even if I'd had the coat on, they wouldn't have noticed. It would've just been nerdy old Kevin in somebody else's coat.'

'I see.'

'Yeah,' he said, 'so I had to sort of borrow it. So they wouldn't laugh at me. I just wanted to try it on.' He returned to the window.

I didn't speak.

'Torey?' he asked without turning back to look at me.

'Yes?'

'Did you think it was a neat-looking coat?'

'Yes. It was a lovely coat, wasn't it?'

He nodded. 'Bryan might have wore it, huh?'

'Mm-hmm.'

I came over and stood beside him. There was an inward sort of smile on his lips and it stayed a long time before finally playing itself out. I thought he was going to say something else; the expectant atmosphere lingered. But he didn't. He only stood with his hands in his pockets. Beyond him I could see the snow falling, and the grinding gray filth of the city below us faded under downy white.

Chapter Twenty-four

Hockey season was well launched, and Hans had promised us tickets to one of the home games. Consequently, there we were, one pre-Christmas Saturday evening, getting ourselves ready to go watch hockey. Personally I despised the game, something I could hardly say to Hans. It seemed like gladiators on ice to me, needlessly brutal and gory. I had been surprised the first time I met Hans to learn that he was a local team hockey player because he had seemed such a pleasant, even-tempered chap and not at all how I had stereotyped men who played hockey. So I had to admit I was looking forward to going just to see Hans play. He could never bring himself to make Charity behave when she was larking about obnoxiously, so I was curious to see him lustily bashing in the skulls of the other team.

Unfortunately, it was not an ideal occasion to go. I was baby-sitting that weekend. My next-door neighbors were a likeable but somewhat odd couple, part of the expired flower-power generation, and they had produced a likeable but odd daughter. Her name was Shayna-Jasmine, she wouldn't eat meat or anything that didn't come out of a sack from the health food store and she had some extremely liberated topics of conversation for a four-year-old. She'd also been born prematurely with a stomach tumor and had subsequently had most of her stomach removed. This meant I had to feed her six times a day instead of three and that she threw up a lot.

But Saturday night was the game Hans got tickets for, so Saturday night, Jeff, Charity, Shayna-Jasmine and I packed up a tailgate picnic and left for the sports arena.

Charity loved the hockey game. All the blood and gore were right up her alley. Jeff, too, was a keen enthusiast. So he and Charity did a lot of yelling and cheering for Hans's benefit. That left Shayna-Jasmine and me to puzzle out a game neither of us understood too well.

'What are they doing?' Shayna-Jasmine asked after half a dozen men swooped down on some poor fallen teammate, all their sticks flying.

'I don't know exactly,' I replied.

'What's that thing for?' she asked, pointing to a strange-looking affair over by one team's goal.

'I'm not sure,' I said.

We watched in silence. The teams skated by and there was a frantic attempt to place a goal which ended in a pileup right below our seats and some nasty hollering, all the words of which were in Shayna-Jasmine's vocabulary already.

Shayna pulled at my arm. 'How come they're fighting?'

'They're trying to get that little puck there.'

'Well, how come they don't just ask for it?'

'The other men wouldn't give it to them.'

'Well, they could say *please,*' she replied emphatically.

I smiled at her. 'That's not part of the game.'

'Oh,' she said and gave a disgruntled little sigh. 'It's a stupid game, isn't it?'

Afterward, after the teams had changed and left and the maintenance men were cleaning the ice, Hans came out of the locker room with pairs of skates in his hands.

'I thought maybe we could all skate a little while they're redoing the ice. Before they refreeze the surface. It wouldn't be so slippery for the girls.'

Hans grinned. He had evidently planned this as a small surprise for Charity and Shayna-Jasmine. The arena was a regular rink during part of the week and had a large supply of skates to rent, so before the game he had gone down and gotten skates from the rental room for all of us.

I hesitated to point out to him that it was after eleven at night and both girls were a little bleary-eyed. Plus Jeff had been feeding licorice to Shayna the entire game, and I was sure she was going to throw up all over us if we jiggled her too much. But naturally, the prospect of such fun appealed greatly to Charity, who came wide awake again and had her shoes off and was tugging at the skates before I found the heart to object.

It turned out to be one of those gloriously crazy little times in one's life when one abandons all good reason and does solely as one pleases. Hans was a lousy judge of small girls' shoe sizes. Charity's were at least three sizes too big and we had to stuff the toes with a pair of Hans's smelly sweat socks. Shayna's were too small and she fussed as I crammed her feet in. But once out on the ice, those things were soon forgotten.

Hans, of course, was an excellent skater and he had both Charity and Shayna-Jasmine up on their feet and steady in no time. I had skated all my childhood on the creek below our family home and on down to the lagoon where the creek emptied. In adulthood I had forgotten the almost airborne feeling and was giddy with it on the huge arena, where I had to swerve and curve around bewildered maintenance men and their long brooms.

For once, Jeff was hopeless. I felt terribly smug when I discovered there was actually something I could do so much better than Wonder Boy. I teased Jeff mercilessly, as he clung unsteadily to the rail. It was late and I was tired. That could be my only excuse for behaving that way.

We fooled around until almost midnight, when the maintenance men were clearly ready to flood the arena and go home. The end came when I missed Shayna-Jasmine. She had left the rink to go get a drink of water, and I found her, skates and all, cuddled up on our coats, sound asleep.

Afterward we returned to my house so I could put Shayna to bed. Charity was also spending the night, so I promised hot chocolate to her and Irish coffee to Hans and Jeff before they left.

We were all exhausted. It was late and the physical exertion only added to it. Jeff made no pretense of vitality. He slumped down in front of the television and flipped it on. Hans came out in the kitchen with Charity and me to give a hand with the drinks. Rummaging around through the liquor cabinet, he decided that Kahlua might make an interesting addition to Irish coffee. We could add some cocoa too, he explained, and create a mocha drink. This launched him, the only person who seemed to be coherent at that hour, into some long story about Germany punctuated frequently by German words I didn't know the meaning of. Not feeling nearly so creative, I flinched at the prospect of coffee, cocoa, whiskey, Kahlua and cream together but dumped them in anyway.

When I turned to take the mugs over to the table, there was Charity sleeping peacefully with her head down on the place mat. So I put her mug back on the counter and picked up Jeff's. In the living room, draped over a chair, Jeff too slept. The national anthem blared out over the television.

Returning to the kitchen, I met Hans waltzing his coffee around the room and humming 'Ach, du lieber Augustin.' With Jeff's mug still in my hand, I grinned at him.

'What a motley crew you all are,' I said. 'This place is like a halfway house.'

A smile spread over his lips. 'Ah well, *Schatzie,*' he said. 'The real question is, halfway between what and what?'

'Here,' said Jeff when I arrived on Monday morning. He tossed a note pad over onto my desk.

'What's this?' There was a telephone number on it. From the area code I could tell it was from the bordering state.

'I've traced Kevin's mother.'

My eyes widened.

'You want to go see her with me? I've spoken to her. I was hoping she might have information she would be willing to share.'

* * *

Jeff and I made the hundred-mile trip to spend an afternoon with Kevin's mother. We found her in a small, dilapidated duplex on the edge of a community just over the border from our state. The place was scantily furnished and absolutely filthy. In the living room there was only a sagging couch, a television and a cardboard box serving as a coffee table. A small boy with wet pants opened the door for us.

While she greeted us with a bashful hesitance, Kevin's mother obviously had intended to make our visit a pleasant one. Even though we had arrived well after lunchtime, she had made a meal for us. It was a heartbreaking thing really. The foods she had bought for us to eat were expensive things—cheeses, pickles, fruits out of season—and must have depleted her benefit check severely. They had to be laid on a card table in the kitchen because there was no other furniture except two wooden benches. She had only bought enough for Jeff and me, not for herself or the little boy, who stood shivering in his wet training pants, gazing longingly at the tomatoes and cookies but never asking for any.

We had to eat it; it was one of those situations where one could in no way refuse, even though we hadn't wanted the food and they could have used it more. But I found myself embarrassed to be eating when she and little boy didn't. Jeff must have felt the same because I could see his cheeks blazing.

'How is Kevin?' she asked shyly.

'He isn't exactly problem free,' said Jeff. 'We were hoping you might be able to give us some background on things about Kevin when he lived with you.'

'He isn't my son anymore,' she said softly. 'Ain't nothing to talk about. You knew that, didn't you? I had to give him up.'

Jeff's brow furrowed. 'I was under the impression he was relinquished willingly.'

The words were too big. I could see her confusion.

'We thought you gave him up because you wanted to,' I said.

Her eyes dropped and there was silence. 'We were having problems.'

'Yes?'

'Couldn't keep him no more.'

'Why was that?'

'Because of Malcolm. My husband.'

'How many children do you and your husband have? Altogether?' Jeff asked.

'Counting Kevin?'

Jeff nodded.

'Well, him,' she indicated the little boy. 'Him and the girls and Kevin, of course.'

'How many girls?'

'Just the two. Barbara and Ellen. Barbara …' she paused. 'Well, they got Barbara in a home, you know. But Ellen, she goes to school now.'

Jeff looked at me, back at the woman. She was a pitiful thing. 'What about Carol?' he asked, his voice gentle.

She studied her hands. 'Just the two girls. Just Ellen and Barbara. Just them.'

There was a moment's silence. The little boy whimpered and she took him into her lap to cuddle his bare feet against her hands.

'Malcolm, your husband, he didn't get along with Kevin, did he?' Jeff asked.

She shook her head.

'And so did Malcolm ask you to get rid of Kevin?'

She did not answer. She pressed her face against the small boy's head. Then slowly she shook her head. 'No, the law did.'

Like Jeff, I had been under the general impression that the parents had voluntarily relinquished Kevin to the state. In fact, I had read as much in Kevin's file at Garson Gayer, so this seemed odd to me.

'The courts told you to get rid of Kevin?' I asked.

The conversation was beginning to bother her. She clutched the little boy closer. Her breathing quickened. Again she shook her head. 'Well, after . . . after, well, you know, that last thing.'

'What thing?' Jeff inquired. Both of us were lost.

She wouldn't look at us. 'You know. The *thing*. That Malcolm did to him, to Kevin . . .'

'No,' said Jeff, 'I'm afraid we don't know. That's our problem.'

'Well, that last time. When he beat him. You know.'

We both watched her. She had the shoulder closest to us drawn up almost to her ear, as if Jeff and I might strike her.

'Malcolm, well, you know, hit him. A bit. He, well, Kevin, he went to the hospital, you know. Well, them judges, well, you know, they told us Malcolm couldn't be around Kevin no more. They said he'd get put, you know, in the slammer. If they ever found him around Kevin again. You know. So . . .'

Silence came and sat beside us. The room was unheated and the little boy in wet pants shivered. He wore nothing else except those training pants, no clothes, no shoes, no socks.

'So, well,' she said, 'I had to put Kevin somewhere. You know. Else I couldn't have Malcolm back with me. He couldn't come 'round, if I'd've kept Kevin. You know.'

In the car on the way home I was angry. What kind of abuse had happened to this boy, that he had been hospitalized and the stepfather had been banned from seeing him again, when the two of them had lived under the same roof? And why the hell wasn't something in Kevin's records? I was really mad. I was almost yelling and, because Jeff was the only other person in the car with me, I was yelling at him. What were the goddamned lunatics in social services doing this time, keeping that kind of information from us? Jeff said nothing. We both knew it wasn't he I was angry with. It wasn't even the dementia that had apparently gripped the interdepartmental reporting of the welfare services. But how did one put into words a thing like a woman loving a brutal man more than her own son?

In the office the next day I started phoning. There had to be someone somewhere in this city who knew Kevin's story. Late in the day I found her, a social worker named Marlys Menzies, who still worked for child welfare.

Kevin was twelve, she said, when it happened. He had just been returned from a group home and had been living with his family for about three months. Friction between the stepfather and Kevin had always been common, Marlys Menzies said, and the major factor continued to be Kevin's refusal to speak to him.

There had been a small incident one night; no one quite remembered what it was. Kevin and the stepfather got into a fray and the stepfather had demanded an explanation from the boy. Kevin, of course, did not answer him. The father punched him. Then locked him up in a broom closet because he knew Kevin feared the dark. Refused to let him out until he answered. And Kevin didn't. The father then took Kevin into the bedroom, stripped him in front of his two young sisters, and tied Kevin spread-eagle on the bed. The girls were then forced to touch and kiss Kevin sexually.

The next morning Kevin still lay trussed up, his sisters having been made to watch him wet himself because he couldn't get up and then to laugh at him, lest they be beaten themselves. When Kevin still refused to speak, to answer on his own behalf, the stepfather became enraged. He cut Kevin loose, dragged him into the kitchen and beat him with a frying pan until the boy passed out.

After the stepfather left the house, Kevin's mother took him into the living room and nursed him. She bound his wounds, and when he bled through the bandages, she changed them and burned the bloody ones. She put away the frying pan and did not dress Kevin, lest he bleed on any clothes. When it became apparent that Kevin was seriously injured and wouldn't recuperate without medical attention, she called in a neighbor. The neighbor then notified the police.

While Kevin's mother made a statement to the police, Kevin was rushed to the hospital where emergency surgery was performed to relieve pressure of a hemorrhage on his brain.

Marlys Menzies had one of those smooth, honeyed voices that one associates with Southern belles. The gentleness of her voice provided a bizarre contrast to her words.

According to the mother, I said, the stepfather was only fined and banned from seeing Kevin. Why had he not been criminally charged?

Ah well, Marlys Menzies said, that was the rub. The mother wouldn't swear out a complaint against him and Kevin, of course, didn't speak. There was no way to put Kevin on the witness stand. And the mother had destroyed all the evidence that there had been any real assault and battery. The stepfather was charged with a misdemeanor.

I thought there were child-abuse laws in this state, I commented.

Marlys Menzies was silent. Well, there are, she said at last. They just don't always work.

The anger I had felt coming home in the car roared up inside me again. What lousy kind of charade was this anyway, where a kid could get half his brain knocked out, and not only was it only marginally condemned, but also collectively forgotten? In a bit of bizarre mental hopscotch, I thought of Hitler's concentration camps. What had happened there wasn't so terribly unfathomable. We had mini-versions of it going on all around us every day. And we, like the Germans, looked the other way and forgot.

Late in the week I mentioned to Kevin that we had tracked down his mother and had gone to see her. He and I were in his room as usual. I had brought him a crossword puzzle book, one of the few old interests he still enjoyed. So he sat on the bed and tried to solve one while we talked.

'Is she coming to see me?' he asked but there was no lilt of hope in his voice. It was a flat question. He didn't even bother to look up from his puzzle when I told him.

'I don't think so.'

'I didn't expect she would.'

I looked up at him. I was sitting on the floor and was even with his training shoes as they stuck out over the bed. 'She told us how they came to bring you to Garson Gayer.'

'She tell you everything?' Still no emotion in his voice.

'No. But I found out. I called a woman named Marlys Menzies. Do you remember her?'

'Yes.'

'She told me the rest.'

'Well then,' Kevin said, 'you should know they didn't bring me to Garson Gayer. You should know Mrs Menzies took me over. I saw my mom last on that day my stepfather beat me up. I haven't seen her since.'

'Do you want to?'

He lifted his eyes from the crossword puzzle and gazed in front of him. For several seconds he was lost in thought. Then he shook his head and went back to the puzzle. 'No, I guess not. Not really. Some things you quit wishing for. And after a while they're gone. They're completely gone and you don't even have the memory of wanting them.'

Chapter Twenty-five

Then Kevin talked.

It was the same as at Garson Gayer. After days and weeks and months of silence, Kevin suddenly decided to talk again to the hospital staff. It must have been hard to do, the way he did it, because everyone had become so accustomed to his silence. It created a terrible furor for the first few days afterward, which caused Kevin to slink around in embarrassment. To me he did not appear to enjoy all the commotion he had created, although to keep doing that kind of thing, perhaps some deep, inner part of him did.

It was very nearly Christmas by then, and he had been on the unit since September. Like the time before, I asked him why he had chosen to talk and why now. Secretly I wondered if it reflected anything Jeff or I had done, but I couldn't tell.

As always, Kevin seemed to run a parallel path of development. While he did improve, there was never any real evidence to link it with something we were doing. Maybe he would have gotten better anyway, without us.

Kevin's reason for talking was less specific this time than it had been the year before. He didn't know, he said, and I believed him. I don't think he really did know. To Jeff he said that he had grown tired of having a single room to himself. And they wouldn't put him in with a roommate if he didn't talk. So he talked. First to another boy on the unit whom everyone called Loopy Larry, who really was crazy as a loon, and then slowly to a couple of the staff whom Kevin especially liked. Within days Kevin was moved in to share a room with Loopy.

While Kevin was clearly happier having someone to share his days with, this change made things unexpectedly difficult for Jeff and me. We no longer had Kevin's private room to work in, and with the loss of it, we also lost that spontaneous, natural sort of interaction we had developed among us. Now we had to go down the hall to the therapy room. It was typical, with a linoleum floor and a table, chairs, a couch and a oneway mirror. The first time I saw it I harked abruptly back to my first encounter with Kevin and again realized how far we had come.

The room was drafty and the floor was not well swept, so that kept us sitting in chairs, something Kevin and I had never done in our whole time together. I failed to realize before then how much time I actually spent working on floors. They seemed a natural place to interact with people, especially children, because I was so tall that otherwise I could never look at them face to face. That certainly wasn't my problem

with Kevin, but because we had started in the very beginning on a floor, we never had changed much. Now here we
were stuck in chairs where neither of us could move surrep-
titiously one way or the other.

More significantly, Kevin's window was gone. His new
room was on the other side of the hall and its window did
not face out on the dramatic panorama of the city below but
rather onto the hospital parking lot. Moreover, Loopy's bed
was under it. There were no usable windows in the therapy
room at all. They were all small, high and frosted over. When
the light hit them right, I could see the fine mesh of wire
embedded in them.

However, we managed, chairs, windows and all. Our sessions became considerably less informal and more like proper
therapy sessions, which may not have been such a bad thing.
Kevin didn't appear to mind the change at all and I was
resigned to it.

Following his decision to speak again, Kevin started to make
progress at a steadier rate. It was still not at the speed it had
been the previous spring but at least we had left the plateau
behind. The paralyzing depression had finally lifted, and
Kevin began to show a rekindled interest in the outside world.

Heartened by this, both Jeff and I were encouraging Kevin
to earn enough points to gain a pass to go out of the hospital. We tempted him with all sorts of interesting prospects.
The amusement park was closed for the winter but there was
still the zoo and the museum and Taco John's with its unlim-
ited supply of tacos. However, out of all the choices, Kevin
came up with one of his own.

Kevin had only one major fear left, or at least only one that routinely interfered with his life. He remained terrified of water. He could bear water running over him, as in the shower, but that was the extent of it. The thought of being submersed in even a small pan of water frightened him.

Yet, it held a horrible fascination for him too. One night when I was there with Kevin, he asked me, would it be possible, maybe, perhaps, if I thought he could, well, if he earned an outside pass, could he, well would I take him swimming?

Swimming? The idea sounded preposterous.

Would I take him? Would I go with him in the water? Where could we go? Did I know a place?

I smiled at the thought. Yes, I supposed we could. If he was sure he really wanted to.

Kevin did. But, he told me, it was just to be him and me. Not Jeff. It was going to be a surprise for Jeff. Kevin would leam to swim and then go out with Jeff and surprise him. Kevin grinned at me when he said that. We'd surprise old Jeff. Jeff would think it was Kevin and it would be Bryan. Even on the outside.

With this secret between us, Kevin managed to earn sufficient points for an outside trip by early January. It was a poignant moment when he met me at the hospital door, his newly purchased swimming trunks still in their paper bag. He was clearly very scared, yet the fire of Bryan was bright in his eyes.

We went in the early evening on a Friday night because that was a night Jeff never came over and because I intended to go to the Y and they held no classes on Friday nights. On impulse I decided to let Charity come along. Kevin had met her on a couple of occasions the previous spring and I knew she would enjoy the pool. I also hoped she might provide some counterbalance for Kevin. This way, when things got too tense, I could turn to her and let Kevin relax on his own.

The Y had two pools, a regular Olympic-sized one and a small kiddies' pool that was only about two feet at its deepest. Since we arrived at 5:30 and there were no legitimate kiddies around, I reckoned we could start there.

Charity came bouncing out of the dressing room all kitted out in a hot-pink bikini, her belly sticking out further than any other part of her. She went into the small pool with a splash, bottom first. Kevin was nowhere to be seen.

I waited for him. Sitting on the edge of the small pool, I stuck my feet in but waited with one ear cocked toward the men's dressing room.

After ten minutes or so I wandered over to the door of the men's. 'Kev?' I called tentatively.

No answer.

'Kev? Kevin? You in there?'

No answer.

'Kevin!'

No answer.

I looked around. There was no one else there except for the towel keeper in his booth beyond the glass partition. Furtively, I took a step inside the door of the dressing room. 'Kevin? Are you ready? Are you in there?'

Nothing.

'Answer me, would you?'

With no indication that he was even in the room, I felt a bit desperate. 'Kevin? Are you having any problems? I can't come in there really. It's for men only, so I can't be much help. Come to the door.'

God, I was thinking, why had I let Kevin talk me into this? *This* was a situation for Jeff.

Still there was no response at all out of the dressing room. I couldn't even hear a noise in there. By now, however, Charity's attention had been caught. She got out of the kiddies' pool and came over.

'You ain't supposed to go in there, Torey,' she said.

'I know that.'

'There's naked men in there.'

'Charity, I know but I'm worried something's happened to Kevin.'

'Do you want *me* to go in there for you?' she asked, clearly relishing the thought.

'No! Go away now. Go back to the water and play.'

'What are you going to do? Are you going in there?' Her evil grin was ear to ear. 'There's stark naked men in there. You ain't supposed to.'

'Just go back to the pool and play, would you? I'll be over in a second. Now scram.'

'You want me to help you? Here, I'll help. Kevin!' she bellowed at the top of her lungs. 'KEVIN!' the entire pool area echoed with the power of her voice. 'KEVIN, COME OUT HERE RIGHT NOW OR TOREY'LL COME IN AND GET YOU!!'

'*Charity!*'

The towel keeper peered around the corner of his booth. Understandably.

'Listen to me and listen good. You go over to that pool and you *play*. Do you hear me?'

She backed off a little way but with a terribly evil grin on her face. 'I'm gonna watch all them naked men come running out,' she said, her voice almost inaudible. She knew I was going in.

Cautiously, I edged around the corner of the entrance. Within seconds Charity was beside me, plastered to the wall like a movie sleuth.

'Charity, get out of here. I don't need your help.'

Her look was a challenge.

'You want to see how mad I can get at people? Is that what you're trying to find out? You want to know if I'm capable of spanking someone nine years old? Because I think I might be.'

A hint of concern appeared in her eyes.

'If you don't want to go home right this minute and not have any swimming at all, I'd suggest you get your tail out of here and back in that pool. This very instant. Understand?'

Just then a man in swimming trunks appeared. He gave us a definitely odd look and went on by and out to the pool. I gave Charity a rough shove in that direction too.

'Get *out!*' I said between gritted teeth. 'I mean it.' She must have realized I did because she retreated.

Embarrassed beyond all description by what I was having to do, I sneaked around the corner of the door and into the room. Like the women's dressing room, there were rows and rows of lockers with benches in between. Obviously there were some men about because I saw a lot of tennis shoes and squash racket cases and the like. And I heard the shower.

'Kevin, answer me. Where the hell are you?' I called in a hoarse whisper. My acute self-consciousness was shortening my temper remarkably. I wanted to scream for him. Or at him.

Finally I located him. Between the very last set of lockers, there he sat on the bench. Dressed only in his underpants, he had clutched the new swimming trunks to his face. He was crying.

'Whatever is the matter?' I slid down onto the bench next to him. At least this far down the chances were probably better that I wouldn't be noticed.

'I don't know how to put them on,' he wailed.

'Hey, hey, hey,' I said and put an arm around him. 'I know it's scary but it's nothing to cry about.' The embarrassment of sitting in the men's dressing room with a weeping seventeen-year-old suddenly melted away and I was flooded with affection for him. Kevin was so innocent. I could feel the dismal despair that must have swept over him in here, alone in a strange place, knowing water waited for him just beyond the door, confronted with an odd bit of clothing that had just proved too much.

I reached a hand out. 'Here, give them to me. Let me see if I can figure them out.'

To be honest, my knowledge of men's swimwear is limited. One of the hospital staff had bought these for Kevin and they were a little tricky looking. From what I could see, there was a white part attached in the middle to a blue part, four leg holes and no way to get in. It was a regular monkey puzzle. Uncertainly, I tried to untangle and then figure out how to stuff the white part back inside the blue part.

That accomplished, I still wasn't sure which was back and which was front. Or if it mattered. Kevin sat beside me solemnly and watched.

Then the worst happened. Around the corner of the lockers came a man with a towel wrapped around his waist. Both of us were alarmed to see the other.

Dead silence.

Still clutching the swimming trunks, I decided candor would be the most valorous approach. I flung the trunks out at him. 'Can you tell which way is front and which is back? We can't.'

Stunned, he took the suit. He looked inside. 'Here,' he said and handed it back to me.

'Well, there we go, Kevin. There's the front. Now you put them on and I'll meet you at poolside.' And I shot out of the locker room without even pausing to see if anyone else was in the place.

Kevin appeared reluctantly a few minutes later. Charity met him and dragged him over to where I was sitting with my feet in the kiddies' pool.

Then started the long, slow process of getting Kevin to the water. Unfortunately, by the time we had finished the nerve-wracking job of getting changed, it had long gone six o'clock, and parents with their toddlers were arriving to use the small pool.

That was too much of a bruising for Kevin's ego, and without ever having touched the water in that pool, he asked if we couldn't move over to the larger pool.

That was a scary-sized pool. Charity, with all her bravado, jumped right into the water to discover that the shallow end came clear up to her armpits. She screamed in panic and flailed wildly over to climb up on my back. I had to hold her in my arms, something I could never have managed on dry land, until she regained her courage enough to get to the steps and then go get a paddle-board from the towel keeper.

There were steps into the shallow end, and I sat down on one that put me into water up to my waist. Kevin sat down at the side of the pool, first on the bench several feet away from the water and then finally he rose and came over near me and sat on the cement. I said nothing about it; we just talked, as two friends might talk, me sitting in the water, him sitting out of it. Both of us knew what was going on below the surface of our words. His courage grew. He came closer.

'You know what?' Kevin said to me.

'What's that?'

'Remember last year? Remember going to the Frosty-Freez?'

I chuckled. How could I forget?

'This is sort of like that, isn't it?' he said and smiled. 'Remember how scared I got?' With one finger he traced the irregularities in the cement. 'It seems silly to me now, when I think about it. I mean, I was so scared. I peed my pants, remember that? God, I felt dumb.'

He looked at me. It was a long appraising gaze. My skin was wrinkling from being in the water so long and I began to inch my way up the steps.

'You like me, don't you?' he asked. There was confidence in the question.

I nodded without looking over.

'That's why you do these things with me. That's why you don't care what kind of idiot I am, huh? It's 'cause you like me.'

'Yes.'

He smiled briefly at me but more to himself, as he bent over and picked at a toenail. 'I knew you did,' he said. 'It's good. It's a good thing to know.'

Six o'clock became seven. Seven became eight. The pool closed at nine. Even Charity, who had continued to play joyfully on her own for ages, was beginning to wane. She grew whiny. She wanted an ice cream. She was cold. She wanted to go home.

Kevin was still on the edge, sitting Indian-style with his legs crossed.

I moved out into the water. 'Here, give me your foot,' I said as I paddled down along the edge of the pool to where it was deeper.

Kevin watched me and did not move.

'Just one foot. Here. Come here to where I am.'

He rose and came over to where I clung to the side of the pool. Sitting down, he carefully extended one foot. I took it in my hand, clasping it gently but firmly. Very slowly, I lowered it toward the water but stopped when my hand touched. With my free hand, I brought water up from the pool to wet his foot. All the time I talked to him of other things and tried to keep the water kind and gentle and without splashes.

For a split second he let his foot remain, then abruptly he jerked it out, sending water all over me. 'I can't!' he cried. 'I can't do it. I just can't make myself.'

'Okay, okay. That's all right. It'll come in its own time.'

Charity paddled her way over to us on her board. Letting go of the float, she transferred herself to me as I stood in the water, wrapping her arms around my neck and her legs around my waist. She was in back of me so she rested her chin on my shoulder to watch Kevin.

Again I took his foot, the other one this time, and brought it toward the water. This time I put water only on my arm above his foot. Still he could not bear more than a moment of it and had to pull his foot away.

'How come you're scared, Kevin?' Charity asked. 'I'm only nine and I'm not scared. How come you are?'

'I don't know,' he replied.

'Do you think you're going to drown or something? I thought I might when I first jumped in. That scared me. But I'm not scared now.'

'I dunno,' he replied.

'You wouldn't, you know,' she persisted. 'That guy over there, he's a lifeguard. He'd save you. Torey might even save you, if she could. Huh, Tor? You wouldn't let him drown, would you?'

I shook my head.

'Or me either. You wouldn't let me drown either, would you?'

'Nope.'

'So, see, Kevin, there ain't nothing to be scared of, really. So why are you? What makes you not even want to put your feet in?'

'Charity, don't nag,' I said. Kevin's head was down.

'I'm not nagging. I'm asking.'

I jabbed Charity with my elbow and that made her hang on to my neck all the tighter.

'I don't know why I'm scared. Honest, I don't.'

'It doesn't matter, Kevin,' I said. 'It'll pass. Just like all the other fears. Look how many you used to have and how almost all of them have passed away. This one will too in its own time.'

Charity held tight to me, her chin still on my shoulder, her long black hair awash in a circle around us.

Kevin reached over to the edge of the pool and touched Charity's hair. He dipped his finger into the water and watched the drops fall off. 'I dunno. I guess I am sort of afraid of drowning. It doesn't matter what anybody says, I know I'm going to drown. It just feels that way.'

He was on his knees now, peering into the water. The water was quite deep where I was standing, maybe four feet or so. Without her float, Charity didn't dare let go of my back. Gingerly Kevin touched the water's surface with one hand and watched the ripples.

'I have dreams sometimes,' he said. 'There's a lake. Did I ever tell you about that dream?'

I shook my head.

'I used to have it all the time but I only get it sometimes now. There's this lake. I don't know where it is. I've never really seen it awake. And I hear my sister calling for me. She's on the other side and she's crying. She's scared. I don't know what of, but I know she is. I just hear her crying for me. And I know I got to go get her but there isn't any way except if I go in the lake. And I know I'm going to drown if I go in that lake. It's black. The water's real black, like night.'

Kevin sat back and looked at me. He looked beyond me to Charity and then back at me. Then on his knees again, he peered into the water without touching it.

'Black water. Not like this. This is green water. It's clear. But I know I got to go in that lake. And I know if I do, I'll drown. I know I'm gonna. But I know I got to go too. I *want* to go. There's nobody going to help Carol, if I don't. Nobody else is there to hear her. And I run up and down the bank and I scream to her. And then I fall in the lake. The water comes up over me. And it's all black. It comes up and I can't breathe and Carol's crying more now than before 'cause she knows I'm drowning. And the water's all over me and I'm fighting to get out and I can't. I'm drowning. I can't get out. I can't help nobody. I can't help Carol. I can't help me.'

'That's a very scary dream,' I said.

He nodded. 'It's a nightmare. And then I wake up and I think I'm going to be sick, I'm so scared. It's like dying, that dream is. Every time I dream it, I think I'm dying and I get so scared. If I ever see that lake, I'm going to drown. That lake's out there and I'm going to drown in it, if I ever see it.'

Charity moved around from my back to my side. She reached a hand up to touch Kevin. 'Don't you worry, Kevin,' she said. 'I got a lake like that in me too. I think everybody does.'

Chapter Twenty-six

When things ran normally, Jeff always got to the office before me. I had an 8:00 and 9:00 session at a nearby school, so I did not check into the clinic until somewhere around 9:30 most mornings. This worked out well because Jeff could then do his morning therapy right in our office without having to book one of the interview rooms.

Because I could usually count on his being around in the mornings when I arrived, I was disappointed to come in on Monday morning and discover Jeff was not there. I had been mulling over Kevin's story about the dream and, while I did not want to give away to Jeff Kevin's secret about swimming, I definitely wanted to talk the dream business over and see if Jeff had heard anything comparable during his sessions with Kevin. But since Jeff wasn't there and apparently hadn't even come in yet, because his coat wasn't on the hook either, I soon forgot about it and sat down at my desk and began to work.

Then I couldn't find my scissors. Standing up, I went over to Jeff's desk and rifled through his top drawer. Bloody hell, Jeff, where'd you stick them this time? I'd punch him, I really would. He was forever running off with my scissors. And he never put them back.

I searched. I searched everywhere and could not find the stupid things. In a fit of pique I stomped out of the office and down to the receptionist's desk to borrow hers.

'Do you know where the hell Jeff has gone?' I asked as she handed me the scissors.

Shirley, the receptionist, and one of the office aides were sitting there, having coffee and sugar doughnuts, our traditional Monday-morning treat from Dr Rosenthal. A funny look crossed Shirley's face when I asked that. She said nothing.

I glanced at the other woman. She looked down. I looked back at Shirley. 'Is something wrong?' I asked, perplexed.

The expression on Shirley's face made it apparent something was, but I couldn't imagine what. The stillness, which must have been only seconds long in reality, expanded to silence the entire room.

'Didn't Dr Rosenthal tell you?' she asked quietly.

'Tell me what?'

This was awful. Something dreadful must have happened to Jeff. He must have been maimed in some accident. Or killed. Jeff was the sort of person you'd expect to have accidents. He lived that way.

'What's happened?' I asked when no one spoke.

Shirley glanced at the other woman and then back to me. She swallowed her doughnut. 'Didn't Dr Rosenthal tell you anything? Not a thing?'

Again I shook my head.

'Jeff was let go.'

'What?'

'They let him go Friday night.'

'What do you mean? They fired him? Jeff? How come?'

'Well, not exactly fired. Just let go. To go somewhere else.'

My confusion was monumental. Jeff wasn't planning to go anywhere. I knew that for a fact. He loved the clinic and he loved the city. Just a couple weeks back he'd been talking to me about a research grant he'd applied for, a grant to come to Sandry Clinic. I knew full well that when Jeff's final training was completed at the end of the spring, he had planned to stay here. He'd told me so.

So what did she mean? Did they fire him? Why on earth would they fire Jeff? He was marvelous at his work. He was better than I was.

Shirley's face was drawn. She fiddled with the remainder of her doughnut before finally pitching it into the wastebasket.

'Jeff's a homosexual, Torey,' she said. 'What with all that's been going on in the city lately, the board of directors . . . well, you know how it goes. They just though it better if he wasn't working with children.'

'He's gay?' I asked, half aloud. I had not known. Yet in the half-conscious part of my mind, I suppose I always had. When Shirley said it, I knew it was true. Hans apparently had been more than a roommate.

Then everything became crushingly clear. The Dade County referendum in Florida had been only months before. Several cities around the nation had begun repealing their gay-rights acts. We had our own referendum coming up in a few weeks' time.

'They found him a place to work,' Shirley said. 'Down in California. He isn't going to be without a job, Torey. They didn't really fire him. It was just because he was working with kids.'

'But he was *good* with kids, Shirley,' I said. 'He wouldn't hurt any kid. No more than I would. He was good. We needed him here.'

'But they found him a good place. Dr Rosenthal gave him a wonderful recommendation. I know. I typed it out. He's going to be working in an alcoholic rehabilitation center.'

'Alcoholics? Jeff doesn't know anything about alcoholics, Shirley. What's he going to do down there? It's kids he's so good with.'

'He'll be good there too, Torey. And they need him there.'

'But what difference does that make,' I asked, 'when I need him here?'

Completely devastated, I returned to the office. I wasn't even capable of thinking. Jeff must not have heard the final decision until Friday night because, as I looked around the office, there was nothing missing to give me a clue of what had taken place. Jeff's desk was still Jeff's desk, stacked untidily with case histories and textbooks and medical dictionaries. Two candy bars and an empty wrapper were on the corner of the desk. Along the back was a collection of Styrofoam hamburger containers that Jeff had saved to keep his paper clips and rubber bands and things in. The only thing on his bulletin board was a long sign with the Pink Panther on it that said, 'This is where Jeff lives it up!' Well, not anymore.

What began to sink in as I sat down at my desk was how involved Jeff and I were professionally. We shared six cases together now. So much for teamwork. So much for the perfect team. What was going to happen to me and the kids now?

And Kevin. *Kevin.* Oh my God. I slumped into my chair. What was I ever going to say to Kevin? How was he going to understand? All it was going to look like to him was that one more man had proved untrustworthy, that one more person had walked out of his life without saying good-bye.

I began to cry, as much for myself, I fear, as for Jeff or Kevin. This business was like trying to build a card house in a drafty room. Half the time was spent desperately building, the other half trying to save it from the drafts. And every time one thought one had finally accomplished it, a breeze would come up from an entirely different direction and knock all the cards down again.

At four-thirty I packed my things and went to see Kevin. He was sitting on his bed when I came in. He had one of the puzzle books out and was intent on it. Closing the door behind me, I came over and sat down on the bed. Loopy Larry was in there too, lying on his own bed and staring at the ceiling.

Kevin looked up. 'What're you doing here? This is Jeff's night.' Then before I could get a word in, he continued, 'Oh well, guess what? I earned twelve more points today. If I earn sixty will you take me swimming again?'

I watched him.

Kevin stopped talking. He searched my face. 'Where's Jeff?'

'Jeff isn't coming.'

He knew something was wrong. Frantically, I was shifting through my thoughts to come up with a viable way to explain what I was going to have to explain to him.

'We've had a problem come up, Kev. Jeff isn't going to be able to work with us anymore.'

'Huh? What?' Alarm ran naked through Kevin's eyes. 'What do you mean? What's happened to him?'

'Well, it's kind of hard to say. Jeff had to go away. He decided to move to California and work in a clinic there.'

Kevin's brow puckered. 'Why? How come? Did I do something? He never told me he wanted to go somewhere else.'

'Oh, Kevin,' I said and sat down beside him to put my arm around his shoulders, 'It was nothing you did. Nothing anyone did. Jeff didn't really want to leave; it wasn't because of us. Not because of anything you did or I did or anything that happened here. That wasn't why he did. Just other things came up. And people at the clinic decided it was maybe best if he would go work somewhere else.'

Tears puddled up in Kevin's eyes and he made no effort to conceal them. 'They're *stupid* people!'

'Yes, I agree with you.'

Kevin snuffled.

'I'm terribly sorry it happened, Kev. I know you liked Jeff a lot. We both did. He was one of our very best friends, wasn't he? And for a while it's going to leave an awful big hole. But I want you to know that his leaving had nothing to do with you or anything that took place here. It was a separate decision Jeff had to make.'

'But why didn't he tell me he was leaving?'

'I don't think he knew until right at the end. He didn't tell me either. But I'm sure he would have, if he'd been able.'

The silence descended on us, rolling itself down off the walls like slime. Loopy Larry was over on his bed, lying there and watching us. He had flat features and I wondered if he had Down's syndrome. When the silence became so complete, he started to make little tiny fiddly noises to pierce it. Crazy as a loon was Larry.

Kevin stared at his puzzle book. I could hear him breathing, and there was something heartbreaking about the noise. It was so pathetically human with its fabric of tears.

'Why did he leave? How come people decided he ought to be other places when you and me wanted him here?'

I let out a long breath of air and weighed what I needed to tell him. It had to be the truth, but how did one say it to a kid like Kevin with his experiences so that Jeff would come out just as he was, neither better nor worse.

'Jeff was a homosexual, Kevin. Do you know what that is?'

'Yeah. Sort of.'

'It's when a person prefers to have sexual relationships with someone of his own sex. So that a man prefers sex with another man and woman with another woman.'

Kevin sighed.

'And that bothers some people. They don't understand it and most people are scared of things they don't understand. They're scared of people who are different from themselves and so they try to make those people go away.'

'Boy, I sure know about *that*,' Kevin said.

'Well, see, Jeff was different in his way, just like you are in yours. And people got scared of him and they decided he ought to go away.'

Kevin's head was down again. *Chirp*, went Loopy Larry behind me. He sounded like a little bird.

With his brow furrowed, Kevin looked at me again, 'But what I don't understand, Torey, is *why?* Why would something like that make a difference? It didn't have anything to do with what he did with me or you or anything. Who would care about a thing like that?'

Instead of going home after seeing Kevin, I returned to the clinic. It was almost six but I knew Dr Rosenthal would still be there. It was his private time with no phones or beepers when he could do most of his writing.

He was expecting me. I had made no arrangements to see him but he must have known I'd come. His office door was open and before I had reached the doorway, he was turned around in his office chair. He gestured for me to sit down. I sat. Still wearing my jacket, still with an armload of books and materials, I dropped down into the chair.

Rocking back and forth in his desk chair, Dr Rosenthal regarded me a long time. He knew my questions before I asked them. I knew his answers. Back and forth he rocked. Finally he reached over his desk and took a tissue. Removing his glasses, he cleaned them, examined them, wiped them again. Then he folded them up and put them in his breast pocket. He rubbed the bridge of his nose. He loosened his tie. I wondered, as I watched him, what made aloof, intellectual men so attractive. He was a compelling man. Then he took out his pipe. Still without saying a word, he opened the tobacco pouch, extracted leaves, stuffed the bowl of the pipe. Did I make him nervous, that he always smoked when I was here? Or did he always have a private little smoke in his office before he went home to the family who believed he'd stopped? Then he pulled open the desk drawer and lifted out the teapot and the tea bags.

'I don't think I want any, thank you,' I said.

He smiled. 'Yes, you do. Come on and join me.' And he rose to go get water.

I was sitting in one of his 'therapy' chairs, a huge, soft over-stuffed rocker meant to relax his clients. I sat with my chin braced on one fist. Tears welled up and came down my cheeks as he gave the warm steaming cup of tea to me. I made no effort to hide them. There was no point. He already knew he had hurt me. I only hoped he felt as bad about my tears as I did.

'Why couldn't you at least have told me?' I asked. 'I never knew at all.'

'It wasn't really your matter,' he replied.

'It was. We were sharing cases.'

'Then it would have been up to Jeff to tell you, not me. It was a personal matter.'

'But he didn't tell me. And I didn't know.'

We fell silent. Dr Rosenthal drank his tea in great, quench-ing gulps. Then he poured himself another cup. The clinic was absolutely silent at that hour, and so I could hear him swallow.

'Why did you do it?' I asked.

'I didn't do it. The board did it.'

'But you could have stopped them, couldn't you? Why did you let a stupid, stupid thing like that, which had no bearing on Jeff's work, matter?'

'Because it did matter.'

'It didn't. No more than my sexual preferences or behav-iors in my own time interfere with my work. Jeff would never touch a kid. You know yourself that's a fact. He'd never hurt a kid any more than I would. Or you would.'

'No, true. But it mattered to the board.'

'But why did you let it? They're stupid, uncaring, narrow-minded people.'

Dr Rosenthal lowered his head and regarded the fabric of his suit. He nodded. 'Yes, they are. But sometimes the stupid are in the driver's seat. More often than not. Because the smart, caring, broad-minded are too busy out doing.'

For several moments neither of us spoke. He rocked in his desk chair, lit his pipe and then sat, contemplating his fingernails and the backs of his hands. I watched him and tried to make thoughts come out of aching confusion.

Then Dr Rosenthal looked over at me. He said nothing at first but just searched my face. 'Were you in love with him, Torey?'

'No,' I replied and it was true. At least it was mostly true. I hadn't really thought about it before, and if it never occurs to you, it probably isn't what you'd call love. But then what is? It's a barren language, English is, for words like that. There's only one to cover everything when the nuances of the emotion could use up a thousand different words. I had never considered Jeff for a lover and he had never given me reason to. But we had had a passionate affair of the mind, and for want of a better word, it had made me love him. I was a great one for loving anyway. It was an emotion that came easily to me. I could do it effortlessly and over such an incredible range of people, big and small, old and young, male and female. I savored the emotion; it made all things bright and beautiful to me when in the hard, cold light of day, I knew they really weren't. But that was always enough, to feel the beauty.

'Not in love with him, no,' I said, 'but I loved him.'

Dr Rosenthal smiled in a sad way and lowered his head.

'You did a rotten thing to me,' I said, 'and to my kids. And a rottener thing to Jeff.'

'I know,' he said and I knew he did.

The worst, perhaps, was Charity.

She was late coming over. Her mom was having troubles recently, and so Charity was having to spend more time minding her young brothers. She arrived after I had already eaten. I heard her coming down the sidewalk. It was a dark, frigid night and Charity came skipping through it, singing 'Silent Night' at the top of her lungs.

'Guess what I did today!' she hollered from the front door as she let herself in. 'Hans? Are you here, Hans? Guess what I did at school today, Hans.'

I came into the hallway from the kitchen.

'Where they at? Where's Hans?' she asked, her voice cautious. She knew already something was wrong.

'Come into the kitchen, Charity. Would you like a mug of hot chocolate?'

'Where they at? They always come on Mondays. Every Monday. How come they're not here?'

Carefully, I tried to explain that Hans and Jeff would not be coming back. Charity was sitting on the stool beside me as I made her chocolate. When I handed it to her, she stared into it, her mouth pulled back in a tight, mordant expression. When I finished explaining, she looked over at me without really raising her head. Consequently, I saw her dark eyes through a fringe of bangs.

'They divorced us, didn't they?'

I smiled in sympathy. 'No, Char, it wasn't anything like that.'

'Yes, they did. Just like my pop divorced me.'

'But parents don't divorce kids, either. Adults divorce other adults. Parents don't divorce kids. Friends don't divorce friends.'

'How do *you* know?'

I studied her face. Her expression was hard and knowledgeable. 'Divorce is something only adults do,' I said. 'It's a grown-up thing. But friends never do it and Jeff and Hans were our friends, Charity. Things might change between us, but it isn't divorce.'

'It's the same thing.'

'No, it isn't.'

'Yes sir. Your pop goes away and you never see him again, really. I mean, he isn't family anymore, like, he doesn't give you baths or play hide-the-thimble when your friends come over. Just like Hans isn't ever going to take me skating again. It's over and I'm never going to see him or Jeff again. Maybe it isn't divorce. Maybe it isn't because they divorced us. But it's the very same thing.'

I paused from hugging her and tried to think of a very honest answer to sort things out. With tears on her cheeks, Charity caught me at my thinking and gave me a small, sardonic smile.

'It *is* the same, Torey,' she said with gentle finality. 'I'm right. I know. Believe me, it is.'

Chapter Twenty-seven

On Tuesday evening Jeff came over to my house with Hans, and we sat around and talked for a long, long time. Interestingly, we managed to avoid the very thing that I think we all meant to talk about, and so our conversation was filled mostly with the future and the past. We all got amnesia about the present.

On Wednesday Jeff came into the office and cleared out his things. That evening when I went to see Kevin, Kevin told me Jeff had been around to talk to him and say good-bye.

'Why should I care?' Kevin said morosely. 'I couldn't care less what happens to Jeff. He can jump right in the Pacific Ocean when he gets to California for all I care. In fact, I wish he would, only it'd pollute the ocean.'

'I see,' I said.

'I hope they have an earthquake. I hope the whole stupid state of California falls in the ocean too.'

I was sitting on the edge of Kevin's bed and I leaned over to rummage through my box of things for a new cartoon book I had brought him. Feeling a little like a weekend parent buying her kid's silence with a gift, I searched in terse, impatient motions through the box. Junk. That was all that was in the box. A bunch of two-bit crap. Why didn't I ever clean it out so that I could find something?

Kevin looked over. There was a poignant moment when he caught me at my frantic searching and both of us knew how vulnerable I was. And he was.

I saw Jeff on only one other occasion, and that time was by accident. After work on Friday I stopped into a local watering hole with some friends. It was one of those convivial places where people gather but was not frequented much by my colleagues from the clinic, which was what I wanted. Apparently Jeff had as well, because as I sat there drinking beer and eating peanuts, I saw Jeff across the room. I rose and went over.

He was at a table with other people whom I did not know but, when he saw me, he got up and met me partway across the room. We went up to the bar and he bought me another beer. Together we stood, side by side, and we said nothing.

'You know, it's a funny place, this world,' he said at last. 'If I were a Nazi, someone would defend my constitutional right to hate Jews. If I were a Klansman, someone would defend my right to hate blacks. It's a funny place, this world. Hate has rights. Love has none.'

And that was it. He left.

* * *

The phone rang at twenty minutes to three in the morning. I had been sound asleep, and it was only after I hung up that I was finally awake enough to fathom what it had been all about.

A nurse from Mortenson had rung. Could I come immediately? Kevin had been locked in seclusion, and even that had failed to calm him down. He was clinging to the door and had a piece of metal railing in his hand.

In the early morning darkness I sat shivering. The telephone still lay in my lap as I sat on the stair. Consciousness slowly fought through to the surface. Rising tiredly, I put all the lights on and went back upstairs to dress. I was cold from waking up in the chilly house, so in addition to my shirt, I put on a woolly pullover, something I never normally wore except when hiking.

The car coughed to life in the bitter midwinter darkness, and I headed downtown to Mortenson Hospital. Only twenty minutes had passed from the time the call came until I left the driveway, but coming out of midnight grogginess made it seem forever to me.

I could hear Kevin screaming. Even before I managed to negotiate the first half of the security system on the unit, I could hear his high-pitched banshee wail. Let me out, let me out, let me out, he was crying. What other patients in the hospital must have thought I could not imagine. It was an eerie, unearthly noise, audible a long ways.

Waiting for a nurse to let me through the second set of doors, I could hear the panic of the staff as well. They chattered anxiously beyond the door as someone fumbled with the keys.

Kevin was in the seclusion room, which was no more than a bare cell. Unlike the room at Garson Gayer, it was not padded. Out in the hallway were Kevin's bed from his other room, his sheets, his bathrobe, his pajamas and a litter of other things he had ripped from the bedstead, the walls, the lighting fixtures and the window.

He was suicidal, said one of the nurses, and showed me things Kevin had tried to hang himself with. She demonstrated how he had tried to stab himself.

Three male personnel were at the seclusion-room door, peering through the small window. Kevin still had his bit of bedstead because he had become so violent that they had been unable to restrain him and get it away. So now they stood gawking through the unbreakable glass, unsure whether he was more likely to kill himself or them.

My adrenaline was up. I could hear it forcing the blood fast through my ears. My hands did not shake yet but I could feel the crawliness under my skin. And as always happened, it made me absolutely fearless. All other stimuli around me were blocked out. I could only think of Kevin.

'Kev? It's me, Kevin. Can you hear me?' I hollered through the seclusion-room door. I pulled the bolt out and let myself in, then I heard it slide back into place behind me.

He was at the far end of the room when I entered. He froze momentarily upon seeing me, then screamed without words. There was a minute's frenzied panic to follow when he tore around the room, doubling and tearing back the other way, all the while crying out. I only stood and watched.

Kevin was far beyond being able to talk. I suspect he was even beyond hearing me when I spoke. His anguish superseded every other sense. So he screamed wordlessly, tore at the walls, bashed himself into the concrete blocks, scratched his bare skin, ripped his hair out in patches.

Yet he never came near me. He never threatened me. I might have been invisible. In one hand he clung to a familiar weapon, a piece of bed. He had a way with knives, did Kevin. Anything could become one. But thus far he did not use it. He only held it as he flailed his way around the room.

In my scramble to get dressed and down to the hospital, I had neglected to put my watch on, so I had no idea how much time was passing. It seemed an eternity to me as I stood there, motionless, but then it would have. Only when my legs began to grow tired from standing and my back started to ache did I realize that the minutes must have drawn into hours. But I remained without moving, just inside the door. I feared to sit because Kevin's motions were so uncontrolled that even by accident he might hit me if I couldn't move quickly enough. Yet I did not think it was wise to move about needlessly. He was too incoherent to perceive things well. God knows what he might interpret my actions as, if I moved around. So I stood. And I stood. And I stood.

Kevin had the strength and endurance that terror gives. For all his crying and bashing, his energy seemed infinite. The January sky beyond the window started to brighten before Kevin finally slowed down. And even then he did not stop. Still wandering restlessly from wall to wall around the room, he wailed, his voice hoarse and cracking, his steps stumbling.

Then he collapsed. Like one of those slow-motion pictures of a chimney being blown down, he crumbled, knees first, wobbling the rest of the way up his body and then falling face forward onto the linoleum floor. There he remained, like a child's discarded plaything.

Cautiously, I lowered myself to my knees. He did not move. I inched closer to him. He had collapsed not far away, only a matter of a few feet.

'Kevin?' I whispered. 'Can you hear me, Kevin?'

Crawling on my hands and knees, I came to him and put my hand on his forehead. He stirred. Gently I stroked back his hair. I found myself flushed with a nameless, primal emotion as I touched him. It rose up from its source deep in secret parts, and I think I could have cried just then for the brutal privilege of being human.

Kevin stirred again, his breathing more of a whine, and I wondered if he had hurt himself in all this fury. Opening his eyes, he looked at me.

I smiled for want of something else to do.

Slowly, painfully, he rose up on his elbows and shoved himself forward until his head was against my knees. Bringing a hand up, he clutched at the front of my wool sweater and then like a puppy, pulled himself up and nuzzled into the soft, Ragg weave. He began to cry, his sobs wet but silent, his face buried in the wool. Because the sweater was large and he was strong, he had pulled it far out from my body and I could not feel the warmth of him against me. All I felt was the rhythmic heaviness of his sobbing.

Gently, I reached over and opened his other hand. I took the piece of bedstead from his fingers and laid it on the floor beside me. The door opened and nurses spilled in, but they did not dare come around us on the floor. Only one did, a tiny little woman with hair cut short and the turned-up nose of an elf. She held a small tray with a hypodermic needle. Deftly she went around Kevin, knelt and administered the shot into his hip. Kevin did not flex a muscle.

Recapping the needle, she looked over at me where I sat with my pullover half strangling me. She smiled sweetly. 'I hope you realize how much we appreciate what you've done,' she said.

Uncomfortable and tired, I only stared at her. How could they appreciate what I had done when I had done nothing?

Chapter Twenty-eight

Kevin sank, curled back up, disappeared once again. He ceased talking, not only to the hospital staff but to me too this time. He refused to respond to anything. Pulling the blankets over his head, he would not budge from his bed. However, the periods of intense depression were now interspersed with outbursts of agonized frenzy, when he would wail for hours on end. During these times Kevin would run from wall to wall to wall of the seclusion room, from corner to corner, back and forth like a caged animal. We could not keep him quiet. His only peace came from a hypodermic.

For the first time since Kevin's hospitalization clear back in September, I came face to face with the consulting psychiatrist who was officially in charge of Kevin's treatment. Before this we had spoken only briefly on the telephone. But now, here we were, soul mates suddenly, standing together outside the seclusion-room door.

Dr Winslow was a lean man, tall, much younger than I would have guessed from his voice on the phone, and he was terribly good looking in a traditional way. He also had an extremely charismatic personality, and the nurses swooned right, left and center when he was on the floor. It was difficult not to fall madly in love with that sort of man. However, if I had had any foolish notions of doing so, he quickly dashed them for me, because in spite of all his sterling qualities, Dr Winslow did not suffer from an overdose of compassion.

He had been thankful for my involvement in Kevin's case. He told me that, as we stood there together outside the seclusion-room door and watched Kevin. The entranceway in front of the small cell was no more than a long concrete arch, made murky by lack of lighting. However, it was a chummy sort of gloom that allowed Dr Winslow and me to talk to one another easily without having to look each other in the eye. Yes, he was glad, he said, thankful I had taken the case. He couldn't afford the time himself. He sighed, his features wrinkling into a frown. After all, he said, there's not much point in working with this kid, is there? It's a sad case but then, where is he going to end up? Rotting away for the rest of his life on the back ward of some state hospital? Most likely. No one wants him. No one cares. No, the doctor said and shook his head. A sad case. He was glad I'd done it. He couldn't afford the time himself. I was less than pleased to realize how valuable he thought my time was.

And why was I there? Dr Winslow asked me on one occasion. Was this for my research? Was I writing a journal article on this case? What was my motivation? I shrugged. A pointless case basically, Dr Winslow had added. He's hopeless. He has no redeeming qualities, not even for research. He's human, I had said, sounding like a sophomore psychology major even in my own ears, but the pause between us had grown too long and I couldn't think of anything else. Yes, Winslow agreed, he was human. And that wasn't so very remarkable, was it? It's a sad case, but the more you get these stories, these bits of human refuse, he said, the more immune you become in the end. They just don't affect you anymore, human or not.

How heartbreaking, I thought, as I stood in the concrete alcove and watched through the safety glass in the door, to grow hardened against real histories of real people's lives, to become inured to real tragedies. There's something more misanthropic about that ability than self-protective. Maybe all Kevin was was human, I said to Dr Winslow, but then that was all any of us were, really, including him and me. Maybe that wasn't much but who were we to judge that it wasn't enough? And Dr Winslow sniggered and patted me on the head and walked away.

After a sufficient number of encounters with Dr Winslow outside the seclusion-room door, I found myself avoiding him. Increasingly, he was only making me angry, and I knew the time would come when I could not hold my tongue. And I knew I had to. Nothing would be accomplished by alienating Winslow, and I couldn't afford to spare the effort anyway. There was too much else to do. However, I was thankful to him for one thing. His comments galvanized my own feelings toward Kevin. Maybe he didn't matter much to anyone else but for the first time I was fully aware that Kevin did very definitely matter to me.

* * *

I came and I came again to the hospital. After Jeff left, I couldn't afford to resume coming every day because I was struggling under the weight of some of Jeff's other cases as well as the ones we had been splitting and of course my own work load. And there were all the emergency calls on Kevin as well, when I had to show up in the middle of the night. But I came when I could and as often as I could.

We didn't do much together. Kevin had been moved into a small single room just off the nurses' desk. It had none of the advantages of either of Kevin's previous rooms: no window, no Loopy Larry. Most of the time Kevin just lay on his bed with the blankets over his head anyway, and I sat on the bed beside him and made inane, one-way small talk. Or if he was in the seclusion room, I did even less. I just came in and stood until either he calmed down or I had to leave. It was a traumatic and draining couple of weeks for both of us but I tried not to let that stop me. I kept coming back. Someone had to. And it looked like someone was me.

After a while even my ability to make one-sided conversation waned, and to fend off the silence, I started bringing books and reading them aloud to him while he lay huddled under his blankets. What a clever idea, Dr Winslow said, when he caught me at it one day, bibliotherapy. Bibliotherapy, hell. I had just run out of other ideas of what to do with the kid and I still wanted to be there. It was a painless time killer. It had worked when I was a teacher, so I reckoned it wouldn't let me down now. Anyway, I don't think it was especially important what I did, as long as I did it.

So there I was reading to him. I had one of C. S. Lewis's books from the *Chronicles of Narnia*, *The Silver Chair*. We were immersed in a world of mugwumps and giants and princes. At one point in the story a witch captures the main characters and forces them to acknowledge that there is no sun. There is no sun. It is all a dream. The sun is just a dream.

Kevin stirred. 'There are a lot of things that are only dreams,' he said. It was the first time he had spoken to me in almost two weeks.

From where I was sitting, I looked up. I only raised my eyes without lifting my head.

'There are so many things that are no more than only dreams', he said again, 'and then there are things that aren't dreams.'

I nodded.

'And sometimes it's hard to tell the two apart.'

He still lay on his side, the blankets up over his shoulders. He stared ahead of him and not in my direction. 'Sometimes I don't want to tell the two apart. Sometimes I don't know if things are real or if they're only dreams.'

Again I nodded.

'Maybe it's just a dream I had. Maybe Jeff's coming back. Maybe he's not gone at all. Maybe I just dreamed it and I'm going to wake up again.'

'I don't think it was a dream, Kevin.'

He looked over the edge of the blanket at me. 'You're not a dream, are you?'

'No, I'm real.'

'I thought so,' he said, and I could not tell if the fact relieved or dismayed him.

We sat together, wrapped up in threads of sinewy silence.

'But I don't really want to know,' he said. 'I wish I didn't. I wish I could just believe what I wanted. I wish I couldn't tell the difference.'

I said nothing.

'I want to stay crazy. It's better that way.'

And the stillness spun up around me, up around my ears like the silk of a caterpillar. For many minutes there was no sound.

Then Kevin peered over the edge of his blanket at me again. For the first time, he looked right at me. He had to raise up a bit on one elbow to do it. 'You don't believe me, do you?'

'I don't want to.'

'It's better being crazy. I told you that before and I'm right. It's better being crazy because if you don't like the way it is here then you can have dreams. And if you don't like the dreams, then they come and give you shots and you don't feel anything anyway and you just drift around. Dead. Half-dead. Alive but like you're dead. You just drift around alive, but dead. And it all seems the same after a while.'

'That's no life, Kevin. What kind of life is that?'

'Who wants life? What kind of life is this?'

'What kind of life is anything, Kevin, when you think like that?'

He flopped back down, unperturbed, and stared at the ceiling. 'Being crazy's not so bad, Tor. People leave you alone.'

'I don't think you're crazy, Kevin. I think you've just been playing one big, long game with everyone. I think maybe you've been playing it so long now that the game seems more real to you than your real life does. I think you've forgotten what it's like not to play the game. But I don't think you're crazy, Kevin. Loopy Larry's crazy. But not you.'

'I'm just like Loopy Larry.'

'No, you're not, Kevin. You're a fox. You're a fox run to ground.'

'*I* seen him do it.'

I paused, baffled.

'*I* seen him. He says, Kevin, come here. He says, see what your sister's done? She peed the floor. He says, you wipe it up. I didn't have anything to do it with.'

'Kevin, what are you talking about?'

He looked at me. 'You want to know why I'm crazy? You want to know why I'm in here, you think you know so much?'

I did not answer.

'I didn't have nothing to wipe the pee up with. And I stood there because I was scared to move in case he'd take after me. And he says, use your hands. So I came over and I tried to wipe it up with my hands. He says, what should I do to her, Kevin, for peeing the floor? My mom was standing there, and he says to her, Josie – that was my mother's name – he says, Josie, go get the hot sauce out of the cupboard. And my mom does. And he takes Carol by the hair. He pulls her over and he says, I'm going to make you drink this, 'cause you peed the floor. This'll make you remember not to.'

The blankets slipped away from Kevin's shoulders. He clutched at them with his fingers but he did not pull them up. His face was pale.

'Carol wouldn't open her mouth, so he put her between his legs and yanked her hair back so she cried. And he shook the bottle of hot sauce down her. Carol screamed, so I screamed too. I screamed at him for doing that and he laughed. He says to me, that makes you talk, don't it? Can talk if you feel like it. I wanna hear you talk some more. And he put her head back and he shook the bottle and he shook it and he shook it. And I screamed. I screamed at him to stop. I screamed at my mother. I said, why don't you make him stop? I hit him and I screamed and he laughed. He let go of Carol and he told her to pee on the floor now. He says you pee when I tell you. He made her take off her clothes and he says, pee. And when she squatted down to pee, he kicked her, hard, right in that private place girls have. And he says, I told you never to pee on the floor. And Carol was crying. And I begged him to stop. I got down on my knees. I told him I'd talk to him. Whatever he'd want if he'd just stop it. I was begging. I prayed to God. I was on my knees and I begged.

'Then Carol sicked up. He was holding her and making her drink the hot sauce and she sicked it up all over him. He got mad. He started screaming and hollering at her. She shouldn't ought've done that, he yells. She'd be real sorry now. Lot sorrier than for peeing on the floor. And he picks her up by the hair and throws her across the room. I ran after her. I ran and he knocked me over and he kicked me. He kicked me so hard I peed blood and it showed on my pants. I was scared he was gonna get me then for it, but he had Carol. By the rocking chair. He sat on her and he held her head by the hair and banged her head against the floor. Over and over and over. Right by the rocking chair.

'I was crying and screaming at him, but my mom, she just stood there. And I yell at her, I say to my mom, *help* her! Make him stop! And my mom just stood there. She says, leave them alone. It isn't any of your business.

'When he stood up, Carol didn't move. She just lay there, and he says, that shows you. Don't it? That shows you who's boss in this house, and it sure ain't some little girl who pees the floor. Some little girl that can't even read. He said that to embarrass her. She was in first grade for the second time and she still couldn't learn to read yet. And I hated him most of all for saying that, for making Carol feel bad. I wanted to kill him.

'Now get up, he says to Carol. And Carol, she doesn't move at all. She just lays there. I see her bleeding. It was coming out of her ear. I kept praying he wouldn't see it, because he'd be mad again for her messing up the floor. And he hollered at her because she wouldn't get up. Get up, Carol, I said, do like he says. And I kept praying to God that she'd hurry up and get up so he wouldn't be madder than he already was. I kept praying. To God and to Jesus, for them to listen to me. I kept saying, *please,* Jesus, make her get up. But she didn't. So he picked up the iron plate from the stove. And he says, get up, Carol, or I'm going to make you really hurt. And she didn't get up. So he threw it at her. And he threw it again.'

Kevin paused. He lay rigid as death on the bed, all his muscles tight, his fingers white where they gripped the blanket.

'You know what. I seen her brains come out all the way across the floor at me. I could have touched them if I'd put my hand out. I could have touched Carol's brains.'

Kevin stopped talking, and in the sudden, short interlude of stillness, the hospital noises came whooshing back in around us like air into a vacuum.

Kevin turned slightly, as if to look at me, but he didn't. 'And my mom seen. My momma seen the whole thing and she just stood right there. She said, leave him alone, it ain't none of your business. And she never once did a thing.'

Chapter Twenty-nine

Back in the office, I went through my telephone file to locate Marlys Menzies's number. I dialed.

Torey Hayden, I said. Do you remember me? I'm Kevin Richter's therapist. At Mortenson Hospital. She didn't remember me, I suspect. Her voice had the hollow ring of false recognition. She didn't remember me from the *Torrey Canyon*.

Was there an abuse incident in his history? I asked. A very serious one, where a child was either badly injured or killed?

Kevin Richter. Hmmm. Mmmm. Let's see. Let me think. After a long pause, she asked if she could call me back. Yes, I said. Feeling angry and disgruntled, I hung up the phone.

At 2:30 when I was down in the reception office, drinking a can of Dr Pepper and chatting with Shirley and the girls, the phone rang.

'Torey?'

'Yes?'

'This is Marlys at Social Services. I found the Richter file for you. I checked. There was an incident. Quite a while back now. About nine years. A Carol Marie Richter, aged seven years, two months, was battered to death by the stepfather during a family argument. He was drunk apparently. Jailed for the offense. Four years.'

'He got four years for murdering a child?'

'Yes, well, you know how those things are.'

'Is there anything else in that file? I mean, are there going to be any other skeletons to fall out of the closet, to make a sick pun?'

She thought that was very funny. I hadn't meant it to be. I hadn't realized what I was saying until it was half out. 'No, no,' she said midst her giggles, 'nothing special. I suppose you could even see the chart if you wanted to get clearance.'

It was an old, old story this, made ugly not only by the principal characters but by the bungling bureaucracy that staged it. Over and over and over again Kevin's stepfather had abused the children. Over and over the children were returned to him and his wife, even after Carol's death. Of the five children, three were now permanently gone from the home.

'How is it,' I asked, 'that social services knows so much about this family and yet there was none of this, neither of the abuse Kevin suffered from his stepfather nor the dreadful thing about Carol in Kevin's file at Garson Gayer? I've been working with him almost eighteen months now and I never knew any of this.'

She did not answer immediately. 'Well,' she said after a bit, 'I think maybe we just thought it might be better for Kevin if he had a completely fresh start when he went into that home. He hadn't had what you could call a really good childhood. He had had so many bad trips already that people were terribly prejudiced about the boy. I mean, you've never seen a youngster who has had more things go wrong for him. If it could, it has. After a point, no one wanted to touch him. It was hopeless. So I guess it just seemed best to wipe the slate clean and start over. To just forget he had a past before he went into care.'

'But the thing is, Marlys, *Kevin* never forgot his past.'

'Yes, well ...'

'Whose decision was it to do that? To not tell anyone at Garson Gayer what his previous life had been like?'

'Just a general consensus.'

'Whose?'

'Ours, I guess.'

'You know, of course, it would have made my job a lot easier to have known these things all along. They explain a lot.'

'Yes, but ...'

'Are there any other surprises lurking?'

She sighed. 'I guess if you've heard that, you've heard the worst.'

It wasn't much consolation.

Things didn't change much between Kevin and me. They went on pretty much the way they had before he'd made me the gift of that small story.

I guess I had expected more out of it. I guess I'd expected that when I finally found myself with all the pieces of the puzzle, I'd be able to get it together at last. But that wasn't so. Instead, Kevin returned to silence or at least to near silence, and his life and my life continued on in a very ordinary manner, if one could take our circumstances as ordinary.

I kept reading. Every day, every hour we spent together, I read. I don't believe Kevin was listening to me read. Hunched up atop the bed or over in the orange plastic chair, he would sit with his arms resting on his knees, chin on them, and he'd stare off. Occasionally, some thought would break to the surface and he would talk to me for a few moments. Usually it was a complete non sequitur to what I was reading. In a way, because I knew he wasn't listening, it made the whole act of reading aloud seem a little ridiculous and I questioned myself for doing it. However, the books gave substance to my being there. They gave validity. And like the window in the other room, they took away our self-consciousness about other matters, the real matters that brought us together.

'I don't think there must be a God,' Kevin said to me one afternoon. I was reading *Men of Iron* and spewing out such lovely lines as, 'Thou art as harebrained knave as ever drew the breath of life,' quoth Gascoyne.

I looked up, relieved for a break. The book was marvelous but it was meant to be read aloud by someone like Richard Burton.

Kevin turned his head to look at me. 'Do you believe there's a God? I was just thinking and I don't think there can be.'

'What makes you feel that way?'

'No God would make a world where there are so many people who got no one to love them. If it had been done to a plan, there would have been enough people to love everybody.'

'There's a lot of people, Kevin. Maybe there are enough.'

'No. No, there isn't. There are a lot of people in the world who aren't really loved by anybody.' He paused and studied his hand. 'I mean real love, where people love you regardless of what you are.'

'Well, I must admit, I don't think that it's necessarily God's fault. I reckon God gave us all the equipment to do it with.'

'Hmmph.' He sneered at me. 'You don't know what I'm even talking about, Torey. You haven't the slightest idea. You've always been loved, haven't you? You always had people to love you.'

I didn't reply.

'Well, you have, haven't you?'

'Yes, I have.'

'Then you haven't the slightest idea, not even the tiniest little inkling of what I'm talking about. You got no idea about never being loved.'

'Perhaps not.'

'You know what most people die from?'

I shook my head.

'Heart rot. It's a kind of invisible cancer. You get it in your heart. You can feel it. It eats you up inside. It's what you get when all you do is get born into the world. Your heart's never got any use. And so you get heart rot and your heart rots away. Sometimes a long time before your body does. Only it doesn't matter because once you're dead in your heart, you're dead.'

I said nothing.

'So the way I see it, there can't be a real God. No God would make such a loused-up world as this one.'

When I continued not to speak he turned to me. 'Do you have any idea what it's like? Do you know how it feels to realize there's four billion people in the world and not one of them cares a shit about you?'

'I care, Kevin.'

'But who are you? Just somebody who's here now and will be gone. You're just here because I'm your job. You're paid to come and care for me. You wouldn't have ever come. You wouldn't have cared, if they hadn't paid you.'

'And there's a lot of times I haven't been paid.'

'Yes. But in the beginning you only came because you were paid. No other reason. You wouldn't have come then if it hadn't been your job. Would you? Tell the truth.'

'But I did come.'

'But you wouldn't have, Torey, would you? Not if they hadn't paid you. Would you? Tell the truth. You wouldn't have come.'

'This isn't fair, Kevin. I didn't know you then. How could I have come?'

'So I'm right.'

I sighed in frustration. 'Yes, you probably are right. I probably wouldn't have come. But I didn't know you then, Kevin. You can't blame me because I didn't know about you. That was hardly my fault. There's zillions of people I don't know and I won't accept any blame for not caring about them. If you don't know something, you can't do much about it. But that's a false argument anyway, Kevin. It isn't whether or not

I came because I was paid to. The important thing is that I came back. And back again. Out of all the kids I work with and have worked with, I came back to you. Time and again I've come back. Sure, I'm paid to, all right, because it's my job and if I weren't paid to, I couldn't afford to come here at all because I'd have to go out and do some other kind of work. But regardless, I still don't have to come here. There's lots of kids out there I could be working with, if I just wanted to earn a salary. And a whole damned lot of them are easier than you. But I came back here. I chose to come back and don't you forget I made that choice. The beginning already happened and if it weren't for my job and the fact someone paid me to do what I do, I would never have been here then and I sure as hell wouldn't be here now. So don't keep harping at me, Kevin. Don't keep telling me I come because I am paid. Yes, I am paid. We both know that. It's old news. But that has nothing whatsoever to do with why I keep coming here. The way doesn't justify the end. I'm here in the end because I've chosen to be. Because I care. How I got here doesn't matter.'

'I thought,' he said very quietly, 'that it was the other way around, that it was the end that didn't justify the means.'

'Oh Kevin, for Pete's sake, don't go looking for what isn't there all the time.'

Bringing up a hand, he rubbed it over his face wearily. He sighed. 'Yeah. Maybe you're right. Maybe it doesn't matter. Maybe it is enough,' he said. 'I guess I was just wanting more.'

Chapter Thirty

The days turned into weeks. The weeks passed. They made up a month. Still I did nothing but read aloud.

It was an eerie time. Kevin talked to me with diminishing frequency and, when he did talk, there was an increasingly irritable note in his voice. But for the most part he just sat, hunched up on his orange chair, and he watched me with an unflinching, brooding gaze as I read. I could feel emotion building up in him, although for a long time I could not tell what it was, partly, I suppose, because I was so busy reading. However, each day he grew a little fiercer, his attitude toward me a little surlier. It was hard for me to gauge whether or not this was all aimed in my direction or if he was just feeling this way generally toward everyone because he hardly spoke to me anymore and of course, he never spoke to anyone else.

But soon I didn't need much of a gauge. Whatever it was, it was growing strong enough to be almost palpable.

Anger. Hate. I recognized it finally. It was the self-same white-hot emotion Kevin had had back at Garson Gayer before Jeff came into the therapy sessions. But unlike then, he didn't acknowledge it. Nor did he direct it. It just sat with us, growing.

I grew nervous in the face of that kind of anger. It had appeared slowly, in a most ethereal way over the passing weeks, on the edge of conversations more than in them, in the shadow of other emotions more than with them. But it fed upon the silence that had come between Kevin and me and soon it was strong enough to be perceivable even over the continuous drone of my voice. Yet Kevin never said a word about it to me. As frightening as his hate had been at Garson Gayer, at least it was there out sitting in the stone cold light of day for me to see. But this time he never acknowledged it at all. Kevin never even gave it the feeble substance of words.

One afternoon I came in late. There had been another boy on my mind that day and I had gotten held up at the clinic because of him.

When I did arrive, I found Kevin pacing in his small room. Hands in his pockets, he shuffled up and down. It was the most activity I had seen in him in ages, and I wondered if they'd been monkeying around with his medications again. He seemed jumpy and distracted.

'You're *late*,' he said accusingly when I entered. 'How come you're late?'

'I got caught at the clinic.'

'It's five o'clock. You were supposed to be here at four-thirty. You're a whole half hour late.'

'I'm sorry, Kev. But I was having problems with another boy. I couldn't get away any sooner.'

'I don't care. What do I care about some other boy? You're late here. Four-thirty is your time with me. Didn't that other kid know that? You are supposed to be here with me at four-thirty and not anywhere else. I had to wait a whole half-hour for you.'

'I'm sorry if I upset you.'

'I'm not upset. It's just your fault for being late.' He flopped down on the bed.

I sorted out the book from my box and began to page through it. 'You want to read today, Kevin?' I suggested. I just wasn't up to reading. The day had been a hard one for me. Too hard, really. Besides, he seemed so edgy. I thought perhaps it would calm him down. 'Here, you read, okay? I'll listen. How about that?'

Kevin took the book from me and studied the page we were on. Then abruptly he smiled. 'This is just like the beginning, the very beginning. Remember that? Way back then? When you first came to see me and you wanted me to read. Remember how I was then?'

I smiled too. God Almighty, that seemed a long time ago. It seemed a lifetime back.

Then just as suddenly he threw the book down on the bed. 'I don't wanna read. What do I want to read for?' Restless again, he paced a few moments.

Going over to my box of materials, he knelt and took the lid off. In rough motions, he went through the contents.

Eventually, he dumped everything out on the bed and then began putting it back, bit by bit. The puppets he pulled over his hands, wiggled, tugged off and threw back in the box. The carton of crayons he opened, tried a couple on the edge of the box, studied the results, rejected. The colored wooden blocks he examined and, unable to figure out their use, pitched them back in. All the paper in there, the pencils, the felt-tipped markers, the sketchpads he riffled through before discarding them with the rest. 'There isn't anything good to do in here any more,' he grumbled. 'You never have anything interesting for me to do.'

'What do you want to do?'

'I dunno. Something interesting. You never let me do anything interesting.'

'Well, give me an idea of what you want to do.'

He shrugged. He thought a few moments. 'I want to paint. I haven't painted in a long, long time. That's what I want to do. But you don't got any stuff.'

Caught completely unprepared for such a request, I pondered it. After such a long period of inactivity, I was eager to comply with anything that might indicate a lift in his depression. And I was desperate to channel his irritable restlessness. Doing anything was better than doing nothing.

'Maybe,' I suggested, 'we could borrow some supplies from the unit schoolroom.' I knew from previous raids that the school program was held in a room at the end of the ward and that there was a large closet in back that held a wealth of supplies. Undoubtedly, there would be materials for painting there.

It was a simple task to get permission from one of the nurses to go back there and get some materials. Armed with the keys, I headed down the hall. Kevin decided to come along and help me carry things.

I let us into the schoolroom. Carefully, I shut the door behind us. I unlocked the closet at the back of the room.

The closet was pantry sized, maybe eight feet long and four or five feet wide. On both sides there were floor-to-ceiling shelves filled with a glorious array of things, every conceivable type of art paper, tempera paints, watercolors, boxes of crayons and chalk and colored pencils. There were books and note pads and workbooks. It was chockablock with all the sorts of things that my greedy little teacher's heart coveted.

'Here,' I said, taking down some paper and giving it to him. 'You can carry that. What kind of paint do you want? Tempera? Or do you want to use watercolor? Here, look these over.'

He stood behind me, between me and the door, while I rummaged around at the far end of the closet getting different types of paint out.

'Kev, which do you want?'

He didn't respond.

'Kevin, come here and decide. Do you want these? Or this kind? Or we could use these and these. What do you think? You're the artist. You decide.'

The lights went out.

I turned in the darkness. 'Kevin?'

There was no sound. I could see nothing whatsoever.

'Did you hit the light switch? Or have we had a power failure? What a place to be stuck in a power failure, huh!'

I could hear him but he said nothing. Suspicion began to build in my head. 'What's going on, Kevin? Did you turn off the light?'

I heard him move toward me. There in the closet, he did not have to move far before we were chest to chest. It remained so black that I couldn't even make out his outline.

'Kevin, move back.'

He pressed against me.

'Kevin, I said move back. I'm not kidding. I mean it. Move yourself back.'

He pressed closer.

'Kevin, I said move *back*.'

His body was heavy against me; his breath was hot. Fear came bolting up into my mouth like bile.

'Don't do this, Kevin. Don't do it. Don't.'

'I hate you,' he whispered back. The words were cold, like a knife blade. His hands were on me. On my shoulder, on my breasts.

'Come on, Kevin, give over. Stop it. Cut it out.'

'I *hate* you.'

I was scared. I was scared like I had never been scared in all my life. No other time, no other situation had ever made me feel the way I did just then. Everything gave way to fear. Even the hyped-up bravado I normally felt in moments of high tension. All was gone from me except for fear. The sickly sweet stench of it hung in the air about me.

His hand was fumbling on my shirt, groping at the buttons. His body was tight against mine, heavy enough to press me painfully against the shelves in back.

And it was the little things that added eerie reality to the moment, the soft crinkling of fallen paper as it was walked on, the waxy odor of crayons, which had always meant warm, sunny classrooms and children's laughter to me before, but never again. Sweat had run down along my body and through my shirt. I felt a piece of newsprint stick to me as I managed to move a little to relieve the pressure on my backbone.

Thank God for small buttons. He could not get them undone in the blackness and I kept wriggling beneath his fingers to make sure he wouldn't. Yet I moved slowly because I was afraid to upset him too much.

Then came the unaccountably loud sound of his fly being unzipped.

'Kevin, *stop* it!'

'I'm a man now, Momma. I'm gonna show you I'm a man.'

'Kevin!'

We fumbled violently in the dark for a few moments, him pressing closer, me wiggling first this way and then that. He had not managed to breach any of my clothes yet, and I was grateful for tough old Levi's and a sturdy bra beneath my shirt.

'I'm gonnna show you, Momma,' he whispered.

'I'm not your momma, Kevin.'

'Shut up. You bitch. Shut up, you.'

Silence. The stink of fear was nauseating me. It smelled like jasmine or orange blossoms, only far too sweet, and under it was a musky odor, like fox.

'Let me go, Kevin. I'm not your momma. It's just me. I'm Torey. I'm not your momma.'

'Shut up, bitch.' His hand came up under my chin. 'I'm gonna make you hurt. I'm gonna make you know what hurt is.'

'You don't want to hurt me, Kevin,' I said. His body was against me; I could hear his breathing near my left ear. I could feel the rock-hard warmth of his penis against my left side.

'It's me, Kevin. *Me.* No one else. You don't want to hurt *me.*'

'I said shut up. Now *shut up!* I mean it. Shut up!' He forced himself against me, pinning me into the corner of the shelves. I could hear him though; I could hear his breathing. He was growing upset.

'Zip up your pants, Kevin. Zip them up and turn the lights on and let's get out of here.'

'*I hate you!* You bitch. You bitch, bitch, bitch, bitch, *bitch!* I hate you, I hate you, I hate you. I hate you so much.' He was almost sobbing, his voice almost incoherent.

'I'm not your momma, Kevin. I'm not her.'

'*Shut up!*' He swung at me to shut me up. In the close space he could not help but hit me fully, and because I had not known it was coming, I hadn't ducked. He hit me squarely on the side of my head. My ears rang.

I hit him back. Immediately. It won me enough space to reach the light switch. I turned it on and what had been a small eternal night dissolved into forty-watt brightness.

I had hit Kevin hard. He'd sunk to the floor with his arms over his face. There was blood, although I wasn't sure if it was his or mine. He was crying, either from pain or misery or both. I stood a moment, my hand still over the switch, and watched him. I had to admit, I wasn't feeling very sorry for him.

Chapter Thirty-one

There had been no choice about whether or not to report what had taken place between Kevin and me in the art closet. While it was over and done with and I had come out of the incident none the worse for the wear, it was not the sort of thing one could shrug off.

I was feeling angry and unsettled. The experience had been humiliating for me, regardless of what might have prompted it and whether Kevin ever did distinguish me from his mother. But reporting it was even more awful. I guess I should have known such a thing was a possibility when working with a seventeen-year-old but up until then I had not given it serious consideration. In my baggy jeans and work shirts, I was hardly dressing provocatively, and Kevin's sexuality had never been a problem before. When it had appeared, Jeff had dealt with it, explaining to Kevin those things he needed to know.

Even in the midst of the turmoil that followed, however, I could not believe Kevin had plotted the act beforehand. A lot of emotions had been building up in him over the preceding weeks. The big breakthrough I had anticipated after he had told me about Carol had perhaps happened after all, although in a way I hadn't expected.

While Kevin was and always had been openly hostile regarding his stepfather, this sudden violence led me to speculate that the hard-core hate he nursed was actually for his mother. It was easier to hate his stepfather. After all, he'd murdered Carol. He had perpetrated all the abuse. And he was an outsider to the family unit. That produced a straightforward, uncomplicated sort of hate. But it was Kevin's feelings for his mother that abruptly began taking precedence in my thoughts. Added to the murky complexities of any child's relationship with its mother was the fact that Kevin's mother had been able to abandon her son willingly in favor of a violent, brutal man. That experience must have hurt Kevin in a way that someone like me with my normal experiences in life had no concept of. And perhaps most important, I now saw the impact that Kevin's mother's behavior on the night of Carol's death had had. She had betrayed Carol by standing there and doing nothing. And she had murdered her relationship with her son. He had not forgotten and he had certainly not forgiven. I had little doubt that by the time she gave Kevin up to the state when he was twelve, he had long since given her up.

So, I could not believe, even in the worst of the chaos that followed the incident in the closet, that Kevin had consciously planned to corner me. It was just one of those things. The weeks had piled in upon themselves and the emotions had just become too much to control. In the dark of an art closet, anyone unfortunate enough to be in the way could have been his mother.

But in the heat of the moment, lucid analysis didn't matter much. My own emotions continued to run high. It just wasn't the sort of occurrence that one could be totally rational about. And I wasn't exactly in a forgiving mood myself, when I had to sit down with Dr Rosenthal and Dr Winslow and then the nursing staff and tell them what had transpired and what I believe led up to it and then answer their questions. I felt nothing but embarrassment and confusion. I was angry with myself for having gotten into such a vulnerable position. I was resentful and suspicious of the other people and their allusions and implications. I was distressed that I had managed to sit behind a book for four weeks and feel all that anger building up in Kevin and still was stupid enough not to do something constructive about it. But most of all I was humiliated, not only because I was forced to sit and talk repeatedly about such personal matters with every passing soul who showed an interest, but chiefly because my professional judgment had taken such a crushingly public blow.

I knew what had to be done. I knew when four-thirty rolled around the next afternoon that I had to return to the hospital and see Kevin. It was like falling off a horse. One has to get right back on again then and there or one never will. So, gritting my teeth to get by the nurses' station, I went back.

Kevin was in his room under the blankets of his bed. He had pulled them so high that not even the top of his head showed. Well, I said, and sat down in the orange chair, that was that. We goofed. But it was over and we were best off forgetting that it had happened. I wasn't angry, I said to him when he still refused to come out from under the covers, and immediately I realized I was. The hurt was too new. When he lay there and wouldn't talk to me and wouldn't even come out from under the stupid blanket and look at me, I exploded. He'd ruined everything I'd tried to do for him, I said. He'd betrayed me, more in heart and spirit than in body.

Kevin for his part let me have my little bit of scream therapy. He just lay there and never moved a muscle.

Back at the clinic the next morning I was called down to Dr Rosenthal's office. He wasn't alone. Dr Winslow sat, like an aging Adonis, and smiled sweetly.

'We've been talking,' Dr Rosenthal said, 'and we've come to the conclusion that it would be best to close the Richter case. Dr Winslow and I have discussed it and it seems the best for all concerned if you and I pull out of it and leave it to them at the hospital.'

I looked at him.

Silence.

'I can get myself out of this,' I said. 'It was stupid. I know it was my fault. But it's over now.'

'No,' he replied.

'The worst of it's behind us,' I said. 'I went over to the hospital last night and Kevin and I, we can survive it. I'm quite sure. If we just have a little time.'

'No,' said Dr Rosenthal.

'Why?' I looked from one man to the other. Abruptly all my emotions, all the anger and embarrassment and humiliation, gave way to panic. Of course the possibility of closing down the case existed when something like this occurred.

The possibility always existed. But I'd never given it much thought.

'Couldn't I just try for a little longer?' I asked. 'Maybe if you wanted to supervise the case … if you wanted to come in yourself personally …' I said, first to Dr Rosenthal and then when he did not respond, to Dr Winslow. Desperately, I searched their faces for some negation of what I now was realizing was inevitable.

Dr Rosenthal shook his head. 'I'm afraid this just isn't the best case for you, Torey. Kevin's had a traumatic life. You're young; you're good looking; you're awfully female, whether you mean to be or not. It makes it too easy for things to happen.'

For the first time since the whole crazy episode had started, I began to cry. Was this going to be it? Was one and a half whole years of my life going to end like this? So suddenly? So simply? So stupidly? Just because of all the millions of times I had had to guess with this kid, this one time I had guessed wrong?

'We'll get a male therapist in,' Dr Winslow said. His tone was comforting and he leaned toward me.

'Yes,' Dr Rosenthal agreed. 'Look how well Kevin did with Jeff Tomlinson. That'd be better. Don't you think? Now, honestly? You yourself were talking about all the bad feelings Kevin had for his mother. Maybe a woman therapist just is not a good idea for him, period. He's too unstable.'

'He's *not* unstable,' I protested. 'It wasn't because …'

Dr Rosenthal raised his shoulders in a shruglike motion. It was a pathetic little movement, and then he looked away. He couldn't meet my eyes any longer. 'It's a tragic way to end a case, Torey, I know that,' he said to his fingers. 'But maybe it'll all be for the best in the end. When everything's said and done.'

'But couldn't I just … ?'

Without looking up, Dr Rosenthal shook his head and I knew it was all over. Eighteen months. And this was all there was.

I went home shattered. I was filled with that sodden, half-sick sort of depression too heavy for tears. Was this it? After all those months of work, was it going to be killed so unceremoniously by twenty unfortunate minutes in an art closet? The horror of what Kevin had tried to do had seemed at the time like the worst thing a kid had ever tried to do to me, but now it was superseded by something that seemed even worse. We could have survived it. Horrible as it was, I knew Kevin and I could have come to terms with it. After all, I was hardly an innocent victim. This was part of the risk one took in this type of profession. I had always known that and I had accepted it the day I chose to go behind the locked doors.

We could have worked it out. But what now? All I had managed to do in the end was to prove Kevin right. No one wanted him and sooner or later, everyone would walk out.

Late that night an old, old friend from my college days showed up. I had not seen Hal in ages, not since the Vietnam War days when we spent our evenings together in dark, smoky coffee houses and planned the Brave New World to the strains of Joan Baez and Peter, Paul and Mary.

Despite its being late and my being terribly out of sorts, I accepted his invitation to dinner. We went to one of those funky, fashionable places where the music is too loud and the hanging plants trail in one's food. We sat in the dark and chatted, a little uneasy with one another because so much had happened in ten years and we were both such different people now.

I went out that evening, I think, to get away from Kevin, away from the present. In his day, I had loved Hal. He'd been the Idealist. Of all of us who'd grown up during those turbulent years with fire in our hearts to change the world, it was he who was really going to do it. No day job for him. No ordinary Establishment life. While I had gone on to graduate school and teaching, Hal had drifted. He'd become an actor, a halfway successful one at that, had been through two marriages and a lot of hard living. But now, a decade on, the smell and feel of the sixties still clung to him. He still spoke with the vocabulary of our lost generation and his dreams were not entirely faded. I sat in the darkness and listened to him and drifted back myself to what seemed a gentler, more hopeful time.

Then Hal began to cry. There had been a reason for looking me up. It hadn't been just a random chance. He pulled out pictures to show me. There was his daughter. And his son, a red-haired, freckle-faced imp. That's Ian, he said to me. Ian was autistic. He had just been committed to a state institution because he had already torn apart two families and Hal just couldn't keep him any longer. Ian was seven.

As Hal wiped back embarrassed tears, neither of us mentioned the irony of Hal's being given a child who had made him leigeman to the most dehumanizing of all society's establishments. Neither of us mentioned the Brave New World either. But the silence yanked me mercilessly back into the here and now.

So in the companionable blackness we quaffed too much Blue Ribbon together and dallied with food neither of us wanted. Finally, I told him about me and Kevin, just to take his mind off things. Both of us ended up crying in our beer, weeping for a world that never was, save dreams.

Part III

Chapter Thirty-two

Life went on. The cold months of winter turned to spring. March came without daffodils that year because it was too dry. April came with the heavy, wet snowstorms, which should have been in February. And May at last brought sun.

There was a new doctor sharing my office with me. He was an older man named Jules. He wasn't much to look at, short, fiftyish, balding and somewhat overweight, but he had such a sweet and self-effacing manner about him that all the women in the clinic were at least a little in love with him at one point or another. In his spare time Jules was quite a serious sculptor and he spent a lot of his evenings and weekends at shows and galleries. Indeed, I suspect Jules had more the heart of an artist than a doctor. So much of our office conversation revolved not around our cases, as Jeff's and my discussions had, but around our artistic pursuits.

While there never was the magic between Jules and me that there had been with Jeff, I liked Jules a lot and was glad someone was back in the office with me. I'd grown very lonely in there with the three phones. Jeff I had heard from a couple of times since he had left, but he never put an address on his envelopes, so I could never write back. I got a St Patrick's Day card from him, for goodness knows what reason, since neither of us was Irish. And I got another card on my birthday in May. Jeff seemed to have settled into his new work in California and sounded happy. But I didn't know. Cards don't say much. He never mentioned Kevin nor the clinic nor whether or not Hans was still with him.

Also during midwinter I met Hugh, and our relationship blossomed over the following months. Hugh was, of all things, a pest exterminator and he drove around in an old VW bus with dead bugs painted all over it. With that kind of sense of humor I couldn't help but love him.

And of course, Charity still provided excitement in my life. She was changing, however. Just after Christmas she was transferred to the other third grade from the one she had been in. I was never sure why the move was made. Her new third-grade teacher, Mrs Thatcher, had taken special notice of Charity and arranged a lot of activities not only to bring Charity's shaky academics up to a passing level but also to provide her with some stability during all her free hours. Mrs Thatcher was an older woman, married and with a family of teenagers. She lived on a small hobby farm to the west of the city, and on weekends she took Charity out and let her feed the goats and help in the barn and clean out the chicken coop. The teacher wasn't the same sort of softy I was; she demanded certain standards of behavior from Charity before she could come, but they were attainable ones. It made all the difference in Charity. For the first time she had genuine 'older sisters' and a real 'mother' who treated her as a mother should treat a daughter. The change was dramatic.

Of course, I could still expect Charity regularly during the week, but it wasn't the same old Charity. She had new clothes, including a pair of genuine Levi's with the little red tag and a jump suit with a fashion-designer's name. She became a regular clothes horse, looking through my magazines and pointing out what she wanted next. She had also begun a diet to lose weight. Apparently Mrs Thatcher was keeping a chart at school and weighing Charity every week. I was very much in favor of this because, while Charity was not grossly obese, she was overweight for her age and the kids teased her. And I admired the teacher for having the power to get Charity on a diet and to make her stick to it, because I had tried and failed several times. However, now Charity had grown quite self-righteous about the whole matter. She knew what she should and shouldn't eat, and because Mrs Thatcher's family ate only health foods, Charity began to sound like Adele Davis as she went through my cupboards. I imagine she must have been a right royal pain at home with her clan, where the meals consisted mainly of junk food.

I was pleased to see the teacher taking such an active interest in Charity, and Charity, in turn, responding so well, but at the same time, I had to admit to feeling a little left out with all Charity's stories of what went on during the weekends at Mrs Thatcher's farm. There had always been a sort of primitive charm to Charity, and now I could see her outgrowing it and daily becoming more and more like the rest of us. Undoubtedly, that was the way it should be and I was happy for her because she was so obviously happy, but it was sad, nonetheless.

Around the time of my birthday in May, I went out to New York on a working vacation, and Hugh joined me for the last of it so that we could drive out the length of Long Island, catch the ferry over to New London and go up through New England. I half hoped to see the battered old VW with all its dead bugs waiting outside my Manhattan hotel but instead I found Hugh in a quite respectable Ford rental car. We took off for a week of walks through old cemeteries, picnics in chilly New Hampshire wayside parks and a diet of fried clams and scallops. We returned home to find May touching June with the worst heat wave in fifty years.

In our small, windowless office the odor of rodents and birds was suffocating in the unnatural heat. Jules sat, sweating over case reports. He had his suit jacket off, his sleeves rolled up and his handkerchief tied around his forehead to keep the perspiration from dripping onto the papers. But the way he had the handkerchief done up, its tail hung down on his nose and he looked like a trainee for Jesse James's gang who had flunked basic bankrobber's kerchief tying.

'Look there, did you notice?' He pointed up at the bulletin board above his desk to where a blue prize ribbon from an art show hung.

I hadn't noticed. What had caught my attention was a memo on my desk. All it said was 'Kevin Richter' and a telephone number.

I sat down immediately and phoned. A secretary at Seven Oaks answered.

I knew what Seven Oaks was; I had had a couple of kids go there before. It was a lock-up program for adolescent boys, sort of a mini-prison before they committed crimes serious enough to warrant graduation to the real thing. The institution itself was spread out over twelve acres of new, low ranch-style buildings, which housed forty boys. It was well run for a program of that sort, but I knew the psychiatric facilities were minimal and I didn't think there was anything in the program geared to deal with serious psychological problems. To my knowledge most of the boys were delinquent, not disturbed, just kids who grew up in the wrong environment and had learned to cope with it too effectively. Seven Oaks's main capacity was in helping the boys unlearn these behaviors and discover new, more socially acceptable ones to put in their place. It seemed like a rather unlikely place for Kevin to end up.

But that was where Kevin had gone. He had been in the hospital for another two months after I'd stopped seeing him. Then had come the hard decision of what to do with him. More by accident than design, he had ended up in Seven Oaks. It was a trial run. There wasn't room available in any more appropriate program, including the state facilities, and so he was given six months at Seven Oaks to see if he could make a go of it. If not, he was to be slotted into one of the long-term wards at the state hospital, because he would have reached the age of majority.

From the account the counselor was giving me, things hadn't changed much. Kevin was still full of his old problems. He talked very rarely and could go weeks between comments. His appearance was poor and disheveled. He refused to participate in things the other boys were doing and in general appeared tired and depressed.

Their main difficulty, of course, was his speech. His silence was impenetrable and it precluded their being able to do anything else with him because he wouldn't even write notes to them. Kevin's file had mentioned me in connection with the speech problem ... There was one of those poignant little pauses, the same sort as I had heard so many other times, harking clear back to when Dana Wendolowski had first phoned from Garson Gayer. Would I be willing to resume therapy? the counselor asked.

I would, I said without hesitation.

Like Big Brother, Dr Rosenthal already knew that Seven Oaks had phoned and why. He met me outside the reception office when I was on my way to lunch, and with neither of us saying anything, we both knew the other knew.

'May I?' I asked.

A smile flickered momentarily across his face. 'If you want.'

'I do want.'

He had his teapot in his hand. It was full of water. He peered into the depths of it before looking back at me. 'You knew, of course,' he said, 'that if it had been my choice, I wouldn't have taken you off the case in February. It was Dr Winslow's decision to take you off. I couldn't do anything about it. Kevin was Winslow's patient. But I don't suppose I ever thought you should have stopped.'

I hadn't known that but I was glad he'd told me.

Then an unexpectedly conspiratorial grin touched Dr Rosenthal's lips. 'He's a son of a bitch, isn't he, that Winslow? I always have thought so.'

* * *

That night was hot and sticky, more like August than June. I lay down with just a sheet over me and stared into the summer darkness. The drone of distant traffic filtered through the blinds. I had no illusions about why I had been asked back. One single quirk of fate kept Kevin and me bound together. If it had not been for my elective-mutism research, my single claim to expertise, I doubt they would have ever bothered to distinguish me from the hundreds of other therapists available in the city. Most likely, I would have left Kevin dancing on that sunny day the previous May and I would never have heard of him again. That was the way it usually was.

It seemed strange to me to think that the only thing that had brought us back together not once, but twice, was something as incidental and undeliberate as my unsuccessful attempt years earlier to understand why a child I'd known refused to speak. If it hadn't been for that spark of interest, which had kindled my research so much later, I would have been no more special than any other psychologist. There would have been no reason to take the trouble to keep coming back to me. The irony was that his mutism had ceased to be the issue between Kevin and me only five days after we had met.

When morning came, I rose and dressed and started the long journey down to Seven Oaks.

Kevin clearly had not expected me. I hadn't even thought to ask if they had told him I was coming. Apparently they hadn't, because when I entered the dayroom where Kevin was sitting, his eyes widened and his jaw dropped, as if I had been a ghost.

'Do you want to go with Miss Hayden?' the counselor asked.

Numbly Kevin nodded and got up. We were led into a small interview room and left alone. I sat down in one of the chairs. Kevin just stood by the doorway and stared at me.

'I never thought you were coming back. I thought you were mad. I thought you maybe hated me now.'

I smiled. 'I was mad for a while. But that didn't have anything to do with it. Dr Winslow and my boss thought it would be better if you and I had a rest from one another for a while. But now it's over.'

Kevin smiled very slightly. It was a disbelieving smile and just touched the corners of his lips. He still would not approach me. He remained at the door and continued to stare at me, as if I had materialized from air.

'So how's it been? Why don't you tell me about what's happened in these last months?'

He just stared. The smile still played on his lips. 'You know what?' he said softly.

'What's that?'

'I knew you'd come. I knew you had to come. I kept praying and praying you'd come back. I kept thinking, if there is a God, please hear me. Please do this one thing for me. I'd do everything you wanted, if God'd only let you come back.'

I sat in silence.

'I knew you would. I knew you wouldn't let me stay like this. That you wouldn't leave me completely.'

He had more faith in me than I did.

The four months had been hard ones for Kevin. My absence had been jolting. A new therapist arrived, but for a while Kevin remained convinced that I was coming back. He worked hard, he said, because he wanted to surprise me with how well he was doing. Then somewhere along the line he realized I wasn't going to return. Jeff and me, we'd both left him. That'd been hard, he said. That was the hardest part.

The new therapist must have been good, though, because Kevin did continue to make slow, albeit erratic, progress, and when a decision had to be made over Kevin's placement, this man lobbied for a less terminal place than some back ward. Seven Oaks was chosen because it had the security features that Dr Winslow felt Kevin needed. Those rages in seclusion must have impressed Dr Winslow, because he clearly did not feel safe having Kevin somewhere without locks. For Kevin it made little difference. He had been behind locked doors so long now that they were taken for granted.

So here he was. He did not fit well into the society of Seven Oaks. The other boys tended to tease and taunt him because he was so naïve. All those years institutionalized with retarded children had left Kevin with a very scanty knowledge of the outside world and he fell easily for the other kids' tricks in this less-protected environment. But those were the good days. On the bad days he stayed in his room, and no one could pry him out from under his blankets. He refused to talk or to participate, and life came to a grinding halt.

Bill Smith, the counselor who had contacted me, did not feel very hopeful for Kevin's chances of survival in the Seven Oaks scheme. If Kevin could not get the hang of their social life there, if he wouldn't cooperate, Bill honestly did not believe he could recommend that Kevin stay on when the six-month trial period ended. While he was willing to give Kevin all the support he could, including bringing me back into Kevin's milieu, Bill was not willing to carry Kevin as a deadweight.

I liked Bill. He was a good-hearted, honest, straightforward man who did not mince words. He would go out on a limb for Kevin, as I suspect he would have done for any of their boys, but he would not saw it off behind him.

So as I caught up on four months' absence, I could see things hadn't changed much. Kevin still lived in the netherland between the outer world and the back ward of some institution, a sort of bureaucratic limbo.

'Is Jeff coming too?' Kevin asked me. He had managed to come across the room finally and sit in one of the other vinyl-covered chairs. The room was warm with June heat and filled with a golden darkness from afternoon sun penetrating pulled shades.

'No.' I shook my head. 'Remember, Jeff left. He left before I did, do you recall? He's in California now.'

'Oh, yeah,' said Kevin forlornly and turned his head away. 'I had been kind of hoping it was all a dream. I dreamed a lot there. I was hoping some of the bad things might have been just dreams too.'

I slouched down in the chair and put my feet on a coffee table. 'So, Kev, shall we give it another try?'

He nodded.

'But some things have got to change between us,' I said.

He looked over. 'Why? Because of what I did at the hospital to you? Are you still mad?' He paused, chewed his lower lip. 'I'm sorry about that. I didn't mean it to happen. I'm sorry.'

'Yes, I know it. But it doesn't have anything to do with that. I just think we need to change some things right from the very beginning. I think we need some goals in mind. You and me, we've been together almost two years now, Kev, and I'm not sure where we've gotten. I felt sometimes like we were floating around like two little boats without anchors, going where we were taken. That works sometimes, but I don't think it has for you and me. A lot of people have been deciding your life for you, Kevin – your folks, social workers, doctors, nurses, counselors, Jeff, me. I think it's time you started making some of those decisions yourself.'

'You're still mad, aren't you?'

'No. Just determined.'

Kevin looked over at me. In the hot, half-light of the room his eyes were fluid gray, like sun on water. 'Torey, can I ask you something?'

'What's that?'

'Do you still like me?'

'Well, yes, of course I do.' I smiled. 'I wouldn't be back here if I didn't, would I?'

'But do you like me a lot? Like you did before? Do you still like me that good?'

I nodded.

'Okay,' he said, 'go on with what you were saying.'

Chapter Thirty-three

And so once again, we started over.

Discomforted by the persistent ambiguity that had haunted Kevin's case, I decided what we had lacked were specific goals. And I had gone out to Seven Oaks feeling very strongly about setting some up, which was a rather unusual feeling for me. I'm not a very goal-oriented person myself. That put too much emphasis on the future and the outcome to generally suit me. Both my work and my life-style were more geared for the present and the process of doing things rather than their ends. However, every once in a while I would feel a lack of direction in what was happening around me and I would resort to goals. It was rather like it was at home when I got fed up with not being able to find something in my usual clutter and launched into a full-scale job of drawer and closet cleaning.

This must happen with Kevin. He must have some tangible goals for himself, I decided. And so must I, so that I could justify to myself that two years' work was not being wasted. I wanted him to go from Point A to Point B to C and I wanted to know from the very start what A and B and C were. And I wanted Kevin to know.

Moreover, it seemed the most viable plan, considering Kevin's living setup. The whole of Seven Oaks was run on a tightly structured form of behavior management. The boys got tokens for appropriate behaviors and for certain tasks, and they used their tokens to buy basic necessities as well as reinforcing activities and items. As with all behavior-management systems, it was extremely goal oriented, and the boys had regular times to assess their behaviors and their progress and to set new short- and long-term goals. So it seemed most logical to hook right into that network for Kevin. That way the counselors and houseparents would understand what I was doing and I would know Kevin's behavior was being monitored when I wasn't around.

Kevin's reaction to this sudden burst of organization on my part was difficult to interpret. I could not tell if he simply did not understand all of what I was getting at or if he was being passively resistant, thwarting me without making it apparent that was what he was doing. Whenever I arrived with all my ideas tucked under my arm and set about discussing them, he pulled a stupid face. I could get no real cooperation out of him, although he gave the appearance of trying.

Setting the goals with him was an exercise in frustration. He could not think of the things *I* thought were important, like interacting appropriately with the other boys. Instead, he came up with things like going to California to see Jeff. Patiently I would explain that, yes, that would be nice, but chances were that going out to see Jeff was not a viable goal, if for no other reason than the fact that neither of us even knew where he lived. So around and around and around we went, sorting out the priorities, trying to make his goals and my goals coincide. All the time Kevin would look dumb and not understand, and I never knew for sure if he really didn't or if he was fooling me mightily.

Regardless, I gained great comfort from having the lists in front of me. I suspect the entire theory of behaviorism and its subsequent manifestations in the forms of behavior management and modification all came about in response to man's infinite need to believe he understands his little bit of existence and can control it. Knowing what one is doing or at least believing one knows, especially when confirmed on paper, gives one a really incredible sense of power.

Kevin was considerably less enthusiastic about this whole matter. 'How come it can't be like it used to be?' he asked me one afternoon.

'Because how it used to be never got us anywhere.'

'Yes, it did. I'm better. Look at me. I don't sit under tables anymore. I'm not so afraid.'

'Yes, but you're still living in some lock-up joint like a thief, aren't you?'

'Yeah, but ...'

'Remember how you were always saying that you couldn't understand how come it was you who was locked up when it was your stepfather who committed all the crimes? Well, I'm trying to change all that. I'm trying to get you out of here and where you belong. You want to get out of here, don't you?'

'Yeah, but ...'

'This is the only way I know how.'

'Yeah, but ...' He frowned and turned away from me. 'I mean, I do want to get out, but, well, it's just that, well, I wish it was like it used to be. I liked it better.'

'But it didn't work.'

'Yeah, but ...'

As it turned out, there was only one real goal Kevin wanted to accomplish. He kept it from me for a long time, until one day when we were sitting in the warm, gold-shaded interview room.

'You know—about goals? I got a goal,' he said to me.

'Oh? What's that?'

He raised one side of his mouth in a self-conscious little expression. 'Well, you wouldn't laugh, would you? If I told you?'

'No, of course not.'

I could see he was considering it carefully, weighing the risks of exposure in telling me. 'I want to make myself into Bryan.'

'I see.'

'I think I decided on a way how. Is it a stupid goal?'

I shook my head. 'No. How do you think you can do it?'

'Learning to swim. I figure Bryan would swim. So I'm going to swim. I'm going to do it. I've decided that.' He smiled gently. 'If, of course, you wouldn't mind teaching me.'

So off we started under the banner of contingency management. I plastered Kevin's room with charts and we colored up graphs with bright Magic Markers, following day by day his progress toward the predetermined goals: personal hygiene (brush your teeth, x1, x2, x3; brush your hair; wash your face; wash your hands before meals; change your under-wear; put on clean shirt; bonus point for everything done), group participation, individual activities, and so on and so on. I dealt in poker chips and gold stars and anything else I could find to motivate Kevin to earn. The payoffs were many and varied, little ones that he could earn through the day, medium-sized ones for the end of the day and big ones to be aimed at over a week or even longer, like going off the Seven Oaks campus. We colored and counted and charted. At home at night I would draw lines on logarithmic graph paper and keep charts in a binder on my desk. At work I would compare what we were doing with old charts I had done or with what the books said. The whole month of June passed that way, with me using up enough paper to kill a small forest and with Kevin dazed into action by the blitzkrieg.

Oddly, the one thing we did do together, the one thing that I had meant most to hitch up to Kevin's management pro-gram but in the end never did, was swimming. There was a pool right there on the Seven Oaks grounds, so three times a week I brought my swimsuit and when we were done with our session, we went over to the pool and I endeavored to teach Kevin to swim. It was a wretched, protracted job but it became a secret communication between us, an act that superseded all the things we were trying to accomplish with words on paper. No matter what happened during the day, no matter how unsuccessful he was with his goals or in his sessions with me, we still went swimming. It developed into a war free zone. Swimming just happened, unconditionally, the way love does in other people's lives.

When the school year had ended in mid-June, Charity's relationship with Mrs Thatcher paled somewhat by virtue of the fact that Charity was no longer her student. Without the daily contact, Charity slipped a little. Her weight, which was almost down to normal, went up a few pounds and her behavior slackened. However, Mrs Thatcher made an effort to still see Charity and not to set her adrift entirely. That helped. Plus, Charity's extended family absorbed her difficulties better in the summer because she frequently went out to see her cousins on the reservation, and the freedom of the dusty hills seemed to calm her down a little. But to compensate for those moments when she just did not know what to do with herself, Charity resumed living at my house.

Hence, when the warm weather of late June stretched out into July and Mrs Thatcher invited Charity out for a barbecue at the farm, Charity in turn invited Hugh and me to come with her. I had never met Mrs Thatcher previously and, needless to say, I was most curious about her. As undoubtedly she was about me. So one hot, hazy July evening we all loaded into Hugh's van and headed out to the farm. With us also was Ransome, a fourteen-year-old cousin of Charity's. He lived in one of the small towns on the reservation, but after persistent trouble with the law there, he'd been shipped in by the relatives to live with Charity's branch of the family for a while. He was a tall, handsome, sullen-looking youth with his hair grown long and a band around his forehead, like an Apache. He wore only jeans, no shirt, no shoes. Hugh and I exchanged looks over his head as we got into the car. Ransome never said a word to either of us.

The Thatchers had a delightful place, a small mixed-animal farm in an area mostly overrun by huge, sprawling ranches. Chickens scattered as we drove up the long, dusty drive, and a goat tied to the railing of the front porch bleated a greeting. Mrs Thatcher came running out to meet us. She had an apron hitched up under her boobs and gray hair tied back in a kerchief. I loved the woman immediately and dearly; she had that warm, unpretentious familiarity of Western women and greeted us like family. Then she brought us around back of the house to meet the other guests as we waited for the beef on the spit to finish cooking.

The children ran off to play in the pasture after we had eaten. Hugh and I stayed a while longer to chat with the Thatchers and with some of the other guests, but we really did not know a soul there aside from Charity. After a decent amount of time had passed, we excused ourselves to go for a walk. Privately, I was worrying about Ransome, whom I had not seen since dinner, and Hugh was just plain tired of all the sitting and the small talk and the barbecue smoke.

Dusk was approaching, although the sun was still on the horizon. Twilight lasted forever during those months, when the day remained suspended between light and dark. Hand in hand, Hugh and I strolled along the small lanes adjoining the farm. They were not much more than Jeep tracks in most cases and ran along barbed-wire fences.

It was not until we got to the far pasture near the river that I finally spotted Ransome. The Thatchers had accepted ten head of wild mustang ponies from the Bureau of Land Management and there among them he was. Ransome obviously knew what he was doing there, barefoot and shirtless, the sweat gleaming along his brown body. He waved the mustangs one way and then the other as they ran by. Then a small mare with a foal at her side broke out from the others. He grabbed her by the mane and bolted onto her back. She was just a wild pony, small and wiry, and his feet nearly touched the ground beneath her. But she wasn't used to being ridden and she galloped fiercely, kicking and twisting. Ransome, his long black hair flowing, lay low against her neck and refused to be unseated.

It was a magic thing to watch, like March hares in the moonlight, and I was beguiled, wanting his shameless, stolen ride to last forever. But he saw us and within moments had slipped to the ground.

For several seconds he paused, clearly weighing the merits of running from us. But he didn't. After a minute or two, he sauntered over.

'I wasn't hurting them,' he said.

'No,' said Hugh, 'we could see that.'

'It's easy to do.' Ransome turned and looked over his shoulder at the horses, still frenzied from his presence. 'It's something my grandfather taught me how to do. He taught me so that I would know what it is to live when other men are just surviving.'

Back at the farmhouse where Charity and the other kids were roasting marshmallows over the embers on the grill, Mrs Thatcher and I sat in the shadows and talked. I was enjoying the company of another teacher, and we relived good times. When the phone rang, I was startled to discover it was for me.

Jules was on the other end. Seven Oaks had telephoned the emergency number at the clinic. 'I was supposed to relay this to you,' Jules said. 'There's been a breakout. Three boys. One of them was your Kevin.'

My Kevin. Those words echoed inside my head as Hugh drove me home to get my car. And they were still in my head when I began the forty-mile drive down to Seven Oaks. My Kevin.

It was almost ten-thirty when I pulled into the parking lot at Seven Oaks. Police cars crowded an otherwise empty lot. All the lights were ablaze in the main office.

Kevin and two other boys, Carlos and Troy, had run off sometime between supper and 7:30 group-activity time. No one knew exactly how they got away or in which direction, but the general consensus seemed to be that they must have walked down the riverbed. Because of the long heat wave, the river was low, and large parts of the bed now lay exposed that normally weren't. It provided one of the few ways off the grounds, if one were small enough or wiry enough to slip between the fencing and the water itself. And it allowed for quite a long run in the protection of the willows, if one didn't mind rocks.

I sighed wearily when Bill told me that. All I could think of was that this was what my efforts at swimming had wrought. Kevin was no longer afraid of water.

Carlos was the kind of boy who ran. He had run before from Seven Oaks and once had managed to stay free for almost two weeks. He was fourteen, tough and streetwise.

Troy, the youngest of the three at twelve, was a rowdy little kid with no conscience and a string of arrests for arson and thievery. He, too, was streetwise and clever at things like purveying drugs and tobacco, so he had a good chance of surviving in the counterculture, if he could make it that far.

And then there was Kevin. An unlikelier member of this trio there could not have been. His inclusion shocked every-body, mostly because he had not been considered a high-risk kid. Why should he run? Where would he run to? They all kept pestering me with variations on these questions. Did I know? Did I have any ideas? No. I didn't. All I could think of was that he had decided to go after his stepfather again but I was praying it wasn't true. As I wrestled a Dr Pepper out of the pop machine and settled into a chair in the office for the long wait, they continued to quiz me. Tell us this. Tell us that. Tell us more about Kevin. And I realized once again how little I really knew him.

I stayed in the office until almost half-past two in the morning. By then even the caffeine in the colas couldn't keep me awake any longer, and I had to give in and go home. Anyhow, nothing was happening. Despite the efforts of policemen and counselors and locals who might have seen the boys cross their land, not a single clue emerged. Thus, I wearily said good-bye to everyone, drank the last of my pop and went out to the car to start the long drive home.

I was full of a kind of listless melancholy as I drove. Undoubtedly it had something to do with the fact that I was overtired and hyped up on too much caffeine, but all I could think of was Kevin going off one more time to do his step-father in. I *knew* in my heart of hearts he had. What was the use? I asked myself. What was the point of working with this boy? Had I accomplished anything worthwhile? Would I ever? Concrete accomplishments didn't usually matter that much to me, but here in the summer darkness, I longed for just one indication that somewhere in all these months with Kevin I had made a difference. In a way, I thought, it would have been much easier to face a rousing defeat than this long, long, drawn-out journey through limbo.

The next day the authorities caught up with Carlos. He was in a town about twenty miles south of the city and had been picked up shoplifting. Carlos was returned to Seven Oaks and upon his arrival was cloistered away with the rest of us and quizzed on the whereabouts of the other two. They had split up almost immediately after escaping, Carlos said. There had been an argument. Then Carlos refused to say more. What the argument had been about, we could not pull from him.

I talked to Carlos later to see if Kevin had given any indication about where he was headed. Did he mention his stepfather? I asked. Did he have any weapons? Carlos just shrugged and gave the sort of half nod kids give to indicate the end of the conversation.

Three more days passed before the police found Kevin and Troy. They were still together. They had made it up to the suburbs of the city but no farther and were discovered hiding in an old tarpaper shack under the bridge by the railway tracks. Both of them were half-starved and dead tired, when they arrived, hauled unceremoniously back in the rear of a police van.

When I went in to see Kevin after he had cleaned up and been fed, I found him lying face down on his bed. The exhaustion showed. They had survived on two cans of pork and beans and a package of cookies Troy had managed to nick from a grocery store. Kevin must have lost at least five pounds. But it was the exhaustion that showed most of all.

I sat down on the chair beside his bed. At first I only watched him as he lay on his stomach, his face half-buried in the pillow. He kept his eyes closed, as if opening them would be too much effort.

I watched him. I had thought I would be angry with him for all the trouble and worry he had caused me. I had expected that when we were alone I would give him a good piece of my mind for what he'd done.

But I didn't. I leaned over and pushed the hair back from his face, smoothed it back. I loved the kid. For the first time since I had known Kevin, it came to me as love. The thoughts I had had during that night when I had been driving home came back to me, but in an academic way, and they seemed unreal. This was what was real. I loved the kid and I was thankful and relieved that he was back.

'How come you ran away?' I asked.

He did not respond. Instead, he only lay there, unmoving, his face partially obscured. I touched his hair again.

'You worried me, leaving like that. Why did you go?'

Kevin stirred. 'I dunno. I just wanted to get out. They were going, so I asked if I could come too. It was sunny. I just wanted to know what it was like to be free.'

Chapter Thirty-four

'I thought maybe you had decided to go up to the prison and kill your stepfather,' I said.

'Who told you that?'

'No one. I just thought it, that's all. Is it true?'

Kevin paused. We had been planning to go swimming, but they had closed the pool to clean it, so we sat under the elms, both of us still in our swim suits. I had my towel draped over my shoulders so that I could lean back against the tree without getting mangled by the bark. Kevin lay on his stomach on the grass.

'Well, Kev, is it?'

'I don't know.'

'I'd think you'd have to. That seems to me like one of those things either you'd plan to do or you wouldn't. So did you?'

He shrugged.

'Is that yes?'

'No, not especially.'

'Is it no, then?'

He shrugged. 'I told you, I don't know.'

'But what do you mean, you don't know? How can you not know a thing like that?'

Another shrug. 'I just don't. Last year I did. Last year I was going to. But now? Maybe he isn't even in the prison anymore. Maybe he's somewhere else. Who knows. I was sure last year. I'm not so sure now.'

I pulled a long strand of hair over my shoulder and studied it. It needed cutting. I fingered through for split ends. 'What we gonna do about your stepfather, Kevin? And your mother, for that matter.'

'What do you mean?'

'I mean, how are we going to lay them to rest? Your mom and your stepdad were part of your life, Kevin. The things they did to you, right or wrong, are part of your life too. And once a thing happens, there's nothing much anyone can do to make it unhappen. It's there. One can never go back. One can never change things that have already happened. You or I or the counselors, none of us can make it so that your stepdad didn't beat you ten years ago or so that your mom would step in and stop what happened to Carol. Or any of that stuff. It happened. It's over. We can't change any of it. All we can do is accept that it happened and then move forward the best we can.'

'I know that.'

'I know you do. But just the same, I know you look back too. And I feel like you still want to go back and undo what's already been done.'

He was watching me.

'Am I right?' I asked.

Kevin shrugged.

'And I keep thinking, we got to do something about that, you and me. Because it's eating away at you, Kevin. They've still got you in their grasp. Your stepdad is torturing you just as much today as he did all those years back and you haven't even seen him in six years. We've got to lay them to rest, one way or another, to get you free.'

Kevin fooled around with a piece of grass. The day was very hot and the wind was warm on my skin. All around us were the sounds of summer and yet between us it was very still.

'You know that lady, Margaret,' he said, 'that lady at Bellefountaine?'

I nodded.

'You know what she said to me once?'

'No. What?'

'She said, "You're never going to really be normal, Kevin." She said, "That's okay. A lot of people aren't, you just got to get used to it. Some people in life, they got the breaks. Some people don't." She said, "You got to accept some things." And afterward, I went upstairs and I looked at myself in the mirror and I thought, you know, I *look* normal. I do. I mean, maybe I'm not so good looking and stuff as some guys are. But I look like I could be normal. So I went back downstairs and said so. I said, "Margaret, I look normal to me. Why can't I be?" She didn't answer me.'

'So you broke her arm?'

'No,' he said. 'That was another time.'

'What happened then?'

'One of the other boys had punched this kid. Hit him really hard. And I'd come down from being in bed 'cause I'd heard them. And I said, "Margaret, you got to help him." And she just stood there. She stood there and done nothing. And this kid was really getting the crap knocked out of him. And I said, "Margaret, why don't you help him? You *got* to help him. You can't just stand there and watch. He might get killed." And she said, "Leave 'em to fight it out. It isn't any of your business." So I grabbed her arm. I was just trying to make her stop them. I didn't mean to break her arm, really. I just wanted her to do something.'

'Kind of like you wanted your mom to do something the time she just stood by when Carol took a beating, huh?'

'Yeah, kind of like then,' Kevin said. 'Only this time I was bigger.'

A bug hopped up on my leg. I watched it for a moment as it crawled along but it made my leg itch, so with my other foot I brushed it off. It hopped back up again.

'But Torey, what do you think?'

'About what?'

'About my being normal. Don't you think I look like I might maybe be a little normal? Just a little even? I was thinking about that. I mean when I ran off with Troy and Carlos. I was thinking I could walk down some street and nobody'd notice, would they?' He paused and looked over at me. 'Would they? I mean, it doesn't show, does it, like I'm wearing a sign or something? Or does it?'

I shook my head.

'That was what I wanted to do most of all when I was out there,' he said. 'I just wanted to walk down the street and pretend I was like everybody else.'

I smiled. 'I think you're normal, Kev. And I don't see why you can't walk down any street you want to and be just like anyone else on it.'

'Then why am I here?'

'Because,' and I stopped. That was a question mostly without answers. He sat, tuned in to my silence like a man on a radar machine. Then wearily he turned away from me. He plucked another blade of grass.

'I told them to call me Bryan. Carlos and Troy, I said to them, "My name's really Bryan, call me that now." But you know, Torey, a name isn't going to do it, is it? There's more to it than just a name. I may be Bryan on the inside. I may be Bryan through and through, but on the outside, I'm always going to be Kevin. Just like Margaret said.'

The following weeks were hell. Perhaps more than ever, Kevin focused on the concept of getting out and leaving behind his many years of institutionalization. At moments like those under the elms, he was desperate to go free and searched the question so thoroughly with heart-wrenching queries that I could have wept for him. But at other times he was maddeningly stubborn about giving up his old institutionalized behaviors and, when reprimanded for them, would retreat back into saying he didn't care, he wanted to stay crazy anyhow.

I went a little berserk. I never knew from one day to the next what he was going to be feeling, and worse, I didn't know what to do about it, other than ride the tide. The two ends of the spectrum seemed farther separated than ever. He could act more normal than I had ever seen him; he could want more desperately to be normal than he had ever wanted to before. But then by the same token, he could refuse normalcy more effectively, grinding his heels in about any little change and be more determined than ever not to do something new. The only real light at the end of the tunnel was that despite his protests and his stubbornness, he never did revert to any really aberrant behaviors, as he had at Garson Gayer and the hospital.

Perhaps this was all a reasonable stage for Kevin to go through. After so many years behind locked doors, the prospect of freedom must have seemed daunting, regardless of its attractions. Perhaps this was a positive sign of growth, this constant seesawing. However, it was enough to drive me around the bend myself on some days.

It was also during this period that my clever system of charts and goals crumbled. I had seen the cracks. Despite the theory of its working, and in fact, the real-life edition's working to a degree, too, it just was not right. Kevin continued to hate it and I wasn't very comfortable with it myself. It was just a bit too organized for me; it regimented my behavior more than was helpful for either Kevin or me. We were spending more and more time in the vicinity of the swimming pool, both of us seeking refuge from the tight little ordered sessions when I ticked off goal sheets and Kevin counted points. In the end, I had to face the fact that for me, personally, it was a more effective backup system and that I functioned better under something less structured for my major approach.

'You want to do away with this?' I finally asked Kevin one afternoon.

'Oh yes. Oh God, yes,' he said gratefully. 'Oh yes, yes, yes, yes, yes.'

'It means no special treats. No prizes for getting your goals accomplished. And it still means we'll have to work hard. No slouching.'

'That's okay.'

'You're sure?'

'Yes, I'm sure. I'm very sure.'

'You really didn't like it, did you?' I asked.

'No. Not at all.'

'How come?' I asked. 'It did work. We did get things accomplished.'

'Because,' Kevin said. He closed his eyes a minute and leaned back. 'I can pretend again now,' he said.

'Pretend? Pretend what?'

'Well,' Kevin replied and there was a wistful smile on his lips. His eyes were still closed. 'Back when I was at the hospital, I used to pretend. The other kids, they always had someone to come visit them. And I only had you. I kept pretending you came for me. That it didn't have nothing to do with you being a psychologist and everything but that you just came for me. I even told the other kids that sometimes. I told Larry. I told Larry you were my sister. So he'd think you were just coming for me.' His head back, Kevin laid his arms over his closed eyes. 'But I couldn't very much do it here, could I? Not with those charts. I couldn't pretend at all, not even to myself.' Cause the conditions just always showed too plain.'

As the warm, warm weeks of July wore on, I could see the growth in Kevin. All the fluctuation was maddening but I was able to see slowly that the ups were higher and the downs were shallower. The growth was snail paced; it had been so much so for a while that I don't think any of us even noticed it at first but now it was increasingly apparent. Kevin was integrating into himself all the parts of him, his anger, his fears, his violence, his depressions, the way those things are in all of us. He still resorted to old tricks occasionally but they were only in short bursts.

Why, after all this time, things were finally coming together for him was one of those basically unanswerable questions. There was no way of knowing, nor in fact, any real need to know. But whatever it was, we all recognized it. For the first time serious discussion was going on in the office of Seven Oaks about Kevin's future placement. We all agreed he did not belong in a state hospital. But where should he go? Should he stay on at Seven Oaks? Perhaps. Perhaps there would even be a less-confining alternative.

Kevin himself was aware of his improvement.

'You know what I want to do?' he said to me one afternoon. We were sitting on the carpet in the dayroom. We were just below the window, and a warm, very yellow sunlight poured over us. It illuminated the dust motes in the air. There were millions of them, drifting down, giving subsance to the insubstantial sunshine. The motes and the light gave an aura to Kevin, like those golden haloes around saints in icons. 'I want to go to high school.'

I looked at him. 'High school?'

'Yeah. If I ever get out. If I do, I've decided that's what I really need to do. Go to high school.'

'Why?' I asked.

'Because.' He shrugged. 'I don't know really. Just to go. To be with other kids. To see what it's like to be real.'

The room was very warm. I lay back on the rug and put my arms behind my head. It drew me back suddenly to the hot, dry summer days of my childhood when I would lie up in the attic, my cheek pressed against the rough boards of the attic floor, and watch the spiders that lived there. The sun would leak through the slats in the attic fan and spotlight the little creatures. The air around me was always palpable with dust, and it had been very hot.

'What do you think?' asked Kevin when I did not respond.

'It'd be hard, Kev. They work really hard in high school and you haven't been in a real school since …'

'Since a long time. I know it. But I could do it. Mr Gomez, who was my tutor at the hospital, he gave me tests. He said I read like a tenth grader. He said I could do everything almost that good. Even math.'

'But that's still two years behind, Kev. Tenth graders are fifteen and you're almost eighteen. But it's not just the work. In fact, it's almost not the work at all. I think you could do the work, if you tried.'

'Then what is it?'

'It's the other things.'

'But what other things?'

'Oh, the going to and from classes. Having to get by on your own. And the other kids. They'd tease you, Kevin, because you're different. Adolescence is a hard time in a kid's life, for all kids, and because of it, they aren't very tolerant. They could make it hell for you without even knowing they were doing it.'

Kevin regarded me. He had gum in his mouth and he chewed it thoughtfully and occasionally pulled part of it out of his mouth in a long string. I think I had hurt his feelings by saying outright that he was different, although both of us knew it. He wanted to refute me, I suspect, but he was too honest with himself.

'I'm just saying that it would be hard, Kevin, that's all. Kids would tease you. They do that sort of stuff without even meaning to be cruel. Kids don't think very much before they act. They'd say you flunked or that you were stupid and that's why you are so much older. Even if it wasn't true they'd still say it.'

'I've had hard times before, Torey.'

'Yes, but this would be different. You'd be all on your own. There'd be no one there to back you up and it would be all your responsibility to keep your act together.'

Still he studied me. Then his shoulders sagged slightly and he looked down at his hands. 'Don't you see, Torey? I gotta do it. I got to know I'm real, if I get out of here. Just for once in my life, I got to know for myself.'

I wanted to agree with him but I couldn't bring myself to. It was more a dream than a plan or even a hope. I suspected he had no idea what an unsheltered place a high school was. 'It would be so hard, Kev. You'd get hurt in so many ways and so badly. There's other things you could do instead. Things just as good, if not better. Maybe go to the community college or something.'

'But it's *gotta* be hard, Torey, don't you see that?'

I said nothing.

'I've done hard things before.'

'Yes, I know you have.'

'I can do it,' he said softly. 'I can do some things even you don't believe I can. Even you don't know how much of me there is. I have to do it. You guys aren't the only ones I got to prove myself to. There's me. Just once in the while I got to prove it to myself as well.'

Chapter Thirty-five

The one issue which kept returning to my mind was that of Kevin's mother and stepfather. If he was ever going to leave places like Seven Oaks and Garson Gayer behind, the authorities had to be assured that he was not going to go around breaking people's arms because of a mis-said word. I found him a predictable youngster. Very little of what Kevin did seemed without reason when I finally got all the information. However, it was apparent that the things that had happened to him in his past continued to influence his present behavior and this made it difficult for anyone to guarantee how safe he was. Knowing why he did something was not the same as knowing if he would or not. And obviously this was going to have an effect on any committee trying to decide if he was fit for freedom or not.

I wasn't one for playing a waiting game. We didn't have years and years and years to resolve these issues in therapy.

Every week or month Kevin spent in an institutionalized situation took him further away from the ability to adjust satisfactorily in the outer world. After such a lengthy incarceration as he had already had, I was worried by each additional day. In a way, Margaret from Bellefountaine was right. Normal might very well be outside Kevin's grasp already. The culture shock would be stupendous, and without the benefits of even a partially normal childhood, Kevin did not have many resources upon which to draw.

Kevin himself was not much help when it came to resolving the issue of his parents. If he felt disinclined to talk about something, nothing I did could get him to. If I hadn't kept coming back to the issue, I don't know when he ever would have. And when I did, he didn't have any answers for me or for himself. What are we going to do? I'd ask. How can we learn to cope with those feelings? Kevin would just shrug and occupy himself in other ways.

Yet, in the end it was Kevin who found the missing piece.

In his regular program Kevin finally earned enough tokens overall to exchange for an off-campus pass. He had been coming up on it for some time and had been very excited because it would be the first time he'd been allowed off the Seven Oaks grounds since the runaway five weeks earlier.

His intention was for me to take him to Taco John's. Kevin adored Mexican food, and I had told him way back when we were running our own behavior-management program that if he hit a master goal and earned enough points, I would take him for a pig-out and he could eat as much as he wanted.

So, pass in hand, he set off with me one August afternoon. It was just the beginning of August, and the nights and the days had run into one, as they do that time of year, without ever cooling down, with the nights so short and the dusks and dawns so long that the heat seems to stretch out over the season like a sleeping lion, powerful but indolent.

We made the journey into the city lazily. Leaving Seven Oaks a little after one in the afternoon, I drove Kevin through the countryside most of the time rather than take the freeway. I think both of us knew that the beginning of the end was nearing for us, whatever way the future went, and there was that unspoken urgency to preserve the small moments of our relationship. Such a long time had passed since Kevin had been out and free that I wanted to make the afternoon good for him, so he would remember it.

We puttered down tree-lined country roads and along the river, sleepy in the August heat. Coming up to a small roadside safari park, I pulled into it and we drove through a large enclosed area filled with local wildlife. There were elk and deer and antelope and a lone moose, as well as smaller animals. In a separate area a bear begged shamelessly for treats, even though a huge, red-lettered sign forbade feeding him. Kevin sat mesmerized, his face against the glass as the bear ambled by, while I told him stories of my childhood, growing up in a gateway town to Yellowstone Park, where bears were part of every child's life. At the end we stopped and went into the little shop and museum and Kevin squandered his meager spending money on a plastic deer statue and six postcards to put up in his room. That left him with only enough to buy seven-eighths of a candy bar, and so I had to lend him the other three cents.

Farther down the road on the way to the city, I pulled over into a small picnic ground beside the river. I parked the car in the shade and we went walking. Taking my shoes off, I waded in the shallows of the river, where the clear water eddied around the rocks. Kevin watched cautiously from the bank, uncertain of the slippery rocks and the moss and the small things that lived under them, to say nothing of the water itself. He had become quite a good swimmer over the summer, but this was very different water. When at last he felt reassured enough that nothing was going to happen, he took off his shoes and socks and came forward to the water's edge with the wariness of a young child. Reaching a hand out for my shoulder to steady himself with, he put his toes in. Kevin jumped in surprise at the temperature, and we laughed together and searched for colored stones and stirred up foam in the shallows with willow wands.

So it took us quite a while to reach the city, probably the better part of three hours. I saw rising in the west the tremendous anvil shapes of thunderclouds, and a hot wind had started to blow, gentle but heavy and warm, like some animal's breath.

The idea to go to Taco John's was an old one, actually, harking back to the days when Kevin was first in the hospital, perhaps even as far back as the spring at Garson Gayer. There had been a Taco John's near both places, but the one near the hospital, you could see from the fifth-floor unit. However, Seven Oaks was almost forty miles south of the city. There was no point in going clear up to the vicinity of the hospital, and Garson Gayer was even farther, an additional eight or nine miles. So I decided to turn off the freeway when I saw what looked like a shopping district.

I wasn't at all familiar with that part of the city. It was way to the south of anywhere my work had taken me. But I did manage to land us in an area full of McDonald's and Burger Kings, so I reckoned a Taco John's had to be nearby too.

'You know,' said Kevin as we rounded another block, 'I think I've been here before.'

'Have you? I don't know this area at all.'

'Yeah. I think. Yes, a long time ago.' His brow furrowed as he stared out of the window. 'Over there. See? If you turn that corner, there's a laundromat. Go that way and see.'

I went down the street and around the corner. Sure enough, there was a seedy-looking laundromat.

'Yeah,' he said, more to himself than to me, 'yes, now go that way.'

So I turned the next corner. The area was quickly degenerating into very run-down houses and boarded-up storefronts.

'I remember this. Hey! I know where this is. We used to live near here. I never knew this was where it was, though. But I remember now. I used to walk to school this way. Go up that street. I'll show you where my old school was.'

Tugging the wheel, I turned us around and took off in the direction Kevin was pointing. In a few moments we were driving past a long, low school building. The playground around it was crowded with aluminum portable classroom units.

'That's where I used to go to school,' Kevin said. 'Stop the car, okay? I'll take you up and show you where my classroom was. Okay? Look at those things. They never used to have all those metal buildings everywhere. Just the brick building. But stop the car so I can show you.'

I pulled the car into the parking lot of the school and we got out. Kevin was trotting now, off in the direction of the brick building. He turned down one side of the school and loped along the row of windows.

'There,' he said, cupping his hands around his face and pressing them up against the glass. 'That's where I went to first grade. Mrs Hutchinson's room. See? Can you see it, Tor? I wonder if Mrs Hutchinson still teaches here.'

I peered through the window, too, into a rather typical-looking classroom. All the doors and shelves were taped for summer. The desks were upended and the floor glowed with a summer's polishing.

'I wonder if Mrs Hutchinson still remembers me,' Kevin said. 'I remember her. I liked her. But I wonder if she remembers me.'

Then he turned. 'Come on,' he said and touched my arm. 'I'll show you where I used to live.' When I headed for the car, he grabbed my arm. 'You don't need the car. It isn't very far. Let's just walk.'

Down a little back street we went, Kevin still half loping, still ahead of me, his body launched forward in anticipation. The streets were shabby, and I was uneasy about being afoot in them, even in the daytime. Many of the buildings appeared derelict, and even those which were apparently lived in looked deserted.

We made another turning and came upon a street of little clapboard houses in dreadful disrepair. They all had been painted hideous colors: pink, purple, green. The windows were falling out, the doors were loose on the hinges. Car parts, dismantled wringer washers and the corpses of old stoves and refrigerators littered the front yards. Most of the houses looked as if no one lived in them, although at the far end of the street a very little boy was meandering about. There was a whole pack of mongrel German shepherd-type dogs lounging on the pavement in the sun.

Kevin stopped dead. He did not speak for a minute or two but only stood and stared.

'There,' he whispered. 'That's my house.' He pointed to one of the houses with dark green paint peeling off its side.

Slowly he walked toward it. It looked derelict to me but I couldn't be sure. 'Momma,' I heard Kevin whisper very softly under his breath.

'Kev,' I said, and touched his shoulder, 'somebody else may be living there now. Maybe we oughtn't to go in.'

'But this is *my* house,' he replied with certainty.

'But that was a long time ago, Kevin. Maybe someone else lives there now.'

He brushed me aside. I leaped ahead of him to knock at the door before he pushed it open, but there was no need to worry. The door gave way easily on rotting hinges. Clearly no one had lived here for a long time. We went in, and the screen door clattered shut behind us.

Kevin stopped and looked around. Knowing I was trespassing on someone's property, I felt vaguely uneasy and wanted out. It wasn't a very inviting-looking place anyhow. Vagrants had camped in one corner of the main room. Rats and mice and birds had taken the rest of it over for their own, and there was a litter of excrement on the floors. The slam of the screen door had startled up bats, and I could hear them shifting nervously over the chimney.

'Momma?' Kevin said again, still softly. There seemed no disparity between his worlds for him. He was aware of me as well as of the long-ago world awakened in his memory. 'This is the living room,' he said to me, 'and this is the way to the kitchen and there's where Momma and Daddy slept. And over there's me and Carol and Barbara's room. Except after Ellen came, Momma made me sleep on the couch because there wasn't enough room in the bed anymore.'

We walked through the house. Kevin scrutinized everything with the thoroughness of a real estate agent, looking at the walls and the floors and the door lintels, as if seeing them for the first time. Having no memories, all I saw was the bird nest in the kitchen cupboard and the pile of rags and food cans, left by vagrants. I heard no sounds other than that of sleepy bats shifting position in the corners.

Kevin had small memories to illustrate each room. 'Our toilet never worked. Sometimes I had to pee out the bedroom window and once the neighbor saw me and she said she was going to call the police if I peed on her house. Gosh, how could I pee on her house? See how far it is? Even my dad couldn't pee that far. But I was always scared anyway that I was going to, by accident or something, so I started sticking my rear out the window like Carol did.' Kevin stuck his head through the broken window. 'We used to save up till we had to go real bad and then see if we could drill a hole in the dirt. But,' he said rather forlornly, 'I guess you can't see any now.'

Then he pulled his head in and turned to me with a smile. 'Me and Carol, when we were little we used to play Chinamen at night. We used to stick both our legs into one side of our pajama bottoms and push our eyelids up like this and hop around going "Ah so! Ah so!" till Momma would come in and tell us we were going to get the shit whipped out of us if we didn't get into bed. And so me and Carol would get into bed and we'd lay real quiet under the covers and every once in a while I'd hear her whisper, "Ah so!" in a real high, squeaky voice and I'd whisper "Ah so!" back and we'd pull the covers over us and pretend we were in the mountains of China.'

He smiled at me again. 'Carol, she was real funny. She could always make me laugh. And I still think of that, of us playing Chinamen. It makes me feel good even now to remember us doing that.'

I was overcome with admiration for him, listening as he went through the house, picking up the bits and pieces of times long past. He had managed not only to survive, but, as Ransome put it, to live. For all the gruesome trauma in Kevin's childhood, he had been happy too.

Then in the living room he paused, his lower lip pushed out over his upper in a thoughtful expression. He stared at the floor. With the toe of one shoe he rubbed away the debris on the wooden floorboards. Regarding the spot, he knelt and brushed back the dust.

'Come here, Torey,' he said. 'Come here and look.'

I came over to where he was and stood over him.

'See? This is blood. A bloodstain. Here. Can you see? Come down here and look at it.'

I remained standing for a moment.

'Come here. Come down here and see it.'

I knelt.

'Feel it.'

I was hesitant. I didn't know what it was he had found. The area was filthy with years of disuse. Bird droppings, rat trails, bat excreta covered the floorboards. I wasn't too keen to touch whatever it was Kevin had located. However, he was very insistent.

'Feel it. Feel it, Torey. It's Carol's blood.'

So I felt the spot, running my fingers over the rough old wood and feeling no more than the grain of it. I could see nothing either. The floor was all spots and dirt and debris, one bit looking very much like any other bit to me.

Outside it began to rain. The sound momentarily drowned out everything, even the heartbeat in my ears.

Kevin shoved back the dirt from another place on the floor. 'What's this?' he said, mostly to himself. 'Is this blood too?' He raised his head and scanned the area around him.

'I think it's just a spot, Kevin.'

He shook his head.

'Just a place maybe a bird was or something. Just a spot on the wood.'

He returned to the section he'd made me touch. He bent to examine it. Then he rose and turned away from me. He went over to the window. The glass on the bottom half had been broken out and was boarded over but the glass in the top half was still intact. Kevin wiped the grime off with his hand and looked out. The silence grew around us, sharp and cold, like the blade of a knife, despite the noise of the storm. Yet it was not a dividing silence. Instead, Kevin and I were bound together by it, like hostages.

I shivered.

Turning back to me, Kevin sat down on the edge of the sill. He said nothing.

I was still kneeling, my fingers still against the wood of the floor.

He studied me, my eyes, my face, the length of my arm, my fingers, until his eyes finally came to rest on the bit of floor I was touching. For a long, long time he simply stared at it.

On the windowsill the rain was dribbling through and running down the wall to form a puddle. Finally Kevin noticed it as the water spread toward where he was sitting. He reached his hand out and touched it. Lifting his fingers, he stared at the pattern the water had made on them.

'They're gone,' he said quietly to his hand. A strange expression crossed his face. His forehead puckered and then relaxed and he continued to watch as the rainwater dripped from his fingers. Then he looked across at me. 'It's over, isn't it?'

I nodded.

'Yeah,' he said and touched the water on the sill again. 'I guess I sort of knew it was.'

Chapter Thirty-six

And it was over. The silence of an abandoned house in an August rainstorm was able to communicate to Kevin what I in all my months with him could not. His ghosts at last lay down.

Between us we never spoke of that afternoon, not then as we drove back to Seven Oaks, not later in our continuing sessions. Not ever. I did discuss the occurrence at length with Bill Smith and particularly with Dr Rosenthal but between Kevin and me it was never cloaked in the insubstantial fabric of words. It didn't need to be. We had shared it. And that had been enough.

Bill Smith and I continued to search for an alternative placement for Kevin. In a couple of weeks Kevin's eighteenth birthday would pass and Bill did not feel that Seven Oaks was the best place for Kevin to remain. Not only were most of the boys there much younger but they were also a different type than Kevin. Because Kevin was so desperate to exercise new-found social skills and make friends, Bill feared he would be taken advantage of by some of the more savvy boys or worse, in an attempt to gain their friendship, he would learn their tricks and we would have traded one set of unacceptable behaviors for another.

I had known Bill was out beating the bushes for another spot, some alternative to a more restrictive environment, because all of us now felt Kevin ought to be given a chance to prove himself. Yet, at nearly eighteen, he was not a good candidate for fostering, mostly because few families would be willing to tackle a kid that age and with his background.

But Bill found one. Mr and Mrs Burchell, they were, a nice-appearing couple, sweet in manner, both rather shy. They weren't very old, in their late twenties or so. They'd been married a couple of years but had no children of their own. When they arrived, we sat around in Bill's office chatting and drinking lemonade. When I asked them why they had decided to foster and why in particular to foster adolescents with problems, Mrs Burchell said they wanted to do something meaningful for society. They had both been fortunate themselves to have had loving and happy childhoods and they wanted to extend themselves to those less fortunate.

It sounded corny, the way they said it, and I must have had an expression on my face that told them that because they both apologized profusely for not being able to say it well. I laughed and Bill Smith told them not to mind me, that I'd been too long in the business to look any other way. I was still chuckling and had to apologize, myself, saying that words counted for naught anyway. Action was everything.

I hadn't seen Kevin between the time I was informed about the existence of the Burchells and their arrival. He had been in woodworking class and wasn't free until four o'clock. The whole affair caught me off balance because Bill had never mentioned any impending fostering possibilities. No doubt he did not want to raise my hopes any more than Kevin's. So I didn't really have a chance to adjust to this abrupt turn of good fortune. The Burchells seemed nice, but I was too uninformed to be much of a judge.

Kevin came into the room, his face wreathed in smiles. He had been told in the morning apparently and now was totally unable to contain his enthusiasm. Mom and Dad. He wanted to call them Mom and Dad right then and there, these people who were perhaps only a decade older than he was himself. However, the old Kevin wasn't too far away either. The excitement overcame him, and when Bill asked him a question, he ducked his head and wouldn't answer.

I was sitting next to him and I kicked him with the side of my shoe. I hissed through clamped teeth. A smile to the Burchells. 'Kevin's a little shy sometimes. But he gets over it. Don't you, Kevin?' I said, and kicked him again.

All in all, the interview went quite well. Kevin did manage to find his voice eventually, after we waited long enough, and the Burchells seemed genuinely interested in taking him. At the end, Kevin and I left together and the Burchells stayed with Bill.

'I'm going to have a family,' Kevin whispered to me as we walked down the hallway. Then as we got outside, he erupted into joy. 'Whoopeee! *I'm going to have a family after all!'*

I laughed. I meant to tell him not to get too high of hopes just in case the worst happened. But I couldn't. When I saw his face, there was no way I could be that heartless.

So after a week of sheer frenzy for Kevin while the Burchells made their minds up, all Kevin could think about was 'his family.' Finally, it was agreed that he would go to spend Labor Day weekend with them as a trial run. This put Kevin beside himself. All we could do was talk about what to take, what to wear and what he might be doing. He had grandiose plans for those four days. Among them was swimming. Kevin had become a passably good swimmer by now, his one monumental accomplishment in everyone's eyes, and he was desperate to show the Burchells, even though I tried to explain that perhaps they would not appreciate the immensity of the achievement for him. But he didn't care. Would there be a pool? Could he take his swimming trunks? Would they come watch him? And on and on and on, ad nauseam.

When Labor Day weekend finally arrived, however, there I was with Bill, standing in the gravel driveway as the Burchells' battered old station wagon with Kevin and his brown suitcase in back finally pulled out of sight around the corner of the Seven Oaks gate. And I could have cried.

Over the latter two months of the summer I saw very little of Charity. We had had the barbecue at the Thatchers' and then I had taken her camping, and there was a Big Brothers/ Big Sisters picnic, but after that, I saw less and less of her.

She had begun spending weekends out on the reservation with her mother's family and then pretty soon it was weeks out there and weekends in town and at last, she was out there all the time.

On August fifteenth, Charity turned ten. I'd promised I would take her shopping for a birthday gift when she got back from the reservation, and over the Labor Day weekend, she appeared on my doorstep for the first time in weeks.

'You wanna go buy me a birthday present today?' she hollered in through the screen door when she found it locked.

I was in the other part of the house, cleaning out closets, a job I detested heartily. Consequently, it almost never got done. But I had finally given in because I couldn't open any of them without endangering my life.

'Can you go today?' she asked when I let her in. She followed me back to the bedroom. 'Will you take me? You know what I want? I want a dress. I want a disco dress. You know, one of them's that's all shiny.'

'A disco dress?' I raised an eyebrow as I settled back down to sort through the junk hauled out from the floor of the closet. When I was ten, I had wanted a horse, a pup tent and a Davy Crockett hat.

'Yeah. You know. Like they got in *Friday Night Fever*.'

'I think you mean *Saturday Night Fever*.'

'Yeah, well, whenever it is. I want one of them.'

'You plan to go disco dancing?'

She shrugged. 'You never know. I might.'

'Yes, that's probably true.'

'So, would you? I seen one. Down at Salvador's Boutique. It's in the window.'

'Char, that's a big ladies' place. No sizes for kids.'

'Well, could we go look at it at least? Could we? You and me ain't done nothing together lately. So couldn't you just take me around to look? Please?'

I sighed. It was not a good day for it. Being a holiday weekend and a Saturday as well, the city would be a madhouse downtown. Worse, I was wearing an ancient, very ragged pair of cutoffs and a T-shirt and that meant I would have to change, my least favorite pastime.

'Please? Haven't you even missed me one little bit this summer? I ain't hardly been over at all.'

'Well, okay, I guess. If you help me put all this stuff away in the closet first.'

'Sure!' she chirped and grabbed an armful. With one swing it landed on the closet floor in a heap.

Instead of hassling in the traffic, we caught the 43 bus and then walked from the courthouse. In an unexpected show of affection, Charity took my hand.

'You don't mind, do you?' she asked when I'd looked down.

'No, of course not.'

'Good,' she replied with a smile. 'Some grown-ups do, you know. They get embarrassed holding hands with you because they think they're too big for it.'

'I see.'

We wandered in and out through all the people on the streets, past B. Dalton's, past Woolworth's and the city's huge main department store, down around the corner and toward Salvador's Boutique.

'You know what?' Charity said.

'What's that?'

'Guess. Guess what's going to happen to me.'

'I don't know. You're going to turn into a green monster and take a rocket off to Mars? Is that it?'

'Nooo! You're silly. No, I'm gonna move.'

'You are?' I was genuinely surprised.

'Yup. Next weekend. My uncle Myron is coming up from Bitter Creek and he's helping us take all our stuff back down there. We're gonna live with him and Aunt Lila and their kids for a while. And I got lots of other family there too.'

'Wow. That's big news.'

'You know where I'm going to go to school? At St Xavier's mission school. I seen it. Ransome goes there. So does Jennifer. So does Tara. It's real neat. It's got a whole new gym built on it. I'll be in Tara's class probably, because she's going to be in fourth grade too.'

'Well, that's super. It sounds like you're really looking forward to it.'

'Yeah, I am,' Charity replied. 'It'll be nicer than here. My grandfather lives near there and I like him a lot. And I got lots of other family. And Jennifer's got a donkey. She said I could ride it sometimes. So it'll be better than living here, I think.'

We had reached Salvador's Boutique. We stopped and gazed in the window. There was a dress there, all right. A really incredible concoction of passionate orange sequins and sleazy shimmer cloth. It looked like what a cheap tart would buy.

'See! That's it. Isn't it beautiful?'

'Mm-hmm.'

'Will you buy it for me for my birthday? That's what I want.'

'Charity, that's for grown-up ladies.'

'Well, I'm getting grown up. I'm ten already. And lookit, I'm almost getting breasts.' She smashed her T-shirt against her chest.

I said nothing because there was nothing there to say anything about.

'Oh, please, Torey? Please-please-please? *Please?* Couldn't I just try it on? *Please?*' She wriggled and squirmed until she looked like she needed to use the bathroom. 'Oh, please? Please-please-please-please?'

I was bending down to peer into the window for a better look at the thing. It really was incredible. 'Look, Charity, you can't even see the price tag on it. That means they've hidden it so you won't know how much it costs. And that means that it must not be worth what it costs or they wouldn't have hidden it.'

'*Please?*'

I looked at her. 'Oh, come on,' I replied and jerked her into the shop.

What a fool I felt like, asking to see the garish dress. The woman obviously thought it was for me, and when I, all 140 pounds of me, asked for a size 3, I could see her wince. Looking over my shoulder to make sure no one I knew was in the shop, I snatched the dress from her and shoved Charity ahead of me into one of the small fitting rooms.

Charity whipped off her clothes and within seconds was shimmying into the blinding orange disco dress. Even a size 3 was way too big for her, despite her pudginess. The string shoulder straps dropped the bodice of the dress clear below her nipples. The waist was on Charity's hips, what hips she had. The skirt came almost to her ankles.

Thoughtfully, Charity looked at herself in the mirror. 'Well, it *is* a little big, isn't it?' she said, woefully.

I nodded, not daring to open my mouth. She looked hysterically funny, and I had to bite the inside of my lip to keep from laughing.

'It's pretty though, isn't it?'

She stood there in front of the mirror and studied her image. A slight smile was on her lips, her eyes were dark and clouded with the secret beauty of her dreams. She touched the dress lovingly, and I could detect just the faintest movement of her hips, as if the music had already begun.

I wondered what she saw. For me there was only a little girl, barefoot and dusky skinned, the outline of her cotton underpants showing through the sleazy material. Her long black hair had been caught back in two uneven pigtails and, although she had lost a lot of weight, her cheeks were still chubby and her elbows were dimpled like a two-year-old's. But I wondered what *she* saw, standing there, gazing at the image in the mirror. The brilliant orange dress glimmered even in the wan fitting-room light.

I smiled at her and she looked at my image in the mirror. 'I think it's beautiful,' she whispered.

'Yes, it is.'

Gently she ran her fingers over the material.

'How much is it, Charity?' I asked, reaching for the tag. The dress cost $15.98, a great deal more than I had intended to spend for her birthday. Charity knew it. She looked at me, she looked at the dress and then back to her image in the mirror. Then without saying anything, she bent over to take it off.

'Hey, wait a minute, babe. Come here.'

She straightened up and moved over to where I could reach her from where I was sitting. I ran a hand along the material. 'You know,' I said, 'I suppose I could buy it for you. This once. Maybe a birthday present and a good-bye gift combined.'

Hope had gone out of her face. 'It's too big,' she said forlornly.

Turning her around so that she could see herself in the mirror, I moved behind her. I pulled on the straps and that hoisted the bodice up under her chin. 'Maybe if I took the straps up for you,' I said softly. It was still hopelessly too long, but once again Charity's eyes were clouding with visions of that inner world I could not see. The faint smile returned.

'It is *so* beautiful, Torey. I think it's the most beautiful thing I ever seen in my whole life.'

'Yes, and it makes you beautiful, too, doesn't it?'

She nodded.

We said no more. Carefully she slipped the dress off and smoothed it out in my lap. Before putting her shorts back on, she paused and studied my face.

'Are you going to miss me when I go?'

'Yes,' I said. 'I'm sure I will.'

'You won't forget me, will you?'

'No, I won't.'

'Say, cross your heart and hope to die if you ever forget me. Say it, okay?'

'Cross my heart and hope to die,' I repeated.

'No, no. You didn't cross your heart when you did it. Do it again. Like this.' She demonstrated. I did it. 'Okay, cross my heart and hope to die if I ever forget you, too, Torey Hayden. Because you really are my best friend. Of anybody, you really are my best.' Then she bent and pulled on her shorts. 'Tor, can I ask you something else?'

'What's that?'

'Well, when the time comes, can I kiss you good-bye?'

'Certainly.'

Gently she leaned forward and kissed me then. 'In case I don't see you when I go.'

She must have known. I never did see Charity again after that day. We went home, I fixed us lunch and she took her orange dress out of the box. Afterwards she put it on and I pinned the straps. I stitched them with white thread because I had no orange, and then she danced for me to ABBA while I sat on the floor of my closet and cleaned. And the last I saw of her was that sunny Saturday afternoon when she disappeared with the shimmering disco dress tucked under one arm, its beauty as lusty as a Las Vegas sunset.

Chapter Thirty-seven

When I came into Seven Oaks on Monday I found disaster. Bill Smith rolled his eyes as I walked by. 'Hopeless,' he hollered after me. 'That kid is absolutely hopeless.'

'So,' I said to Kevin as I sat down in a chair near his bed. 'A little birdie tells me things didn't go so well.'

Kevin was in bed, fully clothed but under the bedspread, nonetheless. He had it pulled up to his ears.

'What happened?' I asked.

Kevin just shrugged and pulled the bedspread higher.

'Now, come off it, Kevin. Talk to me. You don't solve anything hiding under a spread like that.'

He shook his head.

'The world hasn't come to an end, has it? There'll be other families.'

He shook his head again.

'Yes, there will. If there was this one, there'll be others. Now tell me what happened. Maybe it wasn't even that bad.'

But he wouldn't. Bugged by his lapse into this old trick, I got up. 'Listen, I'll be back in fifteen minutes and you better've decided to talk to me or I'll leave altogether. Got it?' So I walked out.

Down in Bill's office I got the official version. Bill was nursing a cold cup of coffee and shaking his head. 'That kid is impossible. I tell you, I've never seen a kid like that one for screwing things up. Holy Moses, he's a walking disaster area.'

'But what happened? What did he do?'

'Nothing. That was what the dumb jerk did—nothing. He just got there and froze. Wouldn't do a damned thing. Wouldn't talk, wouldn't even get out of the stupid car. And can you imagine? They had planned some sort of special picnic for him to meet the other members of the family. And the dumb kid wouldn't even get out of the car.'

'Oh, but Bill, that must have been terrifying for Kevin. Think of it. A big hoopla full of people you'd never seen before when you didn't even know the people you were with.'

'He was stupid and that's all there is to it. Do you know how hard it was to find those people? I beat the goddamned bushes bare to find them. And now they don't want him. What a hopeless kid. He's nuts, that's what he is, a goddamned nutto. Why did they send him here anyway? He's a nutto.'

'Don't make such a case out of it. It's been God knows how long since he's been in a proper family. The closest he ever came was last summer in that group home. He was just scared.

I mean, the boy has a right to be, doesn't he? He doesn't know them. It was all new to him. He just choked, that's all.'

'Hmmph,' said Bill, 'what a lost cause.'

Back in his room, Kevin was still hiding under the bed-spread.

'Get out of bed, Kevin. Get out or I'll pull you out.'

No response.

'I'm not joking. I'll come over and I'll pull you out. Now get up.'

Silence.

'I'm coming. Here I come, Kevin, and I'm not happy. This isn't a joke.' I took a giant step toward the bed.

Reluctantly, Kevin sat up, still keeping the spread around him.

'Now get up. All the way. Get up and put the spread back where it belongs. You look like a grandmother, for pity's sake.'

Wearily Kevin replaced the spread and shuffled over to a chair.

'So what happened?' I asked. I smoothed the bed out and sat on it.

Kevin hunched up in his chair and stared at the floor.

'Look, Kevin, I know you're disappointed. I know you're unhappy. What happened was an awful thing to live through. But it's over and done with and the world still has not come to an end. So let's sort it out so that it doesn't happen again.'

Still no response.

I stood up. 'I'm going. We're past this kind of behavior. It's rude and I won't tolerate your being rude to me. You have the choice of talking to me or I leave. Which is it?'

He shrugged in a half-hearted manner. 'I'll talk.'

'All right. So what's up?'

Another shrug.

'What happened to make it not work out?'

'Their toilet was funny.'

'Huh?'

He had his head tucked protectively down between his shoulders as if some invisible person were standing over him about to smack him. 'I said, their toilet was funny.

'It was funny. It was big. I was scared to use it.'

My heart sank. Were we ever going to come to the end of his fears? I wasn't feeling a whole lot better about this failure than he was or Bill was, and it took hard work to hold my tongue.

'Kev, maybe this just wasn't the right place for you.'

'But it was,' he said sorrowfully. 'It was just me. I messed it up. I was so scared of messing up that I think I tried so hard not to that I did. I just messed the whole thing up.'

'No, it wasn't you, Kevin. It was just the circumstances. They hadn't ever fostered kids before, so they were probably just as nervous as you were. It happens. It isn't any fun when it happens like this but it does sometimes. It wasn't just you. Don't worry about it.'

He stared glumly at his hands.

'There'll be others.'

He shook his head. 'No, there won't be. Who'd want a kid like me?'

'I reckon lots of people, Kevin. They just don't know it yet.'

The placement hadn't been right. That atrocious weekend turned out to be a disguised blessing because we later learned the Burchells were not what they had appeared to be. Unable to have children of their own, they had decided to adopt. However, the adoption agencies unanimously decided that they were not good candidates for adoptive parenthood. The marriage was not working. Their expectations both of each other and of children were unreasonable, and both partners had brought into their relationship some serious personal problems. With this new rejection, the couple had decided to try fostering as their only way to obtain the children they thought they needed to keep their faltering marriage together.

However, it had not been their personal problems that had gotten in the way that Labor Day weekend but simply their lack of understanding of what a boy like Kevin could cope with. The Burchells were well meaning but inexperienced and had drastically overplanned the visit. Kevin, unused to crowds of strangers and the rowdiness of a regular family at holidays, had panicked at all the events and the relatives and the prying questions. This caused the Burchells in turn to panic, and with their own assortment of problems, this spelled disaster. Yet in the end it was probably better. Kevin certainly did not need to get into an unstable foster home.

With this knowledge behind us, Bill and I set off to our separate networks to search for another alternative. It was a bleak job. Who would have the experience and security necessary to want an eighteen-year-old boy with ten years' history of institutionalization behind him? Those types were not too thick on the ground.

Actually, it was Jules who came through in the end. What about a sheltered group home? he suggested to me one afternoon in the office. When he mentioned it, I thought he was crazy. Those types of group homes were specifically designed to cater to retarded individuals who had reached the age of majority. What would Kevin do in a place like that? He wasn't retarded. And I'd had it with group homes anyway.

But Jules was persistent. While Kevin obviously wasn't retarded, he was in no way equal to his peers in the outer world, if not by intellectual difference then by experience. And yet he was no child. He was a man. He had had his eighteenth birthday the week following Labor Day. He was almost six feet two now. And incidents like what had happened in the art closet, Jules pointed out, were there to remind me he functioned as a man, as well. Who would want him in the role of a child? And was that the best role for him anyhow? Kevin could not go back and recapture a lost childhood. Wouldn't it be better just to launch him into a decent adulthood?

All of Jules's arguments were not without a reason. He had in mind a sheltered group home he had worked with before he joined our staff. The place was run by an old friend of his, a retired medical doctor, and his wife. They were both in their fifties and had designed the center several years earlier to meet the needs of their own retarded son.

The place was intended to cater for eight mentally handicapped individuals who were advanced enough to want to live on their own and hold down a small job but were not quite capable of total independence. The home was a huge old Victorian structure, and each of the eight people had a room of his own, which he 'rented' for a nominal sum. They all shared a family dining room, did chores around the place and went out together for entertainment. All the current residents were between twenty and thirty and all had jobs, either in the sheltered workshops or doing menial labor. Evenings at the home were spent learning basic survival skills, such as counting money and doing laundry, with some time off for just plain fun. Besides the doctor and his wife, there were four other paid staff who helped with the residents, including a teacher who came in the evenings to help bolster reading skills and a young man who came on the weekends to teach handyman's skills. The obvious goal of the home was to eventually launch the residents out into a fully independent life, but they were liberal in that regard and, while many of their people had left, a couple clearly were going to be there permanently.

The more I thought about it and the more Jules talked, the more I began to think perhaps this was a viable idea. Kevin was incredibly naïve, and even I had to face that fact. There was just too much for any one person to teach him in his given situation. And yet he was really an adult. Perhaps this *would* be a better solution.

Before bringing the suggestion seriously to Bill, I took an evening off to go see the place myself.

The couple running it were George and Nancy MacFarlane. They were a young-looking pair and very energetic. I arrived at dinnertime, and Mrs MacFarlane had me through the kitchen and into the dining room and down to the laundry room and up to the bedrooms and back to the kitchen before the potatoes were mashed. It was the 'girls' turn to make the meal, and the kitchen was alive with the chatter of the four residents and the staff person. One girl was disagreeing violently about how to peel carrots, and the staff person patiently explained again and again. Nancy MacFarlane leaned over the girl's shoulder, asked what the problem was. The girl wanted to do it this way, not that way. This way, one could cut oneself, Mrs MacFarlane explained, so we all did it that other way for safety's sake. She demonstrated and handed the carrot and knife back to the girl. Show our visitor how it's done, she said, and pushed me up against the sink with the carrots. The girl painstakingly held the knife correctly and peeled. 'Now why's it done that way, Clare, can you tell the visitor?' Nancy MacFarlane asked. Because the other way one could cut oneself, Clare replied.

After the meal, Mrs MacFarlane marshaled the 'boys' out to the kitchen to do the dishes, amidst appropriate groans, while Dr MacFarlane showed me the remainder of the house. He took me on a tour of the residents' rooms and the game room and the little upstairs kitchen where the residents could make tea or soup unsupervised, if they wanted. He also showed me the empty room that would be Kevin's, if Kevin came.

Just as Jules predicted, I liked the atmosphere of the place very much. The couple were caring and dedicated without being condescending. All emphasis was on learning to cope. Did I realize, Dr MacFarlane said, that their own son had managed to make the transition and was now living in his own apartment a few blocks away and holding down an eight-hour job? But for all the emphasis on learning, there was nothing institutional about the setting. It was a home.

My only real qualm was the undeniable fact that all the other residents were obviously quite retarded. Kevin, despite his earlier reports, was not. Would this cause problems? I asked.

No, Dr MacFarlane replied, not from what he had heard about Kevin. If Kevin had been institutionalized that long, he would effectively behave as a retarded individual in many areas, and this would be a sheltered, yet open, place to learn. Dr MacFarlane took me into the living room. Amidst the large photos of the current residents on the piano, he located an album and began showing me pictures. See? This is Benny and now he's living down in Mississippi, working on a truck farm. And there's Norma; she works in a child-care center. And Candy. And Bob. One picture after another of those whose umbilical cords had been cut. Had there been any failures? I asked. With a smile he shook his head. No. If they couldn't make it on their own, they came back. But that was hardly a failure, was it?

I sat down in a chair in the living room, and one of the residents brought me a cup of coffee. Did he realize, I asked Dr MacFarlane, that Kevin had emotional problems and, while they were much improved, he was not by any means problem free? Did he know that undoubtedly the time would come occasionally when the ghosts of Kevin's past would loom up and haunt him again?

'Yes,' he said. 'Don't they for all of us?'

Bill Smith was wary when I first suggested the MacFarlanes' as an alternative placement for Kevin. He had the same volley of questions I had had. Kevin was even more cautious. 'Who are they?' he asked. 'What kind of place is it?'

I explained.

'I don't want to go,' he said flatly.

'Why not? They're very nice. I went over myself and had a look. I think it's great.'

'I don't want to go,' he reaffirmed. 'I like it here just fine.'

On his next green pass, I took Kevin into the city to get a hamburger. We could have gotten a hamburger much closer and needn't have driven forty miles for the privilege, but I had other thoughts.

'You want to drive by the MacFarlanes'?' I asked as we sat in the McDonald's parking lot and ate our food.

He shrugged.

'Come on, I'll take you. We'll just go by the front before we head back to Seven Oaks.'

As we went by, Kevin put his head out the open car window. 'It's big, isn't it? Stop a little bit, so I can see it better.'

I drove around the block again and stopped on the opposite side of the street. Kevin stared out the window. 'It's real big. How many people live there? It could be a hundred by the looks of it.'

'No, just eight. Just eight people about your age and the MacFarlanes and a couple of people helping them. There's maybe ten or twelve altogether.'

'Well,' he said with a derisive tone, 'that isn't a real home, anyway. It's a group home, like at Bellefountaine.'

'Not exactly. It hasn't got any houseparents. Just the MacFarlanes. And the residents all have their own rooms and stuff. It's more like a family than Bellefountaine.

And besides, it's not a kids' place. It's for adults. Like you are.'

This thought clearly had never occurred to Kevin before. He sat, digesting it. 'Yes, I guess I am, aren't I? Hmm.' He fell silent as he studied the house. I started up the engine. 'Well,' he said, 'it's not such a bad-looking place. I might consider it.'

When the MacFarlanes came out to Seven Oaks, Kevin did decide he would go down and see them. It was a much different interview than with the Burchells. Clearly Kevin was determined not to get burned twice. He was polite and shy but he had questions and none of them were about whether or not he could call them Mom and Dad.

Then came the first visit, a weekend away. Bill Smith and I did not even dare voice our worries to each other. It was already the middle of October and Kevin's six-month tenancy at Seven Oaks was very near its end. This *had* to work out. Seven Oaks just was not an appropriate placement for Kevin.

But where else would he go? Neither of us dared think about the weekend. When I got home that Friday night, I took my phone off the hook. I didn't even want to know if anything went wrong. But when Hugh took me out for a meal on Saturday night, I made him drive me across town and by the MacFarlanes'. Not for any reason. Just so I could look.

I think Kevin and I both knew the end was approaching for us. It wasn't something either of us said to the other but, when he came home from the first weekend and plans for the next weekend were being discussed, I knew it was almost over.

I came in late one evening to find Kevin sitting in his room, doing his schoolwork. He turned as I entered.

'You're late,' he said. 'You're awfully late. It's almost suppertime.'

'I'm sorry. I couldn't get away earlier.'

'How come?'

'A kid at work. I have a little boy in therapy. I think he's schizophrenic but I don't know. They want to send him up to Medicine Rock, and so it took a while to untangle.'

'Was he upset?' Kevin asked.

'Yes, you bet. He's scared. He's in a foster home now and he's scared of being sent away from it.'

'How old is he?'

'Ten. He's got some real problems. But anyway, enough of that. I'm sorry I couldn't get here.'

'You weren't here yesterday either,' Kevin said.

'They told you, didn't they? I phoned and asked them to tell you.'

'Yeah,' he said, 'they told me.'

'Listen, Kevin, I'm sorry. I really am, but if you could just see this kid—'

He was smiling at me. It was a soft, enigmatic sort of smile and it caught me off guard. When I stopped talking, he continued to watch me for a moment longer without speaking.

'You did that for me, didn't you?' he said.

'Did what?'

'Well, when I had problems, you used to take time away from other people, didn't you? Just like now. When that other boy needs you more than I do.'

I nodded.

'I'm better, aren't I?'

'Yes. A lot.'

He looked down at his homework and then again at me. 'I decided I'm going to go, Torey. Over to the MacFarlanes'.'

'You did?'

He nodded. 'I asked Dr MacFarlane if I came, if I could go to high school. And you know what he said to me?'

'What was that?'

'He said, "Yes, son. I think that's a good idea."'

Chapter Thirty-eight

The move to the MacFarlanes' took place smoothly. While Kevin settled in over the next weekend, I spent my time with Dr MacFarlane, trying to find a high school in the district willing to take a chance on a kid like Kevin.

In the beginning, the idea still sounded harebrained to me, fraught as it was with so many built-in chances for disaster. However, Dr MacFarlane seemed to find it much more reasonable, and Kevin nursed it like a babe. So I did my best to put what expertise I had had in education into finding a suitable placement and helping devise a viable school program. Soon I found myself haunting old territories, meeting child-study teams again, chatting up principals, visiting special-education classrooms and guidance counselors, all in an effort to construct an educational plan for a boy who had been out of public schools for ten years.

God bless them, there was a school willing to try. Two weeks later Kevin was registered as a sophomore. He was to take four classes, English, math, social studies and art, plus a study hall. The rest of the time he would spend in the special-education resource room where the teacher would make sure he was keeping up on his work and coping with things.

On the very first morning, one of those dark misty November days, I came to pick him up and drive him to school. He was outside already, waiting for me. He had a cowboy shirt and new jeans on. His hair was a little longer around his ears, and I wondered where along the way he had become handsome to me, because he was. He reeked of Brut as he climbed into the car.

'Here, look at my notebook, Torey,' he said. 'Mrs Mac took me to the store last night to get it. Look at it. And look here. I got pencils. And three pens. I wanted a cartridge pen. That's what Dale, this other guy there, has. But she said, later on. See, Tor? Look at all I got.'

He was spilling the guts of the notebook over the front seat as I drove. His voice was rapid and cracked with excitement. And then he stopped. The car fairly exploded with silence after all the chatter.

'What if they don't like me? I might get lost. It's pretty big. What if I get lost?'

I smiled over at him.

'I must say, I *am* a little scared.' Then he smiled back. 'But I am going, aren't I? I really am going to high school.'

Kevin's new life fit him. For all the other times that even small changes devastated him, this major alteration in the pattern of his life came naturally.

Being the only nonretardate in the MacFarlane household was a kind of blessing to him. For the first time in his life he was the best at almost everything he tried. The other residents respected him and openly admired his prowess. Their esteem mattered greatly to Kevin. Quickly he learned to do accounts. His math had never been strong, but in comparison to the others, he could learn even that rapidly and soon he had gained the necessary skills to acquire a checkbook and a small savings account. He mastered cooking much more easily and invited me over for a Saturday-night meal, which he had planned and cooked himself with help from the other male residents. It was spaghetti, and I wondered if he remembered, as he served it, what meaning spaghetti had first had for us. He asked and received permission to paint his room a new color. He chose a ghastly shade of lavender and was delighted with it.

Dr MacFarlane soon became 'Pop' and Mrs MacFarlane remained 'Mac' forever and they did treat him with the tenderness given a natural son.

His greatest pride, however, was his job. Because Kevin went to school and all the other residents had some sort of work during the day, Kevin quickly found himself considerably short of cash in comparison. This caused problems, especially on weekends when the other residents wanted to go to movies or bowling or engage in other activities Kevin couldn't always afford and had to ask the MacFarlanes for. However, Dr MacFarlane found a solution. Kevin had learned the basic survival skills so easily and well that Dr MacFarlane began to pay him a small sum to be a 'teacher.' Each evening for an hour Kevin would sit down with another of the residents and teach and practice basic math and reading skills. Kevin loved it. What it did for his self-image was far more than it ever did for his pocket.

But perhaps the thing that pleased me most was not Kevin at all but another resident named Sally. She thought Kevin was handsome. Pretty soon, Kevin wasn't thinking Sally was too bad either, and under the watchful eye of the MacFarlanes, Kevin suffered the joys and sorrows of his first romance.

The first few weeks of school were traumatic, to say the least. It was the schedule that nearly killed him. He had had no idea what he was getting into, being at school all day, and he came home exhausted enough to sleep for the first few afternoons. The classes, too, were much harder than he had expected, even the art class. He didn't understand many of the things presented, simply because he lacked the basic background. He was crushed at the first midterm to discover that he was not getting the best of grades. But he wasn't failing either, we pointed out, and that was all that mattered. There were some other rocky moments. He was the only resident saddled with homework, and this meant that he missed out on a lot of the home entertainment and even some outings. And of course some of the kids at school did tease him.

But in the end, it worked. Mrs MacFarlane sat down with him every night until the routine was established and Kevin could carry on on his own. He was bolstered at school by an excellent special-ed teacher. And he did his own part. Never once did he fail to answer a question in class when asked. Never once did he lose his temper or rage or act strange. In fact, the kids teased him over adolescent things, over his age, over his shyness with girls. They didn't appear to suspect that there was anything else very unusual about this boy, other than that he was new and he was a little slow on the uptake. For all intents and purposes, Kevin was like everyone else. And finally, I too had to agree that Kevin's idea to go to high school was a good one. Because of the nature of the MacFarlane home, this was his main opportunity to associate with his peer group, with youngsters who were normal. Like he was.

I never failed to be awed at this final transition from Seven Oaks to the MacFarlanes'. It had proved to be so flawless.

Unlike when I was a teacher, there was no clear demarcation of the end. No June arrived that forced stock taking of one's successes and failures and then a final parting. It was kinder here in the clinic, where one went timeless after a while and worked without worry about the start or finish of a thing. I seldom regretted the ends here the way I had in teaching because here they usually came when both the child and I were ready. It was a natural parting, slower and less hurtful.

The end for Kevin and me was almost here. He had found friends at school and he was busy at home. By mid-January our sessions were tapering off. For quite some time we had only seen one another once a week anyhow, and he had been coming to the clinic. I hadn't been out to see him at the home for four or five weeks, except once at Christmas to take him a gift. But now we were even missing our weekly sessions occasionally. We both knew the end was nearly with us.

* * *

We were in my office. Usually we used the therapy room down the hall where there was more space, but Jules had a client interview there, so Kevin and I came instead to the office. Kevin sat in Jules's chair and spun it around.

'You know,' I said, 'I think it's maybe time for you and me to finish.'

'What do you mean? It's only 4,15. I'm here until ten to five.'

'No, that's not what I meant.'

He was not happy when he understood what I was talking about. Indeed, he was angry with me, rising from the chair, pacing back and forth before sitting down again.

'You see?' he said. 'It's just the way I always said it was. You never really cared. You came to see me just because they pay you to. And now you're going to stop.'

I tried to explain, to defend myself at first, but then I stopped. It wasn't like that and I knew Kevin knew it wasn't too.

He fell silent, an angry silence wherein he frowned and grimaced, turning his head away from me. I couldn't get him off the subject for the rest of the time, nor could I diminish his anger. In the end we had to leave it over until the next week so he could simmer down.

But Kevin knew, as I did, that the time had come. He paused at the doorway as he was leaving. 'I guess this means I'm well now,' he said without smiling. 'I guess that isn't always good.'

Our last day was a cold, snowy Thursday in February. Kevin came in breathless and red cheeked from the sub-zero temperatures outside. He sat down in Jules's chair in the office without taking off his coat or boots. Only his ski cap had been jerked off, leaving his hair standing up in rumpled confusion. During the week he had gotten contact lenses and, although I had known it was coming, it was somewhat of a shock to see him without his thick glasses. Against the rosy redness of his cheeks, his gray eyes were shimmery like quicksilver.

We chatted about his plans, about things at home, about the future. I couldn't tell what Kevin was thinking beneath his cheery exterior. We had decided this would be our last day some weeks earlier, so we had both known it was coming.

When an unexpected pause wandered into the conversation, tears gathered abruptly in Kevin's eyes. He leaped to his feet. 'I got to be going. It's pretty late and me and Denny Crenshaw are going swimming at the Y tonight.'

I nodded.

Backing away from me, he watched me. I could still see the tears, still see him ducking his head to keep them from showing. All the seconds and minutes and hours of the last two and a half years folded in upon themselves accordion-style, and the distance between us filled with unsaid things. I looked down at my fingers and listened to the silence.

'Torey? Can I ask you one thing?'

'Sure.'

'But don't answer, okay. Just let me ask it.'

'All right.'

'Here it is. Well, I want to know if you would, I mean, if I ever got in trouble again … I mean, if I *really* got in trouble again, would you come? Would you be there?' Then as I leaned forward, he threw up a hand. 'But don't answer that. Okay? Don't tell me your answer.'

'Why not?' I asked.

'Because, you see,' he said, paused, then smiled at me. 'You see, I want to go away from here always thinking that you would. I don't want to know if you would or not. I just want to know I asked you and you didn't say no.'

I nodded.

'I won't forget you,' he said.

'Nor I, you, Kev.'

'Will you come see me sometimes?'

'Of course I will.'

'And I'll phone you sometimes. Just to see how you are. Okay? I won't forget you.'

'I know you won't,' I said.

'Well, I have to be going now. Denny's waiting downstairs and he's going to wonder where I got to. Did I tell you, I might get to go on the school swimming team? If they don't think I'm too old, I might get to.'

'Yes, you told me.'

The tears were there again, and the last moment passed between us without words. I had risen and come to the door of the office with him. I smiled. He smiled. I smiled again.

'Well, I've gotta go. See you around, okay?'

'Yeah, Kev, see you around.'

And he turned and walked down the long corridor, where the lights were very bright even on a winter's afternoon, and so he cast no shadow behind him. I stood motionless in the doorway and watched him. At the very far end of the hall, he paused, turned and waved. 'Bye, Torey,' he called before disappearing.

Good-bye, Bryan.